Winter's Tales

NEW SERIES: 6

*

EDITED BY

Robin Baird-Smith

St. Martin's Press
New York

Winter's tales (New York, N.Y.: 1985)
  Winter's tales. – New ser, 1- – New York: St. Martin's Press, c1985-
  v.; 22 cm
  Annual.
  Continues. Christmas feast.

  1. Short Stories – Periodicals.
PN6120.2.W56   808.83'1-dc19   89–62382
                    AACR 2   MARC-S

Library of Congress [8703]

ISBN 0-312-05299-5

First U.S. Edition
10 9 8 7 6 5 4 3 2 1

CONTENTS

ACKNOWLEDGEMENTS

The stories are copyright respectively:
© 1990 Clare Colvin
© 1990 Peter Benson
© 1990 David Plante
© 1990 Patrick Roscoe
© 1990 Laura Kalpakian
© 1990 Norman Thomas di Giovanni
© 1990 Janice Elliott
© 1990 Joyce Carol Oates
© 1990 Rasaad Jamie
© 1990 Paul Sayer
© 1990 Anita Mason
© 1990 Haydn Middleton
© 1990 Carlo Gébler
© 1990 Francis King
© 1990 Simon Mason

EDITOR'S NOTE

Seán O'Faoláin, one of the great masters of the short story, called this form an 'essential art'. 'A short story', he wrote, 'is like a child's kite . . . if it is good, the main thing a story writer wants to do is to get it off the ground as quickly as possible, hold it there, taut and tense, playing it like a kite.'

True enough, for if it is to be successful the author must convey, in a limited number of words, all the elements of characterization, drama and situation, which will grip the reader and achieve the writer's purpose.

In each of the stories in this book these elements are present, though they are combined to very different effect. There are stories which chill (Patrick Roscoe's 'My Lover's Touch'), stories of the supernatural (Clare Colvin's 'Something to Reflect Upon'), stories which at first appear merely to entertain – though on closer inspection they contain a deeper resonance.

Thus the themes, the style, the very voices of the authors are distinct, giving each story its own 'personality'. They cover not only a wide range of cultural traditions (the Argentine, Canada and the United States) but vastly differing cultural backgrounds, and they range from the sharply and intimately depicted Parisian flat that is the setting of Clare Colvin's haunting tale, to the windswept flatlands of California (Laura Kalpakian) and the unplaceable yet sharply focused setting for Paul Sayer's police state of 'Judpara'.

Yet there is a unity in this collection as well. All these stories deal with the human condition, and with human relationships in particular – displaced, disturbed, unlikely or unrealized as these may be. These are stories set in the real world, but where the participants in the action are hovering on the knife-edge between sanity and insanity, where the fantastic and the unexpected are likely to break through the familiar.

Winter's Tales relies on its readers for its continued existence. I hope this year the readers will be pleased with the selection of stories on offer, dictated as it is, by the quirks of editorial taste

Robin Baird-Smith, 1990

SOMETHING TO
REFLECT UPON

Clare Colvin

The Villa Mozart is one of the finest turn-of-the-century apartment buildings in the Seizième, possibly one of the finest in the whole of Paris. You go through mahogany and bevelled glass doors to the main entrance hall. At the end of the hall a curving stone staircase winds round a glass elevator and the stone walls meet the ceiling in a carved frieze of grapes and pomegranates. On the stained glass window a pre-Raphaelite nymph in semi profile yearns towards the heavens. Her auburn hair snakes out behind her to merge with the surrounding leaves.

The apartment itself is on the third floor and protected by a double front door with an elaborate lock that sends metal bars into the door frame at an extra turn of the key. I unlock the metal bars and step into a world of polished parquet and double doors. Two sets of glass doors lead into the dining room and sitting room, which are linked by more doors. Both rooms have French windows leading on to narrow iron balconies. I stand in the centre and see in the sitting room, in front of me, a marble fireplace surmounted by a looking glass which is framed by white plaster garlands. Turning towards the dining room, there is a twin fireplace and glass. I am reflected in the reflections of the mirrors *ad infinitum*. The image is of a woman with a pale face and long fair hair tied back with a black ribbon. She is wearing a dark grey coat and a light grey patterned cashmere scarf. Her clothes look expensive, but unobtrusive.

[11]

My aunt, whose apartment it is, is called the French aunt, though she is English. She is married to a French diplomat and they are abroad most of the time, letting the apartment to other diplomats. This is why it has such a formal, unlived-in air. The table, flanked by the elaborately simple curves of art nouveau dining chairs, is a dark, polished mirror, untouched by spilt wines or carelessly placed knives and forks, all the marks that an ordinary table acquires as its patina. The pale colours of the sofas divulge nothing of evenings past, of cigarette smoking, coffee drinking, not even an indentation to show that they have been used. The air of impersonality is such that you hesitate to make a mark, but just drift through the double doors, touching nothing.

I am here because a diplomat who should have taken the flat did not, after all, get posted to Paris, and I am staying until they find another diplomat. I am also here because I need to recover from, no, to recover *myself*. I look on my leaving Robert as an escape, a declaration that I will no longer live a sub-text. It should be a triumph, but everyone extends sympathy to me, as if I am ill. So perhaps it is a defeat, after all. The first old friend with whom I had lunch here, who took me to a panelled restaurant near the Place Vendôme where we had a wild mushroom salad and scallops poached in seaweed, suddenly became terribly solicitous and asked me how I felt. I couldn't speak, and he pressed my hand and said, 'Of course, you feel numb.'

'Yes,' I said, and we talked about something else. It is not only numbness, but a vacuum. The person you were has melted away, leaving a non-person, about whom others make their own judgements, assigning you a character, feelings and motives you do not

[12]

possess. On my own, all that seems left is a bank of memories. I cross the road to the Jeu de Paumes and meet myself many years ago, walking from the gallery with nymphéas in my eyes. Straight ahead of me is the Crillon, like a formal Government building. One of those windows overlooking the Place de la Concorde was where we spent the first night of our honeymoon ten years ago. It was there, after months of being drawn into marriage by all the pressures which eventually make people marry, that I sat up in bed in the early hours of the morning and thought, *What have I done?* The Place was a moving pattern of weaving and dipping car headlights, illuminating in their rays a drizzle of rain. I watched them from the window until the sky began to lighten. We returned to England a married couple, Robert and Alice. Robert's name was always in front, to do with the way they sounded together. I lost my surname, too, and with it my sense of identity.

I am growing cold as I stand in the Place de la Concorde, and I remember it was cold then, as well. It is New Year's Eve tomorrow and some friends of the aunt have asked me to a party. Memories of New Year's parties stretch back for years, the prospects for each year judged by that moment at midnight when you find whether you are where you want to be. This is the first time I have spent New Year in Paris.

I return to the quartier of the Seizième. It is a strangely quiet and self-contained part of Paris. You walk through canyons of late nineteenth century apartment buildings designed for the haute bourgeoisie. Each apartment block has a large carpeted front hall, polished brass fittings, and an office for the conçierge. The area is inhabited only, it seems, by women of a certain age, wearing calf-length black mink coats and

[13]

walking their dogs. I stop at the traiteur to buy pâté, olives and céleri rémoulade. As the assistant wraps each portion, he says inquiringly, 'Et avec cela?' I order an oeuf en gelée which I had not originally intended to do. My French seems to have deserted me totally, and I am pointing at things like a tourist. I am glad to get back to the apartment where I can think fluently, rather than fit into the role of the quartier's mental defective.

In the apartment, the silence is profound. The front looks on to a cul de sac ending in a garden, and on to a similar turn-of-the-century stone building opposite. The bedrooms on the side look into a quiet street with little traffic. Opposite the bedrooms are more apartment buildings, less distinguished architecturally but still bearing the stamp of money and position. The silence is broken by shouting in the street – mad, furious shouting. I open the window and see, on the pavement, a bearded man in an anorak who is so beside himself with rage that he is practically falling into the gutter. 'Espèce de con!' he shouts, and 'Je vais vous tuer!' I cannot quite make out what he is on about, but he uses the verb *tuer* a great deal. The concierge in the apartment building opposite comes out in a patterned frock that spreads across her hips. She stands there impassively, watching him. Obviously she knows he is not going to *tuer* her. If anything, he is going to *tuer* the women in their black mink coats. Perhaps he is protesting at his anonymity. I shut the window again. Metal rods slide into both ends of the window frame.

Here in the apartment I am protected, living in a hermetically sealed vacuum. How quiet it is, and how different from the place I first stayed in in Paris, an attic room in one of those hotels where you were

[14]

afraid, as you ascended the slanting stairs, that they might fall away from the walls and cascade you into the basement. It was on the Left Bank, and there was noise at all times, until four in the morning from the late night people, and beginning again soon after five with the dustbins and the streetcleaners. I suppose I must have had a certain courage to have come to Paris that first time, at about seventeen or so, but when I come to think of it, I did quite a few brave things when I was young. I grew cowardly as I grew older, afraid of the unknown, and then I married Robert. At seventeen, after taking a modelling course, which was an accepted finishing education for girls at the time, I had gone to work for the house of Duparc in Faubourg St Honoré. I spent three months sitting in a changing room with another English girl, occasionally being asked to parade in the salon in one of M. Duparc's dresses, hand stitched by shortsighted seamstresses in the basement. It was a small House and it was like being part of a tense, temperamental family. M. Duparc flew easily into a tantrum, and a few years later he had a heart attack and retired. No one carried on his name, he was not that important a couturier. And I, who had had barely acknowledged fantasies of taking Paris by storm, left at the end of three months. M. Duparc decided to return to having Parisiennes as models, and Mme Duparc told me with sympathy and tact that there was no more work for me. 'You are charming, my dear, but you are too self-effacing with the clothes. They must be worn with panache. Ma petite, you must make a production of yourself, if you are to be successful. Otherwise no one will notice you, and the world will go on without you.'

One way of not being noticed was to marry Robert, for he demanded all the attention and did all the talking. It was easier to say nothing than to compete, and so Robert began thinking for me as well. He would tell other people what was in my mind and although I did not necessarily agree, when he said it with such an air of decision, it seemed to become fact. So my thoughts became Robert's too, and when I left, I found it hard not to ring him up to find out what I should think. Whenever I bought clothes in neutral shades, I heard Robert's voice ringing in my mind, 'For God's sake, why don't you wear some bright colours? No one will notice you dressed like that. You'll just fade into the wallpaper.'

I felt bruised when I arrived at the flat, but now, as long as I stay indoors, I feel an expansiveness and calm. It's going out that is the problem. Simple things like buying a loaf of bread are difficult when the slightest contact with another person makes you wince. I left my skin behind when I left Robert. I expect he shows it to people as proof that I will return. Until I grow another, life is bound to be painful.

Oddly enough, going to a party is less difficult than everyday life. It is to do with the preparation. I prepare myself like an actress in a dressing room. I sit in front of the mirror for the ritual of making up. First you prime the canvas with foundation, then you add colour. Pale eyeshadow overlaid with grey, eyeliner, carefully blurred, lip gloss, masses of mascara, and a touch of what they used to call rouge and now call blusher. There, who's got a pretty mask, then? The model training was not for nothing. Now I decide on the clothes. The grey blouse, no, that's wallpaper dressing. Finally I wear the black dress with a low back, long earrings and beads. I hear Robert's voice saying, 'I hate you wearing black.'

I am now ready to go into the street. I close the

door behind me and lock the iron bars into place with a turn of the key. No fumbling with mortice and Yale. One flick of the wrist and the door is secure as Fort Knox. I walk down the stairs and into the street. The world outside is not as frightening at night because the dim lighting shields you from the stranger's gaze, and in the quartier there is no one around anyway. The women in their mink coats have locked themselves into their fortresses.

A taxi pulls up and I get in and am suddenly transported into a world of window curtains with bobbles, and boogie music. The taxi driver has a collection of big band music from the forties and fifties. He holds the tapes up for inspection at the traffic lights. He doesn't trust modern music, he says, because it destroys the ears and the mind. He is going to celebrate the New Year in his cab. At midnight, the time when no passenger will be there, he will turn the boogie music up and clash a spanner against his spare hub cap. It sounds as good a way of spending New Year's Eve as any.

We boogie along to my aunt's friends' apartment near the Parc Monceau. I don't know them, but they heard I was in Paris on my own, so they told me to come to their party, because to be alone on New Year's Eve is a bad omen for the year ahead. A maid opens the door and takes my coat, and a shy young man, my hostess's son, shows me into the salon.

I am in a high-ceilinged room, even higher than the Villa Mozart, with a gilded mirror on one wall that reaches to the ceiling. The parquet floor is covered by a deep Aubusson carpet, and cream and gold leaf Louis Quinze chairs are placed at strategic intervals. Two women sit, straightbacked, conversing with each other, their chairs too far apart for the conversation to

[17]

be private. The young man has disappeared towards the front door, and the women are looking at me in an expectant way for an introduction. I shake hands with the fair-haired woman in a billowing pink dress, and she smiles graciously, then I shake hands with the dark-haired woman in black. She, too, smiles and looks friendly, but neither of them move from their chairs and there are no other chairs nearby, so I move on. In the far corner four men in dinner jackets are having a conversation and, from their lack of interest in a new arrival, it is evident that they wish to continue without interruption. On such occasions, a drinks table can save you, but there is no drinks table here. I stand in the middle of the Aubusson carpet, reflected in the mirror, in a slim black dress, and behind me the two women on their gold leaf chairs at a distance from each other, still conversing. I think, if I walk across the carpet I shall hear the crunching of gravel.

The shy young man returns and asks what I would like to drink. Some wine, I say, and when he scurries off, I follow him. There is the drinks table in the hall, with its comforting array of bottles, so now I know my escape route. Madame, my hostess, is there too, smiling, gracious, slightly distrait, for she had set herself the task of preparing a four course dinner of the sort you would expect in a restaurant. Several times during the course of the evening she emerges from her hutch of a kitchen to supervise arrangements and then returns to the stove. The taxi driver in his cab and Madame in her kitchen have both, in their separate ways, decided to spend New Year's Eve alone.

I feel better for a glass of wine and more people are now arriving, noisier and jollier than the earlier guests. I am still the outsider, but that, after a couple of glasses, does not seem to matter as much. The room

[18]

is warmer, less intimidating, and the pendants of the chandeliers sparkle like leaves in a heat wave. The mirror reflects people weaving in and out of groups, and the Louis Quinze chairs have been abandoned. The party is going to be fun, after all.

In the dining room with its magenta walls, the candles on the tables cast flickering pools of light. The central dining table, polished and dark like the one at the Villa Mozart, has a selection of dishes of smoked salmon, cray fish and pâté de foie gras. I am sitting next to an enthusiastic and friendly man, whose dinner jacket seems incongruous with his untidy thatch of hair and gold-rimmed spectacles. He is not at all worried by my lack of French, and launches, for no apparent reason, into a dissertation on the virtues of Akhnaton, the first reformist Pharoah. A monotheist, too, he says, as if that were a further sign of virtue. The dissertation is fascinating and everyone listens as though it is a lecture on their chosen subject. What do French women do during their men's displays of virtuosity, I wonder? An Englishwoman would have been watching her husband's face with an expression either of maternal anxiety or of distaste. Mme Akhnaton, who has a Nefertiti profile, is doing none of these things. She is narrowing her Anouk Aimée eyes at a middleaged admirer who is still crazy about her after all these years. Everyone here has known each other since they were very young and they are still carrying on the same interchangeable relationships. Mme Akhnaton knew Edouard de Truc when he was a smooth young man with dark hair, but she married her enthusiastic Egyptologist. Edouard de Truc now has grey, thinning hair, though he is still smooth, and he fans the memories of their earlier affair.

It is midnight and the tables are abandoned, as

everyone performs the first task of the New Year, circling the magenta room to shake hands with and kiss their fellow guests, murmuring 'Bonne année.' At the last stroke of midnight, a tall, wasted-looking young man with large eyes, whom I had not seen before, says to me, 'Happy New Year,' in a perfect accent, and kisses me on both cheeks. I feel like someone who has been struggling in the rapids of the French language, and who has now come to dry land.

Jean-Marc, our hostess's son, puts on a Stones record and someone rolls up the Aubusson, leaving a wide expanse of parquet. Jean-Marc has a veritable archive of English records – Rolling Stones, Beatles, Bill Haley. Edouard de Truc dances to the memories of his youth, and so do most of us, apart from Jean-Marc, who is too young, and possibly the man I am with, who may be too young, but I am not sure because of the damage he has done to his face. It reflects lack of food and sleep, and the possibility of drink or drugs. His name is Philippe and he has arrived late from another party with a similarly ravaged-looking woman and a pale young man who has taken up residence at the drinks table.

Philippe and I sit on the broad Directoire sofa, watching the dancers. They have mostly dispersed, except for the fair-haired woman in pink, whom I had first seen sitting straightbacked in a Louis Quinze chair, and who now dances by herself in front of the mirror, with an undulating body and balletic movements of the arms. She enjoys the way her body moves with an innocent shamelessness, and her face – she must be about thirty-five – has the pleased expression of a schoolgirl showing off. Whether people are watching is irrelevant to her, for she loves music, she loves dancing, and she loves herself. The floor is her stage, and this is her show, choreographed on the spur of the moment. After a while, she pirouettes away through the door with a final flourish, acknowledging the applause. Philippe offers me a truffle from a silver dish. I choke on the cocoa dust with which it is coated, and try to blow if off the chocolate. The fine dark dust goes all over my dress.

'That's why I wear black,' I say, then notice that the cocoa dust has also settled on the cream brocade upholstery. I think, I won't be invited here again.

The pale young man, Lucien, and the woman with the ravaged air, whose name is Brigitte, join us after circling the rest of the party. Brigitte has red hennaed hair, intense eyes and talks a great deal about herself. She says she is a photographer and had an exhibition a while ago in a small gallery in the Marais area. The photographs were of women in different walks of life – a well known writer, a film director, a dancer, an alcoholic prostitute in a café, a lavatory attendant.

'Who buys the photographs?' I ask.

She regards the question as insulting, as I would not have thought of buying a photograph as a work of art. It appears that, so far, the writer and the film director have bought their own photographs, but the alcoholic whore and the lavatory attendant have not. Lucien disappears to the hall again to refill his glass and Philippe discusses Lucien's drink problem with Brigitte, who seems if anything more drunk. I am not sure about Brigitte, but I like Philippe. He has sympathetic eyes and a way of drawing me into the conversation, and he seems to like me.

At three in the morning, the party is beginning to disperse, and Brigitte says she will give us a lift, as there are bound to be no taxis. Lucien insists that we go back to his place for coffee, and we drive towards the Place de L'Etoile, a land of fir trees covered with false snow and white fairylights, like the glittering domain of the Snow Queen. Lucien's flat is a former chambre de bonne's rooms at the top of a large apartment building off the Avenue Foch. He is clearly one of those drinkers who hates to be on their own. He pours a whisky for himself and makes some Nescafé for us. Brigitte, in whom drink has unleashed a streak of aggression, is angry that he does not have real coffee. How can he possibly live in a place without coffee? How dare he offer his guests Nescafé? She bullies Lucien as if he is the owner of an indifferent restaurant. Philippe tries to intervene and she tells him to shut up. Lucien says in a quiet, flat voice, 'There is either whisky or Nescafé. The whisky is real.' Brigitte has a whisky and begins a monologue on photography. Her face is square-jawed, her eyes fanatical. I think, I have drained the dregs of this particular New Year's Eve. It's time to go.

Philippe says he will walk me home, but I say, No, I'll take a taxi. Outside it is raining, and there are no taxis, only an occasional late partygoer swishes past, sending up a spray from the road.

'I'll walk you home,' says Philippe. 'I have an umbrella.'

It is not really cold, just wet, and we walk along the avenue. Philippe's arm rests lightly on my waist, and after a few minutes I put my arm round his waist. He is so thin you can feel his ribs through the jacket and I think, It is so long since I walked with my arm around someone. Although we are both tired, we are still talking. I learn a little more about Philippe. He is only half French. The other half is Polish which is why he accepts with fatalistic grace the walk through the rain. It is nearly five by the time we reach the Villa

Mozart, and we are the only people awake in the neighbourhood. I realise that Philippe cannot be left on the doorstep, with his sodden shoes and his hair in rats' tails dripping onto his collar.

'I'll stay until the Métro begins running,' says Philippe. He takes off his shoes and puts them beside the sofa, and I drape his jacket over a chair by the radiator where it emanates a dank smell of wet wool. I make a pot of tea for us, and Philippe sits on the sofa, his eyelids half closed. His white shirt hangs loosely on his body, the cuffs rolled back. I tell him a little, though not much, about why I am here. He listens, his hand resting lightly on my shoulder, then he says he must sleep for a while. It seems entirely natural that he should sleep in my bed. He takes off his shirt and climbs into one side of the bed. He closes his eyes, and his face, in profile, looks exhausted. I get into my side of the bed and lie quite still. Then his hand reaches out for mine.

'Are you asleep, Alice?'

'Almost,' I say.

'Goodnight, then, Alice,' he says and is asleep a few minutes later.

After an hour or so, there is a grey light through the shutters and I lie there, too tired to move, aware of the body next to me. He is still sleeping and in the faint light he looks at peace. The wasted look about his face has gone and he looks younger than before. The eyelids stretch over the large eyes, like a marble angel in repose. I think about his sympathy and knowingness last night. He asked me very little about myself, yet he seemed to know more than I said. I think, None of this would have happened if I had not been in a strange city, dependent on other people's

[23]

whims. I have been too long on my own and now I have made a connection.

I leave him to sleep and stand under the bathroom shower waiting for my mind to clear. Then I go into the kitchen to make some breakfast. There are croissants, which I warm in the oven, and orange juice in the fridge. I leave the coffee on the stove and return to the bedroom. The blankets have slipped halfway down his chest and he is lying on his back, one arm stretched behind his head. I sit on the edge of the bed as he begins to stir and then I notice, as he moves the arm, a mark like a bruise or perhaps more like a dark discoloration.

You would have to be out of contact with all newspapers for the last few years not to be wary of these marks, I think. Nowadays there is no looking for kindness from a stranger, no love from someone whose history is not known to you. A whole way of reasssurance has gone. I exist because I am loved. Now that way is closed. We are all locked in our separate bodies, hardly daring to touch each other. Last night I had forgotten the new set of rules. I had been going back to the days of chance, when chance was safe. Now the plague is spreading through the land and the Masque is ended.

Philippe opens his eyes and sees me looking at him. He says, 'Good morning, Alice. Tu as bien dormi?' Then he gives me a warm smile full of affection. 'I smell coffee. How kind you are.'

We have breakfast in the sitting room and Philippe sits on the sofa, wearing his dried clothes again. He seems content simply to watch me, looking at me with his large, grey eyes. For him, it is the beginning of something new, a special friendship. For me, this breakfast is a disengagement.

'I must get home, but I'll ring you later,' says Philippe. He writes my phone number on the pad by the phone, tears off the page and then writes his own number on the next page, writing underneath 'Philippe'. At the door, he puts his hands on my shoulders and looks intently at my face, as if he is trying to read it. Then he says, 'A demain,' kisses me softly and fleetingly on the mouth, and turns and walks away. I shut the door and stand in the hall for several minutes, listening to the silence. There is an awareness in the apartment that someone has been here, that the emptiness has been momentarily filled. In the sitting room, I look at myself in the mirror. My face seems different, more the way it was a few years ago, a little softer, perhaps. I take the coffee cups into the kitchen. The flat is closing ranks around me again, as the hushed impersonality returns.

New Year comes quietly to Paris. For the past two or three weeks, the French have been sulking. They have been frightened out of shops and restaurants by terrorists' bombs, and they are furious about the train strike. I hear on the radio that the Métro may be next, and decide I must visit the Bibliothèque Nationale first. The state of the Métro reflects the fury with which the French regard their inefficient Government. Once it was neat and clean, but now there is litter, which no one clears away, as if in a dirty protest, and the interconnecting subways are lined with beggars and buskers.

On my way home from the Bibliothèque I stop by at the traiteur and buy some rillettes and a salade de tomates. The weather has turned colder, and the central heating in the flat does not seem as stifling. I pour myself a San Raphäel blanc with ice and soda water. I know from the times when Robert would go out without me that you have to be disciplined about drinking on your own. Only one before dinner, maybe more if you are cooking.

The phone rings and it is, as I thought, Philippe. No one else has my number here. I have a momentary feeling of dread, that fear of involvement brings, but it is not difficult to deal with the call for, after ten years of being married to a man who tried to control my thoughts, lying comes easily to me.

'I'm terribly sorry. I would have loved to have seen you, but I am going back to London tomorrow.'

He sounds surprised and says he thought I was staying here for longer.

'I rang my husband, and we decided it would be a good idea if I went back now.'

A pause at his end of the phone. Then he decides, obviously, that changes of plan are a natural part of life, and the fatalistic element re-asserts itself.

'I'm sorry you're going . . . Well, let me know when you come to Paris again. You have my telephone number, don't you?'

I do. It is still on the pad by the phone.

Two days later it begins to snow and the Métro goes on strike. Now I have all the time to myself in the world. I look out at the white-blanketed street from my window. No one is going anywhere, least of all me. The central heating insulates me, providing a world of warmth that denies the natural elements. The phone remains silent. I lose the desire to go out, even to the traiteur or the boulanger. I eat less and less, but I read a great deal, I listen to the radio, I make some notes, I rest. At night, occasionally, I take a sleeping pill, for though I am tired I find it hard to sleep. I spend much of the time thinking about how each step in my life has taken me to this still centre, this place of stasis. Each time I was given a choice, I took a path that led to a lessening of choice. Now I am at the centre of the maze, with no choices left, but a sense at least that I still desire to exist. On my way into Paris, along the Périphérique, I saw a cemetery of neat, crowded graves, with little stone houses to which the bodies were confined, and I had a sudden sense of claustrophobia. How terrible to be confined to that space, never to go anywhere again. My own confinement to this apartment is not a wish for non-existence, more a wish for non-feeling until I gain my strength. Things will take their course, I realise, if I have time on my own. In the middle of the night the phone rings, a loud, insistent ringing. It would not be Philippe at this hour. I let it ring until it ceases. How oppressive a large flat becomes when you are on your own. You begin to feel previous lives going on in other rooms. Space has to be filled and if you do not fill it yourself, the past returns and gains possession of its territory.

The next day it snows again. I stand at the window and watch it swirling down and sideways, so light that it sometimes spirals upwards again. It is dizzying, almost hypnotic after a while. I open the window and look down at the street. An ambulance is drawing up at the Villa Mozart, and after a while the ambulance-men carry out from the building a covered figure on a stretcher. One of the black mink coats has lost its owner. I switch on the radio and hear that the Métro strike is still going on, and there is now fury at the police because they do not have any snow ploughs with which to clear the streets, only battering rams with which to knock down demonstrators. A government minister is making an emergency broadcast on the subject.

Some days I stay in bed most of the time, because I feel curiously tired, and if I am not going out I may as well stay in bed as sit on the sofa. But as the days go by, I am aware of having turned a corner, of beginning to feel stronger. My legs no longer ache as if I had been walking for ever, and I need less sleep. I have just been tired, that's all it was, and now I'm getting better. The weather is improving too. It is lighter and brighter, and the snow is beginning to melt. When I open the window there is a mildness in the air. It is almost time to go out again.

I begin to think of food, quite ravenously, and then, the next morning I awake with a feeling of purpose and determination. The time has come to put my house in order, to do some cleaning, to stock up with food, why, even to cook a meal. I have found a new purpose in simple household matters. But there is just the business of getting out of the house. This is going to be difficult, because I am simply not used to exercise any more.

It feels good to be in the fresh air again. The pavement is clear of snow, apart from the slush wedged against the wall. It is really quite an effort to walk the slightly upward rise to the traiteur. In his window the massed oeufs en gelée glisten invitingly, framed in chopped aspic. The shop assistant looks at me oddly. He has not seen me for a while, and I know I am pale and underweight. He inquires after my health and I say that I have had the grippe, but I am better now. I look at the dishes of the day, but he has only an insipid blanquette de veau. Time to do my own cooking again. I buy the first course from him, freshly cooked langoustes with a mayonnaise verte, and the final course, a crème brûlée with a smooth crust of caramel in a heartshaped dish. Then I see that

[28]

he has pink champagne on special offer. No, he says, they have no half bottles, and so I take a whole bottle. I don't care what they say about pink champagne – I love it. I buy a bottle of Bordeaux, some mineral water, and pâté and olives.

Next door the butcher has laid out pink and red flesh on the marble slab. I still think in terms of two rather than one when I am cooking, and I ask for two fillet-steaks without thinking, but I do not correct my mistake. I shall do a Tournedos Rossini, with some of the pâté. At the boulangerie I buy a baguette and croissants, then fruit and salad leaves at the green-grocer. Even if the rest of Paris has fallen apart, the shops in the Seizième hold fast to their standards. I am out of breath when I return to the Villa Mozart with my shopping bags. I am also short of cash. I unload the various packages into the fridge and then rest on the sofa.

Evenings are always reassuring. You draw the curtains and any obligation to be active has gone. At this time of the day it is quite natural to be sitting at home. People working, people going to the shops, taking clothes to the laundry, all those obligations have gone and it is quite all right to do what I have been doing most days, which is nothing. But tonight I have something to set my mind to. I have a dinner to prepare. I go to the Dutch bureau in the dining room and find some linen place mats in the drawer. In the glass cabinet are some fine champagne glasses shaped like flutes, so I take one and then ease the cork off the champagne. It is more robust than white champagne. I have one glass and immediately feel lighthearted. Now to get the dinner together.

I really do not need more than the langoustes. I had not realised how your stomach adapts to lack of food.

[29]

It does not want more, but on the other hand, I am hungry for different tastes, so I shall go on. I bought a raspberry feuilleté in the boulangerie, when I wasn't looking, which I shall have with the crème brûlée. In the meantime there is the fillet steak, underdone, the bread cooked in the juices of the meat and coated with pâté. One last glass of champagne – I did need more than half a bottle – and I go on to the Bordeaux.

I pour it into a large wine glass. In my head a conversation is beginning with my companion for dinner. It is Philippe, and I try to explain why I have been here on my own for so long. It is, I tell his sympathetic eyes, to do with finding out if anything is there after all the responses to other people are gone. When you only see yourself reflected in other people's eyes, you are not sure if you exist without them. Once the self that responded to others in the way that others expected, once that self is gone, you wait to see what will emerge in place of the mirror image. And there is someone now who is different, someone who enjoys life and wants to talk and laugh and love. I am not Robert's person any more, closed into a mould that constrains me, aware of the closing walls of circumstance. Now that is sorted out, I am ready to build a new life. Everything is beginning to fall into place and I have a need for new places, new experiences. I am ready to leave the apartment.

Well, the raspberry feuilleté was a little too much, but never mind, what I shall have now is a digestif. That should settle matters. I pour myself an Armagnac and watch the news on television. Around midnight, the feuilleté strikes again. I have an awful stabbing pain in my chest, which continues after I have gone to bed. I take some Neutrose Vichy and a couple of sleeping pills, to sleep off my indigestion.

[30]

I am awake now, it is morning, and I feel better than ever before. The doubts have gone and the cloud has lifted. An intense love overwhelms me and focuses on Philippe. I forget my fears, and that I don't really know who he is. As in a fairy tale where the heroine is indissolubly tied to the first living creature she meets when she wakes from her sleep – so I feel tied to Philippe. It will be easy to telephone him, now that I feel lighthearted and warm again.

I have been lying on the bed, and I must have been very tired. It must be late in the day, too, because the light through the shutters is bright. A fine day, and there is a warmth that is not just from the central heating. I stretch my arms and look up at the ceiling and – that's curious – I can't think why I haven't noticed it before, a large discoloured stain, and some of the paper is peeling. It looks as if there has been a leak from upstairs but why did I not notice it before? I walk along the corridor to the sitting room. The shutters are closed, but bright shafts of light slant across the floor. It seems dusty. Then I see something alarming, or rather, I see an alarming absence. The Dutch bureau has gone and so has the glass cabinet. Someone has been in and taken the furniture. Not all of it, for the sofa is here and the dining table, but the valuable pieces have gone. And the vase with dried flowers on the mantelpiece has gone, too, so have the magazines on the coffee table. The flat, always so impersonal, is now denying that anybody lives here at all. Someone must have come here last night, but why have they done it? Have there been burglars, or has my aunt sent in someone for the furniture? Is she telling me to leave? I look at the telephone and the pad with Philippe's number on it has gone as well. I walk towards the front door, and that, too, seems

different. Have I somehow got into the wrong flat? I
hear voices outside and now there is a key turning in
the lock. Either it is my aunt or one of her agents
come to tell me they want the apartment back, or else
I am in the wrong apartment and am about to be
accused of trespass.

The door opens and a woman steps into the hall.
She has long, blonde hair and an attractive, suntanned
face. She is wearing a cream linen suit and everything
about her is well groomed and cared for. A man
follows her, bulky with short hair, a dark blue suit and
slightly piggy eyes. Behind them, just closing the
door, is my aunt's agent, M. Maurice. Why couldn't
he have telephoned, the rude young man? I say,
Bonjour, m'sieur, but he walks past me, and so do the
two people he is showing around. They are, as I first
guessed, Americans. I follow them into the sitting
room and when Maurice opens the shutters, letting in
a flood of sunlight, I say, 'Excuse me, M. Maurice,
but I am still living here, you know.' He is looking in
my direction, but he does not seem to have registered
what I have said.

'This is the sitting room,' he tells his Americans.
'You will observe the symmetry of the two marble
fireplaces at either end, and the matching mirrors. An
excellent room for entertaining, you will agree. With
the double doors open, so, it is perfect for a large
reception.'

'It's really beautiful,' says the woman. 'One of the
prettiest rooms I have seen, and so much space.'

'Yeah, very nice,' says the man. He obviously leaves
domestic decisions to his wife. He looks around the
room, his eyes sweeping past me, and says, 'Let's see
the rest of the apartment.'

I wait to confront them when they return. It is quite

[32]

extraordinary, just at the moment when I feel ready to meet the world again, the world refuses to acknowledge my existence. As I wait, I begin to feel angry about the furniture. It is all to do with M. Maurice. He must have removed it, and he doesn't want to speak to me about it. Perhaps he is stealing the whole flat from my aunt. I go and stand by the window, so that he must see me as soon as he comes in. I hear them returning and M. Maurice ushers them back into the sitting room. The Americans sit on the sofa and M. Maurice draws up a dining chair. The tapestry armchair, I notice, is also missing.

'Really, M. Maurice,' I say, tapping him on the shoulder, 'may we please speak about the furniture.'

M. Maurice is looking inquiringly at the couple. 'Well, m'sieur, madame?'

'The trouble, as always, is the price,' says the woman. 'Paris prices seem to be way ahead of the States.'

'Mme Lavalle has not been anxious to sell in the past, but it seems they would now rather live outside Paris when they retire and will sell at some point, but they are prepared to wait for the right price.'

'Then there was that unfortunate business with her niece,' says the woman. 'That can't make her want to keep the apartment.'

'An accident,' says M. Maurice with a shrug of regret. 'She had not been in good health for some time, and was taking too many medicaments. Fortunately, we found out quite soon because Mme Dumas upstairs was worried when there was no reply from this apartment after her bathroom had flooded. Otherwise it might have been a matter of weeks.'

'How very sad,' says the woman. 'What a waste.'

I do not believe them. Today, more than ever, I

want to leave the apartment. I can see the trees outside, the new leaves ruffled by the breeze. I now know, more than anything, that I want to be part of life again. I can hear the pigeons in the nearby garden, and I am aware of the warmth of the sun on my skin. All this energy, all this love that I have been feeling, is evidence that I am still here. I am more alive than I have ever been.

'I think perhaps we ought to go on to 53 Rue de la Tour,' says the woman. 'Not that it's much cheaper. What do you think, Jack?'

'I'll see whatever you say,' says Jack. M. Maurice smiles and nods and they get up to go.

'No,' I cry out. 'Don't go. Look at me. I'm still here.'

How can they leave without even seeing me?

'Look at me! For God's sake, look at me!'

I have moved from the window to the centre of the room and am standing in front of the mirror. Reflected in it is the mirror opposite which reflects back the view of the room. That is all there is, an empty room.

'Please look at me.' My voice has become faint and there is a chill going through me, a feeling of absolute coldness.

'I'm not sure I like this area, anyway,' says the woman. 'I want somewhere with more life going on.'

By the door, she looks back and stares towards the fireplace. Her eyes are momentarily confused, then she turns away.

'What is it, Linda?' asks Jack. He is impatient to get on.

'That's odd, I thought I saw something move, for a moment. But it was only a shadow on the wallpaper.'

They left the apartment and locked the door behind them. It was eleven on a fine morning in June.

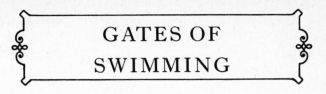

GATES OF
SWIMMING

Peter Benson

The summer of 1969 produced some hot spells between periods of cloud and rain, and though the rain was always warm, it was uncomfortable to swim in, so we never did until the last two weeks of the holiday, when the weather was dry and clear for days.

It was a two mile walk from my cousin's house to the swimming place on the river. For a while, we walked around the edge of a field, before meeting the river at the bottom of it, and then we followed a path that meandered along the bank. A dog called Bob went first, Rachel next, then me, and behind me, Cathy. She was Rachel's friend, and liked to stop and stare, so after half an hour of walking, we were strung out along the river bank. Bob had smelt rabbits in a hedge. While Rachel encouraged him, I looked down at weed as it swayed beneath the surface of the river, and at a group of willow trees on the opposite bank. Where the sun broke through the branches of the other trees that grew all around us, little coins of light were spotted on the bank. I turned around and watched Cathy as she picked some flowers. She was wearing a loose yellow shirt and white shorts; her legs were brown and glossy. As she bent down, I could see the straps of her swimming costume.

I was an only child, and was being raised in an atmosphere of modesty and civility. I lived in Manchester; my annual holiday in the country had, over the years, exposed me to more life than I saw for the rest of the year at home. Maybe my parents understood that I should not be cossetted, and mother's brother's farm was the perfect place for me to let off steam and see a different life. Rachel was effusive, and had an anarchic attitude that never failed to take me by surprise. I was fourteen; she and Cathy were sixteen. In any other group walking along a river bank, this age difference would have meant nothing, but to me, then, it meant a lot. I was a baby, and the girls winked at each other.

The swimming hole was at a bend in the river where the current had carved out a small beach and a deep pond of still water. Trees hung over it, so the sun warmed the water for only a few hours each day, but the walk had made us hot, and it was a relief to sit on the bank and dangle our toes in it. Bob ran onto the beach for a drink; when he'd had enough, he jumped onto the bank and nuzzled in Cathy's lap. She stroked his head and then cupped his chin in her hand and looked into his eyes. 'Who's a good boy?' she said, and for some reason, Rachel laughed.

We had brought a picnic – rolls, cake and squash – made and packed by my aunt. She was a quiet and solitary woman. My uncle was quiet too. Whenever I think about them now, I have a vision of them lurking in barns with handfuls of hay, or disappearing across fields in search of sheep – it was strange that Rachel was so extrovert. 'Come on!' she yelled. 'Let's eat!'

'That means we won't be able to swim for a bit,' I said, being sensible.

'So what?' she said, sitting down and spreading a table cloth on the grass. 'We've got all day.'

Cathy smiled, nibbled the corner of a roll and whispered 'All day . . .' and then lay back. She had short hair, cut like a boy's. It would not have suprised me to have seen her with pointed ears, but they were small and delicate, like shells. I wanted to touch.

[38]

Rachel tossed a piece of bread at me, and though I didn't throw any back, she flicked another piece. Cathy didn't join in; I said, 'Stop it. There're people in Biafra . . .'

'So what are you going to do?' Rachel said, 'Post it to them?'

'Don't be stupid,' I said.

Cathy didn't say anything, and though I hoped she would agree with me, and even felt that she did, she concentrated instead on making a daisy chain. When it was finished, she hung it around her neck, opened her arms and said 'I'm going in.'

She stood up, unbuttoned her shirt, took it off and let it fall on the grass. As it fluttered past me, I smelt it. It smelt of apples and talc. Then, above me, she unzipped her shorts and stepped out of them, flexed her legs and bent upwards, with her arms in the air.

She was wearing a blue swimsuit made of finely stitched, bubbly material that shone in the sun. In places, it had rucked up, so she looked plumper than she really was. Her calves were creased from where she had been sitting on the grass, but the skin on her back was smooth and brown. I watched her step off the bank and cross the beach to the water. Bob barked, and when Cathy whistled, he joined her in the river.

While I watched them, Rachel came to sit by me. 'Want a drink?' she said, and showed me a small bottle. 'It's sherry,' she said, and took a swig.

'Should I?' I said.

My parents didn't keep alcohol in the house.

'Why not?'

I took a sip.

'Have more than that!' she said, so I did, and I liked the taste. I didn't feel it go to my head.

'She's grown since last year,' I said, pointing to Cathy.

'Yes,' said Rachel. 'I suppose she has.' She laughed. 'I suppose we all have.' I didn't look at her, but I nodded.

I wanted Cathy to be interested in me, and though she didn't ignore me, I felt that I was just a kid to her. When I looked at her, she was floating on her back in the middle of the pond. The daisy chain around her neck was breaking up, and as it did, the flowers idled around her. When Rachel and I joined her, I was left to one side while they swam together.

The water was cold, but after the walk and then lying in the sun, it was refreshing. I grabbed the branch of an overhanging tree and swung from it, dropping down to splash between the girls. As I did, Cathy jumped out of the way, but Rachel grabbed my head and pushed me under, so I was faced with the sight of her thighs through the murky water, and had to gulp. I felt a mixture of joy and fear, like a telephone ringing unexpectedly. I was only under the water for a couple of seconds, but time seemed to slow down. I swallowed a mouthful of water, and then she raised her knee and hit my chin. I tipped back and then surfaced, spluttering. Rachel was laughing, while Cathy was floating on her back again on the other side of the pool.

I got out, sat on the bank and drank some squash. It was at this moment that an old man came walking along the bank, carrying a fishing rod. I expected him to be angry with us, but he just smiled and mumbled something about getting old. He stood next to me, and when I offered him some squash, he took the bottle gratefully.

'It's a hot day,' he said.

[40]

I nodded.

He looked at the girls. 'Those two,' he said, 'I remember when they were babes in arms . . .' He passed the bottle back to me. 'Are you their friend?'

'I'm Rachel's cousin,' I said.

'Then you're a lucky boy.'

'Yes,' I said, but didn't explain that he didn't know half of it. Even if I had, he wouldn't have heard me, because he walked on without a word, or a look back in our direction.

When he'd gone, the girls climbed out of the river, and Rachel said 'What did he want?'

'Nothing.' I pointed to the squash. 'I let him have a drink.'

'Urgh!' she said. 'I hope you wiped it before you put the top back on.'

'Why? He was all right.'

'He gives me the creeps. He's always lurking.'

Cathy didn't say anything. She picked up a towel and dried herself, and then spread it on the grass and lay down. From where I was lying, I could see her feet and her legs as far as just above her knee – I couldn't see the rest of her unless I craned my neck. A wasp buzzed over me, and rested on top of the squash bottle.

When Rachel had dried herself and laid down too, the only noise came from the river and the rustling of the leaves and branches. A few birds sung; as we rested there, staring at the sky and counting flying insects as they passed over us, even Bob was quiet. He had found a shady spot beneath a tree. The atmosphere was charged with an electrifying peace, as grains of sugar are swirled into candy-floss. I heard Cathy sigh, and I remember the sound carried to me and turned in my heart as if my arteries and valves were

[41]

being flooded. Walls of mystery shuttered my eyes, and the sensation of drowning made my whole body creep. I bent around to look at her, and though the sun was in my eyes, I could see and almost reach out and touch her swimming costume. She was breathing shallowly and quietly; I put my hand up to shade my eyes – as I did, she said, 'What are you looking at?'

'I . . .' I stumbled. 'No. There's a wasp in your hair . . .'

'Oh!' she cried. 'Where?'

'Don't move,' I said, and I leant towards her, and looked into her hair. The wasp was in panic, struggling against the strands, drowning. I reached towards it, and after two attempts, managed to pick it up by the wings. 'There,' I said, holding it in front of her before flicking it away. 'Gone.'

'Oh . . .' she said, and smiled, with relief, I think. 'Thanks.'

'That's all right,' I said.

'I hate wasps.' She moved onto her hands and knees, bent towards me and kissed my lips before standing up and walking towards the swimming hole again. 'Nasty things,' she said, and dived into the water.

The kiss was so sudden that I hardly had time to notice it, but I could still feel it. I sat on the bank in a trance, and had even forgotten that Rachel was there. She sat up, saw Cathy swimming and yelled 'Wait for me!' I think all this happened in 1969, but when I saw Cathy last week, she swore it was 1970. We agreed though that it didn't really matter when it happened, because she didn't recall the events as I did, though their details have occupied a corner of my mind for twenty years, like the gates to a world I don't think I have ever seen.

MATANTE CORA

David Plante

One Christmas when I was a boy I was given as a gift a toy log cabin set which consisted of different lengths of brown dowel notched at each end so that they could be interlocked to form corners and walls, and, if the builder was good at it, doors and windows. The roof was made of flat green pieces of wood, and there was a red chimney. I made a log cabin in the middle of the living room, in the midst of aunts and uncles who had come to visit. After I put the roof on, I had a curious sense, lowering my head to floor level and looking into the cabin through the small door, that very little kept me from being able to actually go inside and live in that dim interior. It seemed to me I had lived in there. Inside, I would look out the doorway, not at a huge eye staring in at me, nor at the legs of chairs and the toes of my aunt Cora's shoes, but a landscape under snow.

My aunt Cora, whose French was greatly more grammatical than her English, said to me, 'Hey, you done a good job.'

I turned round and smiled at her. She always wore a green visor to protect her eyes, filmed by cataracts, from the light, or so she said. She refused to have an operation, however much pain her eyes gave her. To see, she had to open her eyes wide and stare, so those whitish eyes seemed to bulge. She kept her hands clasped in her lap and her feet crossed. She said, 'They could have used you in the old days.'

[45]

I smiled again, which was what a nephew was supposed to do towards an old aunt rather than speak.

Then she told me the story of how her *pepère*, my *arrière pepère*, had just managed to slam the door to his cabin before an Indian tomahawk hit him.

She was a big woman, with large shoulders and arms, but she sat like a well behaved girl. Her hair was white, with two white, artificial braids pinned to the sides of her head just above the black band of the visor. Her face was grey-white, and she had long black hairs just below her chin. The bodice of her blue taffeta dress was cut low to reveal the slopes of her great breasts, and she wore a necklace like magnified, rhinestone studded lace over her exposed flesh. The dress was long, with a very full skirt. Below it, her legs were in orange stockings and her black shoes with laces were the kind old women wore.

When she reached for a glass of soda that was being passed around on a tin tray, she made a kind of arabesque with her wrist as she slowly raised her arm, then delicately extended her long fingers to take a glass. At the same time, she uncrossed her feet and separated her legs so her knees rose sideways into her taffeta skirt. Her smile was large and strained.

It would not have been unthinkable, given the slow and deliberate way she moved, that she was wearing under her dress something, this something unthinkable, to bruise her flesh and cause her even more pain than her eyes did, if her eyes did cause her pain.

It was as though she brought to the surface of her big body the greatest attention possible to it, as though she, with her extravagant dress and jewellery, wanted others to be as aware of her body as she was. Of course, she knew her body was nothing and that no attention should be given to it. But if she made so

[46]

evident, with a sensuality that beamed about it, the presence of her flesh, she made even more evident her denial of her flesh. She knew that the first condition of a body – that is, the primary reason for anyone to have a body – was that it should suffer, that it should be subjected, in its suffering, to being nothing. Matante's attitude towards the body was like that of the image of a saint having her breasts cut off within a heavy gold frame, the frame making all the difference to the suffering endured. Her clothes and jewellery were the golden adornments of her religion on a body in agony.

She bored everyone with her detailed talk about her pains, which took up almost all her side of a conversation, but we never stopped her from talking, we listened.

Only with my father did she not talk. When she and my father sat together alone, they remained silent. This was not because they didn't have anything to say to one another. With all his sisters, with his mother too, even when making a visit to their homes, my father sat with them in silence. I would stand, unmoving, by his chair until he said it was time to leave.

Matante Cora's greatest longing, since she was a girl, was to enter a convent and become a nun. God had given her a vocation, she was sure. She wanted to wear the true clothes of her religion, the nun's black habit. But this was denied her.

She had, when still a girl, been accepted into a convent as a novice. The job assigned to her was to wash floors and clean toilets. The lower panes of the windows were painted so no one could see out, or in. After a year of washing floors and cleaning toilets, she was told she didn't have a vocation and she must leave the convent.

[47]

She told this story as more evidence of what she had suffered, not only physically but spiritually, for it was a great spiritual suffering to be denied the fulfilment of her greatest ambition. She nevertheless believed she did have a vocation, which might have been, it occurred to her as she prayed, that of suffering the denial of every single earthly fulfilment. She was not elected to be a member of her Church on earth as she wanted to be, so this left her with the heavenly Church, which she would, she dared hope, become a member of on her death. She knew in her soul she had a vocation, but this would be fulfilled only by her wearing the heavenly habit of a nun in God's unearthly Church.

I thought of Matante Cora when, in a catechism class, which was usually given in French by Mère St Joseph de Nazareth, a nun on a visit from Canada spoke to us about vocations. Whenever we were addressed by someone other than our regular teachers, we listened in fear. The nun, tall, stood before us, and, swaying a little, described to us the feelings we'd have if we did have a vocation, feelings which we should recognize because they were inspired in us by God, who Himself gave out the gift of a vocation: a feeling of being chosen for something special; a feeling that you were not like others, though the sense of feeling different didn't mean you thought you were better than others, but often meant you thought you were inferior; a feeling of wanting to devote yourself to something larger than yourself, though you knew that this something was so much greater than you you were not worthy of devoting yourself to it; a feeling of wanting to do something, something that was great, something that had never been done before, but that you knew couldn't be done without the help of a power greater than you; a feeling of wanting to give in, give yourself up totally, to that greater power. This tall nun from Canada swayed more and more with the ecstasy of her talk. When she finished, the class was so silent I could hear birds chirping outside in the school yard. We were in the seventh grade. After a moment, Mère St Joseph told us all to stand and, in chorus, thank the nun for coming from Canada to speak to us. Before leaving, the nun said that if anyone wanted to have a word with her, she would be in the office of Mère Superieure after the last class of the afternoon. No one had ever spoken to us as she had. She had spoken to us as if she knew what our feelings were.

In the school yard at recess, I was sitting on a stone wall with classmates. Another classmate came towards us and said, 'Pauline is going to see that Mother.'

'Oh?' I said.

'She thinks she has a vocation.'

I looked across the bare, sandy school yard, glinting with fragments of broken glass, to where Pauline was standing with other classmates, all girls. Like the others, she wore the school uniform, a dark blue shift over a white blouse with a pale blue ribbon at the collar, but she appeared to me to be suddenly essentially different from anyone else of us.

I didn't understand Pauline's vocation, and I never understood Matante Cora's. It was as though she was inhabited by an inner being, her true being, which belonged to a world different from her outer. A vocation made a person strange. Certainly Matante Cora was strange to me, though, at the same time, completely familiar, her talk about her sufferings as boring to me as it was to everyone else.

She never explained why she wasn't allowed to stay

[49]

in the convent and be professed. I wondered if it was
because she didn't wash the floors and clean the toilets
well enough, but, from something my mother told me,
which was, 'She was too avid,' I suspected Matante
Cora was asked to leave because she washed and
cleaned too well, fanatically.

It wasn't difficult to imagine her, a novice, so
fervent in her devotions that the Mother Superior
thought she was going too far: she recited her prayers
in a voice higher than the others, bowed her head in
adoration of the host lower than the others, kept
silences, her lips pressed together, with a greater
strictness than the others. And she insisted on suffering more than the others. She might have been
thought to be putting on an act, and was not sincere
in her devotions, so was not sincere in her vocation.

I understood my aunt believing she was sincere. To
her, the grander the demonstration, the grander the
sincerity. She could not really understand how a vast
proclamation of love should be thought by others to
be affected, when, in herself, she felt, felt with a depth
and width, the vastness of it. She sang out a sense of
that vastness, she bowed to it, she kept the rules of
silence, kept all the rules, in obeisance to the power
over her. She couldn't have been more sincere. She
replaced her positive body with a negative one, suffering her subjection to that vastness, but the more she
suffered the more insincere she was considered to be
by the Mother Superior, who, seeing her red, scalded
hands, told her that she must use less hot water in her
bucket when she washed the floor, whereas Cora had
thought that the hotter the water the more convincing
her mortification of the flesh would be, or so I imagine.
She never understood, never, that she could in any
way be insincere, and it bewildered her when she was

told she was, and that she only thought she had a vocation when in fact she didn't. Her love was great, and, to be equal to it, she should have shouted out her prayers, prostrated herself in the aisle, taken a vow of life-long silence along with vows of chastity and poverty. Her love was so great she should have to renounce her physical body for the attainment of the spiritual, which body alone could be united with her loved One, thrown herself into thorny, tangled rose bushes, and she should have found approval from the Mother Superior for this. She wanted a demonstration as great as her love. There was no way she could go too far.

To me, what was most amazing about Matante Cora was that she was incapable of being embarrassed. She embarrassed my mother, who, unlike my father, listened to her talk about how she had been, years before, denied the only thing she had ever really wanted in this world, her mystical marriage, but that she had had to accept God's will that she was not worthy of such a marriage. My mother would say, 'I'm so sorry for you,' and blush. Matante Cora never blushed. She'd press her open hand to her bosom and say, 'I accept all the unhappiness sent to me.'

Shortly after she left the convent, she married. She knew before she married that the man was an alcoholic and ran around with other women. Marriage didn't change this. He would leave her alone in their tenement apartment for days, and come back drunk, dirty, and smelling of perfume. He'd be too drunk even to undress, and Cora would do this for him, and as she'd undress him he'd vomit. If he were really drunk, he shit (my aunt used this word, which my mother never did) in his pants, too, and Cora would have to clean that up as well as the vomit. He'd lean on her and she'd stagger getting him into the bathroom. Sometimes he'd fall, and she couldn't get him up, so she'd have to wash him where he lay, then cover him with a blanket and let him sleep where he was until he woke. In the meantime, she'd wash his clothes. This happened over and over, and after each time he'd say he'd never do it again, but he would, he'd go off, sometimes for a whole week, and Matante Cora always had him back.

She'd tell my mother this, and my mother's face would be pink with a blush.

'What could I do?' Matante Cora said. 'He was my husband.'

'What did your mother say?' my mother asked.

'She said just that: I married him, I had to live with him.'

My mother bit her lower lip.

Matante Cora said, 'He lived off the women he picked up in bars. When he was out, I'd lie in bed wondering what woman he was in bed with, where, and how long it would take her before she'd finally throw him out. I could always count on that: that the woman he was living off would throw him out. And then he'd come back to me.'

My mother winced. 'He must have smelled of those women.'

'He smelled. He smelled of more than cheap perfume. Sometimes the smell that came off him made me want to vomit. He'd say, Give me a kiss, give me a kiss.'

'You didn't.'

Matante Cora raised her large hands in a gesture of: what could she do? 'He was my husband.'

'You should have left him.'

'But he was my husband.'

[52]

'Yes,' my mother said.

If I, standing by my mother, had heard all this before, my mother must have heard it many times before.

My mother said, 'It makes me realize how lucky I am having the husband I do.'

Matante Cora said, 'When he started to beat me up, my mother told me to leave him, to come back home and live with her. I was always black and blue. Hey, once he threw a knife at me, but it missed. I wouldn't leave him. I wouldn't leave him because I knew he was my penance.'

'A penance for what?'

As with her whole body, which rose a little from the chair, Matante Cora said, 'For my life.'

My mother drew back.

'Hey,' Matante Cora said, 'sometimes he'd come back from being away with some woman, maybe a lot of women, and, drunk, he'd want me to go to bed with him, and I'd push him away, but he was stronger than I was and pushed me – '

My mother said, 'I've got a husband who doesn't even drink.'

'You're lucky.'

'I know I am.'

'He'd leave me when I became pregnant, too, he'd go off for weeks, a month. When he'd come back, he'd never tell me where he'd been. If I asked, he beat me up – that is, if he wasn't so drunk he was throwing up and shitting and not able to hit me. And when my daughter was born, he became worse.'

'For the sake of the baby, shouldn't you have gone to your mother?'

'No. And my mother refused to see me because I didn't go to her. Everyone refused to see me because I

[53]

wouldn't accept help. But I had chosen this life. I knew what he was like when I married him. My marriage was no one else's fault but mine. I was alone, I was alone once for a period of three months, and I had no money.'

'He brought you money?'

'He always brought home some of the money he got from the women.'

'Oh, Cora,' my mother said, and raised a hand to a cheek. She hadn't heard this fact before. 'You didn't take it?'

'I took it. We needed to eat, the baby needed to eat. When he was away for those three months, I didn't have money to buy food, and my baby starved to death.'

My mother raised her other hand to a cheek.

'I watched her die,' Matante Cora said. 'She was in her crib, a tiny, skinny girl, and suddenly she began to grow, to grow and grow, her arms and legs especially, and then she cried out and died.'

'And you didn't kick him out after that?'

'Well, I couldn't keep him out. If I did, he would, I knew, be lost, and he would die outside the Church. He was my penance. I had to save him. He would have been lost for eternity, my husband, if I didn't save him. I couldn't let that happen.'

'Yes,' my mother said.

'And I did save him. When he came back after the death of our baby, he was in a worse state than ever. He was covered in sores.'

'You slept in the same bed with him?'

'I slept in the same bed with him. I took care of him.'

'Where did you get the money?'

'He came back with enough money.'

'Cora, my God.'

'He died in the Church. He confessed and received
Extreme Unction, so he was saved. He died in our
bed.'

My mother lowered her hands into her lap.

Matante Cora said, 'And a short while after he died,
I found out that I was pregnant again.'

My father, who might have been sitting at the same
table over which this conversation took place, would
not have said a word, but would have stared into
space.

When we were alone, my mother asked me, always,
'Did you believe what Cora said?'

I'd shrug.

My mother would go on, 'Well, true or not, she
should have left out that part about her baby dying.'

The other big topic of conversation – conversation?
– for Matante Cora was the job she had in a laundry,
which she'd got after the death of her husband some
thirty years before and still had.

After her husband's death, she moved in to the
apartment of her mother, who took care of the baby
while she was at work. The laundry was a half hour
walk away, and on the way Matante Cora said prayers.
By the time she was at the junction she would have
said her first prayer, by the bottom of the hill she
would have said ten prayers, with meditations separ-
ating them. Most of these prayers were Our Fathers
and Hail Marys, but some she made up herself, and
these were pleas to be relieved of her suffering, but
only if it was His will. If it was His will that she
should suffer, she would submit. She offered up all
her suffering to Him.

Her job at the laundry was to sort out the dirty
clothes that came in canvas bags. She would sit on a

[55]

low stool, in the midst of these bags, and she'd open one, take out dirty, stained sheets, dirty shirts, dirty underwear and socks, some of them so dirty you couldn't believe people had used them up till the time they sent them to the laundry, and make sure they had indelible laundry marks on them, then separate them out into baskets. She would find diapers filled with shit, from a mother too lazy to do anything but wrap them up and throw them into the bag.

My mother, who, again, would be the listener, would say, 'How could a mother do that?'

Matante would answer, 'You don't know what people are like out in the world. You don't.'

That was true. My mother didn't. Matante Cora did.

She would describe, in detail, some of the more disgusting states of items received to be washed and ironed. Sometimes I didn't understand. My mother would explain, 'No, Cora, no, that isn't possible.'

'There it is,' Cora would answer. 'That's what human beings are like.'

'Oh no.'

'But they are. They are.'

'How can you do such a job?'

At times, my mother said she wished she could have a job, it would get her out of the house, but my father wouldn't allow her, partly because it would have been humiliating for him, a worker, for his wife to work, and partly because he, who knew the world and what human beings did in it, wanted to protect her from it. My aunt Belle, my mother's younger sister, who thought my father and his sisters came from a more primitive background than she and my mother, said to me once, 'Your father has always wanted to protect your mother. If she couldn't cope with the world, it was because he wouldn't let her try. He wanted to keep to his God-darn backward ways, in the back woods.'

Matante Cora would say to my mother, 'I have to work.'

'Couldn't you find another job?'

'This was the job God gave me.'

Matante Cora described the state of an undershirt in a way that made my stomach turn over, and yet I listened: the undershirt must have belonged to a man with a terrible disease, because the shirt was stiff, *stiff*, with dried blood and pus and whatever else had leaked from his sores and dried on the cloth. One of the colored women who also worked sorting out the dirty laundry found it, and swore and wouldn't take it out of the bag. Slowly, elegantly, Matante Cora took it out, held it up by its short sleeves, and to show the others that she had no fear of what was merely human, with a smile, for a moment raised it and pressed her face into it. The other women screamed, or some of them did. One told her she was crazy. No one in the laundry would have understood her doing this even if she'd explained. No one would have understood that, so sure of the uncorruptibility of what protected her, she could put herself in the midst of corruption, and feel, after, totally pure. Nothing, nothing upset Matante Cora. She didn't have to explain that to anyone in her family.

Only my mother, red faced, would bite her lower lip hard.

Then Matante would describe her prayers on her way home from work. Sometimes, she would have to stop walking, because suddenly, there where she was on the sidewalk, she would be so taken over she could feel herself, or some self in her, being raised, raised

[57]

high, and the self that had been walking didn't know how to move.

My mother said to me later, 'I wish she hadn't told us about that undershirt.'

To her sisters, Cora couldn't talk about religion, as they, like my father, wouldn't listen, but she told them jokes she had heard at the laundry, crude jokes about shit. She never told any of these jokes to my father, and not to her sisters when my father was present. In telling them, she would stick out her large, wet tongue through a wide, strained smile, her cataract-white eyes bulging. When one of her sisters told a joke, she would listen with that expression, too, repeatedly and excitedly nodding her head so her earrings swung.

She accepted miracles in the parish with as much ease as she accepted the basest of what was human. It did not surprise her that someone saw the eyes of a statue of the Virgin move and fill with tears, or that someone else heard his name called out when praying alone in church. More miraculous events occurred in other Franco parishes, as far away as Pawtucket and Woonsocket, towns with Indian names. In one parish blood spurted from the floor when the curé accidentally dropped a consecrated host (the spot had to be washed over and over by the nuns, and all the cloths that were used had to be burned). And if she took it for granted that God manifested Himself in such ways, she took it for granted that the devil manifested himself also. She herself had seen the fingerprints of a man burned into a wooden post in the cellar of his house, a post the man had grabbed on to when the devil had appeared to take him away, but the man hadn't been able to hold on, for the burning devil was stronger than he was and pulled him away.

[58]

Sometimes my mother would say about Cora, 'Well, I admire her. She has great faith.'

Matante Cora believed in the most miraculous without having to overcome any doubt, without even wishing she had more evidence for believing in the miraculous than she had. I more and more felt that she and I belonged to different Churches. I would have been embarrassed, impossibly embarrassed, to belong to hers. She wasn't.

The miracles she most believed in were cures. She had never met anyone who was cured, but there was no question that many had been, by prayer and adoration. She implored to have her illnesses cured by prayer and by placing holy images in odd places in her apartment, in drawers, under mattresses, in the pockets of coats hung in closets. She longed for this miracle: *'ma guerison'*. Whenever she said *'ma guerison'* she pressed her bosom and bowed her head a little. She wouldn't go to a doctor. When my mother asked her why not, she said, 'Doctors rob you.' My father, too, never went to a doctor. It never seemed to discourage Matante Cora that her miraculous cure didn't occur. She needed no signs, no revelations. Her longing to be cured wasn't really a longing, but a heart-felt accommodation that she wouldn't be, and for my aunt to accommodate this fatality required a greater expansion of spirit than to hope. It must have been because of her expecting no revelation, nothing, that I, though on one low level fascinated by her faith, was, on a higher level, bored by it. Matante Cora, in a strange inversion of positive longing into negative accommodation, believed that miracles didn't, couldn't, happen to her, and her fate was to offer up forever the illnesses God would not cure, which she did ecstatically.

What came to me at the time when I thought about

Matante Cora's faith and its difference from mine was
that all offerings to her God were of her sufferings.
This didn't strike me as odd, it simply struck me.
Even to me, to sacrifice was to cause yourself a degree
of pain or discomfort, such as to walk up the stairs
rather than to take an elevator, or to deny yourself
pleasure, such as candy. Walking up the flights of
stairs, denying myself the piece of candy in the glass
bowl, I would say within myself: I offer this up.
Matante Cora's list of pains was much more impressive
than any I could impose on myself – and, in any case,
I never did think that pains really should be imposed
on yourself, but should be visited on you, and I wasn't
certain if Matante had imposed her pains on herself or
they had been visited upon her. She offered up her
painful eyes, she offered up her tired feet, her head-
ache; she offered up everything she had to endure at
the laundry, and everything she had had to endure in
her marriage; she offered up her disappointment in
not being accepted as a nun; she offered it all up,
kneeling and holding it up on a great, round, golden
tray, as a sacrifice to her God. I wondered why it had
never occurred to her, as it did to me, that God might
have been more attentive to pleasures offered Him
rather than sufferings, so your offering of the candy
melting in your mouth might have been received by
God with much less indifference than He received an
offering of a canker sore.

Certainly, Matante was aware of sensual pleasures.
I suspect her marriage survived on them. She was
aware of her body. In the country where she would
come to visit us, she'd emerge from the house in her
old fashioned, woollen bathing suit, her stockings
rolled down to her knees, and she would stand in the
midst of her nephews and smooth the clinging woollen

material over her breasts, her large nipples showing, then would place her hand on her hips, her pinkies sticking out wearing, as always, the green visor to protect her eyes from the light. But Matante never realized that her very sensuality, in which she must have taken at least the pleasure of her awareness of it, could ever, ever be of interest to God.

Well, I know why she and I were made to believe that our offerings to God should be of our sufferings. At least, I know why she believed this. What else could she have done with her pain? Compared to it, her pleasures were nothing. The great pleasure of her childhood was oranges at Christmas. Because she had no toys, my father, older than she, made her a small doll's house, and because she left it hanging about – *une trainerie*, which no Franco household could tolerate – her mother burned it, and the last Cora saw of it was the black hot plate of the coal range close down on its burning roof. This wasn't cruelty. My grandmother simply did not understand the pleasure of a doll's house, and I should think Cora didn't, either, which was why she left it hanging around and never played with it. I don't think I understand pleasure, though I also don't think I understand pain in the way Matante Cora did. Her life was made of pain, and the only significance she could give what her life was made of was to plead to God to accept it. She said, 'I offer up my pain, because that is all I have.'

Because it was all she had, she exaggerated it to make it more than what she had. She exaggerated her sufferings so, they seemed false. And perhaps they were false, if what my father, who never expressed the sympathy towards her my mother did, said was true: 'She brought all her sufferings on herself.' My mother

[61]

asked, 'Why would she do that?' My father shrugged one shoulder.

I thought: If she did bring them on herself, they are false, because only what comes on you and takes you over and is much more powerful than you, however much you fight it, is true.

But were my devotions true? All I was ever over-whelmed by, and had resisted until I gave in and offered this up as a prayer, was the pure pleasure of the body. But that ended in my feeling ridiculous. To be overwhelmed truly, I would never, after, if there was an after, feel ridiculous for having given in. I felt ridiculous after the solitary pleasure of the body because I knew I could have resisted. All my giving in showed was that I had a weak will. For it to be true, you could not *want* to be overwhelmed. It had to be forced on you against yourself, against your will. You had to fight it and fight it, and, most likely, it would be something you did not want, had never wanted. But nothing, nothing but my own sensuality pressed in on me. Against my will pushing out, pushing out with a passion almost equal to the one pressing in, nothing tried to possess me truly, purely. And yet I kept up my devotions, expectantly.

I thought I was essentially different from Matante Cora, but, like her, I believed, without ever saying so to anyone, that the only true life was made up of suffering, and as God, in His infinite wisdom, only accepted what was true, it was only a life of suffering He would accept. But if Matante Cora had brought her suffering on herself, which falsified it, what could I, who, in relation to her, had had a life of pleasure, claim as suffering? I couldn't claim anything. Perhaps the only real difference between Matante Cora and me was that she went on with her devotion with no awareness at all that she might be false in it, expecting nothing, and I was beginning to think I was incapable of true devotion.

I rejected, and then objected to, Matante Cora's superstitions.

If I was to be truly overwhelmed, I would have to be by something I could not imagine. It would have nothing to do with what Matante imagined as religion, even though that something were great suffering. Such suffering was itself unimaginable.

I did not believe Matante Cora's religion was true, because it was based on her willing, wilfully willing, her religion to be a religion of suffering. At the same time, I, too, believed only suffering made religion true, and I could understand Matante's incomprehension at being thought insincere in such suffering. How much more must she suffer for it to be sincere? Not even my mother really believed her. I knew that my own, my entirely spiritual suffering, was false. To the degree that you could help yourself – as Matante, a big boned, strong woman, could, and as I, healthy and having years before attained the age of reason, could help ourselves – your personal suffering was false. Only the truly helpless could suffer truly.

At one time, perhaps, her ancestors in the woods, and, more remotely, mine, had truly suffered, and had had to offer this suffering to God as the only way of relieving themselves of it, for if they couldn't make sense of it, He did. But Matante and I were not living in the woods.

Because I was so much like Matante Cora in my disposition, and because I saw so much falsity in that disposition, I wanted to be completely different from her. When she started to tell my mother about the death of her baby, I, who used to listen attentively no matter how many times I had heard the story, would leave them, or, like my father, look away, pretending I was not listening.

Privately, I wrote poems, secular poems, about the great, suffering world.

I wondered if Matante Cora ever thought about the world. I doubted she did. I doubted she ever prayed for the world.

The last time I saw her before I went off to college was at the lake house where my parents spent the summer. She had asked if she could come on a certain Sunday when she said the lakes were blessed and had special curative powers. I didn't know what of her beliefs were derived from the Indians, though I hardly thought of Matante as a quarter breed (she said, Blackfoot) Indian or even as a Catholic: she was simply Matante Cora, who had her own beliefs. In the house, she put on her old bathing suit, came out, posed for my older brothers and laughed, a deep, primitive laugh, then went down to the lake along a path through the pine trees. She didn't have her visor on. I, in my bathing suit, followed her. She was wearing her black granny shoes, the laces undone, and her white legs were riddled with blue and purple veins. At the lake edge, she asked me to stand by her so she could lean on me to take off her shoes, then, slowly, with calm, solemn ceremony, she walked out into the water, holding her hands, palms down, just over the surface, and when she got to her waist she stopped. I stayed on the shore and watched. Her mouth was moving rapidly: she was praying. As she brought her hands together she submerged them into the green water and, with a continuous, round gesture, raised them, palms up and dripping with water, towards her face, which she at the same time lowered.

[64]

She pressed her dripping palms to her eyes and held them pressed while she prayed, her jaw as if jerking in spasms. After her ritual, she came out of the lake and leaned on me to put on her shoes. I let her go back up the path alone, and dove into the lake to swim.

When I got back to the weed grown, mossy lawn before the house where there were chairs among the birch trees, I found her sitting on a settee, made of wooden slats, with my mother. My father was sitting on a chair at a distance. My brothers had gone. Matante was wearing the blue taffeta dress she had worn for as long as I could remember on special occasions, such as a visit to her brother in the country. She again wore her green, transparent visor.

I, wet, sat in a chair across from my father, my mother and aunt between us.

Matante was telling my mother about the pain she suffered in her eyes.

Then she began to talk about her dead mother, and my father turned his head towards her with attention. She said that one year, she and her mother hadn't been able to get to a lake on the day when they were blessed, but, as it happened to rain that day, they put pans out in the back yard to collect the rain water, which they considered would be even more curative than lake water as it came directly from God. Mémère had saved some of that water in a bottle.

'Do you still have some?' my father asked.

'I can give you some,' his sister said.

'I'd like to have some.'

'What's wrong?'

My father raised his strong chin and didn't answer.

Matante Cora said, 'I saw her, I saw our mother, last night, she appeared to me when I went into her bedroom – '

[65]

Quickly, my father said, 'Enough of that.'

He looked, I thought, alarmed, though my father never expressed much in his face except when he was being photographed. (Unlike his sister, he seemed to have a very high tolerance of pain, so, if wounded, as he once was at his work when he caught the tip of a finger in a machine, he did nothing but breathe in and fill his lungs, but he didn't utter, and his face remained stark. Perhaps his sister was similar, which made the suffering of her pains all the more pretentious. I don't know if this high tolerance of pain, the lack of expression, was Indian. Nor do I know if it was because of our Indian blood, that my father and his sons were not allergic to poison ivy, which I, knowing I wasn't, used to pull out by the roots, my mother, who was allergic, shouting at me. And I don't know if my father's alarm at his sister's recounting the appar-ition of their dead mother, and his immediately stop-ping her, was Indian.)

Matante Cora turned away from my father and said to my patient mother, 'I pray for my mother, too, to intercede for me in my offerings. I have a special prayer to my mother.' She pressed a hand to her bosom. 'I say, *"Ma chère mère, vous qui avez connu tant de souffrance dans votre vie, vous qui –"*'

My mother glanced at me, and I saw, as the blush rose into her neck, her slight smile. I smiled back.

I avoided Matante Cora on my visits to the parish after I left for college, and when, during the summer after my Freshman year, she came to the lake, I went out in the rowboat or stayed in my room.

My mother wrote to me, when I moved away from America to live in Europe, that Matante was, by a special dispensation from the bishop, professed a nun on her death bed, and laid out and buried in the habit of a nun.

MY LOVER'S TOUCH

Patrick Roscoe

One night, when I am six years old, I fall asleep in my bed in the house where my mother and father also live, but wake up somewhere else. I am naked and hungry and cold. The room is bare and dark. There are no windows, and the light socket on the ceiling is without a bulb. The door is locked. I know, as I am certain my heart will beat again and then again, that my mother and father will not unlock the door, and will not bring me food and blankets, and will not comfort me. They do not know where I am, they cannot come to me, they do not wish to find me: the reason is not important. It doesn't matter why I live in this room, and others equally dark and bare, for the next eight years.

My sense of time is imprecise, and marked only by the ticking of my heart. After waiting several days in darkness, I am old as the ancient man who has searched one thousand years for love. He has crawled across the world, and I between these four walls, to find the holy places where He might appear. Only the desperate are truly hopeful.

If you stood outside the door and listened through the keyhole, you would hear me say: sky is blue, grass is green, God is good. These are the old songs I croon, my arms wrapped around myself tightly, tightly. I wonder if anyone hears me. Listens but does not answer.

At the beginning I sometimes wish for a bed. On the cement floor I lie pressed against a wall, trying to warm the cold stone with the heat of my body. The stone soaks up my heat but offers none in return. I attempt to recall sensations of softness and warmth with such strength that there might appear beneath my head a pillow, against my skin a sheet of silk. The more frequently and vividly a vision is remembered, the sooner it fades, as though inside ourselves are stored, like money in banks, impressions which must be added to and not only drawn from. Or we become a vault as cold and empty as this room. Stone is hard and cold, I must repeatedly remind myself, while the darkness blurs all definition. What is soft, warm? I grope blindly around the room, until I realize there is only one such thing. I touch my bare skin.

My skin is porous, and as the chambers beneath it empty of old impressions of colour and light, darkness seeps inside to replace them. It fills me until, if you opened a flap of my skin like a window and peered inside, you would be unable to discern any difference between the outer and inner darkness. In this way my body, swallowed up by the lightless room, seems to float in a big black belly. I savour all feelings of pain and hunger and cold which suggest my continuing existence. I would be grateful for any touch upon my skin, no matter from what emotion it was born.

My ears learn to listen. I see sounds and hear shapes. Those that reach through my walls are never loud or clear enough to permit me to see a person, a car, a bird. They are indistinct as strangers' faces in the night. By their quality, however, I sense that somewhere there is day as well as night. Periodically a needle is sunk into my arm and I fall into deeper darkness, wake in another room. Except that its temperature is slightly higher or lower, air staler or fresher, sounds more or less muffled, the new room might be the old one. Then I discover countless minute differences between textures and flaws of this cement and that of my previous home. But the darkness is constant and may be relied upon. A thousand secret quirks in its character I alone know and cherish; like any true and loyal ally I will not reveal them, though you beat me. I will only say that sometimes I believe I have been taken to a room just beside the last one. At other times, sounds that come to me suggest I am now higher above the world or deeper inside it, nearer or further from the heart of a city. Yet there is never a line of golden light beneath the locked door, and without this crack of illumination I have no proof that the globe is not a black egg, twirling somewhere beyond the warmth of the sun, the light of the stars. The moves from one obscure void to another have no meaning or purpose I can discover, except to teach me: every room is dark and cold and bare.

Always the only article in the room is a bucket in which I expel my wastes. When it is not emptied for several weeks, the air I breathe smells so strongly of decay that it feels to me like a heavy substance, both liquid and solid, like a swamp, into which I sink. I spit on my skin and try to wash it clean with saliva. The bucket makes me more thankful for the darkness, which conceals the tireless journeys of roaches toward and from their pail of food. When I am most hungry, I view my excrement with appetite. I drool.

Every three or four or five days footsteps approach my door. The sound is purposeful and loud, suggesting its source is a large body and firm mind. Sometimes the steps pass my door, fading into silence. Maybe they stop just outside, and if my heart were not beating so loudly I might hear through the inch of iron the sound of another's breathing. A body listens, then walks away in the direction from which it came. Or perhaps a key grates in the lock. What I call food is thrown inside my room; anyway, I eat it. Soon I begin to wonder about the hand that throws the food, then I become curious about the heart that throws the hand. My need to know consumes me, and on the first occasion that the mass of flesh and bones and blood enters my room, I welcome it as explorers greeted their original sight of a new world. I feel warmth and weight strike me strongly, and treasure the discovery. Like the wheel and gravity, the act of love has always existed, though upon finding it for ourselves we insist it is our invention alone.

As his footsteps draw near, my heart pounds more and more loudly, and in their rhythm. A thin, mechanical cry, like that of a baby bird in a nest, swells through my throat. I do not know if I will be beaten or fed, and my emotion is an equal measure of fear of hurt and hope for comfort. Slowly this feeling becomes one inseparable thing, and I find pleasure in pain. I take satisfaction from the blows of his fists and feet against the surface of my skin, and this feeling enters me more deeply when he fills my body's openings. His generosity touches me. Sometimes he feeds me after it is over, sometimes not. Eventually food becomes as unimportant as light and warmth; when my belly grumbles, it is calling hungrily for his hands, and the only taste I savour is the salty richness of my blood. If I were not hungry, he would not feed me, I realize. If I were not cold, his body would not warm me; if there were light, he would not illuminate the darkness. His visits are unpredictable and always expected. Over the years, I notice, they occur with gradually increasing frequency and possess a more intense, powerful character. I wonder where they will lead. Feel him push further into me, like a brave explorer daring to enter more deeply the dark labyrinth from which he might not emerge alive.

He has never spoken to me, nor have I heard him moan, grunt, cry. I do not know his face except as darkness made solid. If I were free and walking down the street, I would not recognize him though he bumped into me and apologized at length. I would look into every face that passed and wonder if it were his. Strangers would glance quickly away from the small boy with staring, starving eyes. I would believe every face his face.

Alone. Waiting for his next visit, I try to imagine him. I consider whether his face is lined or smooth. Is his hair dark or light or turning grey? By his strength, I know he is not old. But I picture his eyes as old, and sad. I conjure his presence until he becomes as clear to me as someone I have once known, but forgotten.

Does he miss me when he goes away? Ache for me as I ache for him? I see him walking from this room, straightening his tie, smoothing his hair, with his handkerchief wiping away a spot of my blood that trembles like a tear upon his wrist. He drives home, stopping at a supermarket to buy the loaf of bread his wife has asked him to pick up on the way. His blue car pulls into a driveway before a pretty house. A small boy is sitting on the front steps. He looks hungrily at his father, who tosses three pennies to his son as he passes into the house. The husband kisses the wife. The family eats supper. Afterwards, the man sits in the living-room with a newspaper held before his face, like a shield. The woman gazes at the man, but sees only headlines that scream war, murder, accident. As she turns to him in bed, he moves away. I should check on Rickie, he says. He stands above the bed in

[73]

which the small boy lies with closed eyes though awake. The father's fists are hidden in his pockets. He looks down upon his son's face, which is smooth and white as a fresh, unmarked piece of paper. The father does not touch his son, the boy's eyes do not open. When he sleeps at last, the boy sees things that make him wish he dreamed pure darkness.

He has been beaten and kicked until filled with pain completely, I know. My body feels his desperate attempts to free himself from this old and lasting hurt. There is anger and sadness when such release does not occur, and steadily growing violence in his efforts to achieve it. I feel inadequate when he leaves me, as troubled as he was before. I would like to kiss away every tear in his eyes, stroke his back with tenderness. I believe I can save him. But I find myself protecting my eyes and kidneys and other vulnerable places from his blows; however much I want to, I cannot give myself up to him completely. He tries to smash through my skin so he can curl his whole body inside my dark empty room, and float there like a fetus that knows only warmth and comfort. The words of love I wish to utter emerge from my mouth as a very high loud squeal, which resembles the noise made by a pig being slaughtered and which continues until he forces my head into the pail of waste or fills my mouth with some part of himself. When he is gone, the cuts and bruises left upon my body burn with warmth and I feel, in the cold darkness, a hot bright fire near to me. My skin throbs and aches, remembering my lover. I feel his touch still upon me and I am not alone. The emptiness of his absence, my room, is filled. Yes, I wait for him with longing and pray that when he returns I can heal him at last.

Three times an angel has appeared to me – or that

[74]

is what I call her, since she resembles my memory of
that ornament that stood on top of the Christmas tree
in the pretty house. She floats down from the darkness
above me and illuminates my room with her presence.
My eyes are not used to such light. It dazzles, blinds.
She wraps me in her wings, which are warm and soft
as all feathers. Milk and honey are what she feeds me
during long, sweet kisses. She kisses the sores on my
body and they are healed. She bathes me in scented
water and rubs my skin with fragrant oils, murmuring
soft sounds which might mean: one day the darkness
will turn to light; or, the darkness is not so bad; or,
the darkness is for the best. Then, with a wave of her
wand, she is gone. I hate her. Not because she doesn't
carry me away on her strong wings; I do not wish to
leave my room, and would not go with her if she
begged. But I have been familiar with pain and cold
and dark hunger. They were my good friends, and the
brief visitations of my angel only turn them into bitter
enemies whom I must fight until I am conquered.
When I am beaten, they are on my side again and tell
me, warningly: we are constant companions, we are
not fickle friends, it is less painful to lie always in
darkness than sometimes in light. We will win every
war.

The time of waiting can pass slowly. I repeat my
prayers: bless him, save him, bring him back. Dragging hours are filled by recalling his last visit. Replay
that act of love over and over until it becomes a film
in my head I can start at the flick of a switch. Crouched
against the wall, I watch the same scenes recur. There
are certain favourite ones. Play them in slow motion,
make the pleasure last and last. Touch my skin and
feel the unique imprint of his hand. The tender
bruises. Happy.

[75]

But in the darkness my touch is sometimes clumsy. I fumble with the switch and by accident start a film I do not wish to see and cannot halt. I see a boy of five years sitting on the front steps of a pretty house. He sits there because the sunlight is warm. He wears a pair of short blue pants and a white shirt with short sleeves. He wraps his arms around his bare knees and rests his head upon them. Through the open window behind him floats music. His mother is listening to the radio while she cooks supper. Tonight there will be macaroni, baked soft and warm. The cheddar cheese will be melted creamily throughout, the blood-red tomatoes sudden bombs of flavour, the top a crust of golden crumbs. The scent of cooking food and the sound of music are ribbons that twine around the boy. He narrows his eyes until sunlight enters them like a crack of golden light beneath the door of a dark room. He is waiting for his father to come home from work. Then they will eat. The blue car will turn the corner and approach slowly down the street. The boy will watch it steadily, because if he glances away even quickly the car will turn into another driveway and his father will go into another house, pausing to toss copper pennies to another boy, who will bury them like pirate treasure.

After the wrong film plays and the strong images fill me, I cannot feel my lover. There is no dark space inside me for him to enter. I see him brutally loving another boy, who is smaller than me. Who cries and cries. He still sobs after my lover leaves the room. Shut up. I tell him, because the sound irritates me and because I am jealous. The boy weeps until he melts into a pool of tears. I lap up the salty puddle greedily, and he is gone.

A month later I can feel my lover's touch again. His

[76]

gentle, tender caresses. Afterwards I am surprised to find my skin sore, my heart bleeding. Two words twist and coil and wrap around each other in my mind. Love hurts.

My ears become more sensitive to sound the longer they are surrounded by immediate silence. I come to believe the muffled sounds that pass through my walls are cries of other boys who also await a consoling lover. They weep when he is with them and when he is not there. Every cry uttered through time and space is the echo of one voice, I think. Listen to my voice escape from a boy who walks the tightrope of the equator and from one who leans his back against the Great Wall of China. From one who treads on air, above the new moon. Their cries bounce between my four walls, echo in the hollow space inside me. Or is this sound the beating of my heart?

I hear the turning key. Although it scrapes in the lock, the door does not open. Footsteps move away, leaving silence behind. He has not come to me in a week, my skin holds no stinging memory of his touch. I need to feel him upon me, against me, inside me. My fists hammer on the door and my voice calls out. I turn the doorhandle. It opens. After one thousand failed attempts to open my door, I believed it useless to touch it again. At once I know that since the moment I ceased trying, years ago, the door has been unlocked. The sound of a turning key has been, always, the protest of my rusted heart upon his entrance.

I am afraid to leave my room because it is my only home, and for a moment fear that I will lose it forever holds me there. But I must find him. Suddenly, I doubt he will come to me again, for I have failed to swallow all his darkness, so he is going to another bare room where another boy waits hungrily. I leave, walking down a long, dimly lit hallway. On both sides of me are closed doors like the one I have just opened. They are scratched and marked, but without numbers. Through them comes the sound of crying boys. As my footsteps approach, the cries stop; and I sense breath held, pulses racing in hope. When I pass by, the cries begin again, in a higher key. I could open any of these doors, fall upon a waiting boy, soothe him with my loving blows. But I need such comfort myself and walk on in search of it. The empty hallway bends. I turn a corner, then reach a flight of stairs leading down. I descend them to a door below, open it, and find myself on a street at dawn. Night is leaving the world, a red planet is rising in the sky, I am falling into darkness.

Warm. Soft. White. I presume I am lying in the arms of my angel, then see I am in a bed in a white room. The sheets are also very white, and so are the bandages that cover various parts of my body. A tube runs from a glass tank filled with clouded liquid and into a vein in my left arm. My lungs cannot breathe this thin, odourless air and my eyes cannot bear this bright light. My skin cannot breathe beneath these bandages, blankets, sheets. The pillow and bed beneath me are not solid or hard enough, I am sinking into softness. Drowning, suffocating. I gasp and struggle until hands appear to hold me down. They are not his hands. They belong to bodies clothed in white, to faces bearing expressions I do not remember how to read. Do they convey love? Hate? Sounds issuing from their mouths speak a language foreign to me. A needle sinks into my right arm, and I am filled with joy because I will wake in another dark room, and my lover will come to me there. Before falling into blackness, I see the sky outside the window. It is white. The air that enters the open window stings my eyes and hurts my throat with its freshness. It flutters the white curtain, like an angel's wing.

I waken to the same white room, the same bright light. Disappointment. The light drains the darkness from me, illuminating the empty space beneath my skin, leaving me weak and weary and sad. I lie very still and silent, becoming familiar with the routine around me. I wait, but only women in white visit me. When they touch my forehead or wrists, their hands are as light as fingers of air. The tube is taken from my left arm, my right arm is injected less often. My hair is cut and I am bathed. Later the bandages are removed. I watch mouths open and close, sometimes suspecting the noise they make is meant for me. It has no meaning. I strain to summon sensations precious to me – cold, darkness, hunger – but the bodies that bend over me refuse to let me live in my former state of grace. They are enemies who plot to kill me with attention. No matter how tightly I close my eyes, some light seeps inside their lids. Even at night scattered lights glow around me. Wounds on the skin of darkness.

A man comes once each day. By my bed he sits and moves his mouth. I wait for fists to strike my body, which aches more painfully as each sore heals, each bruise vanishes. When the man does not touch me and when I remain silent, we are both disappointed. I wonder what wrong I am doing that he does not lovingly hurt me. I struggle to speak. Lay me on the hard floor and love me with all your strength, I will say when my clumsy tongue learns to move again. I make sounds and the man's head nods. The first word

[79]

I correctly form is not the one I expected to say. Darkness, I beg.

They ask my name and age and place of birth. They desire to know what happened before I was found on the street. Who did this to you? What was done to you? Where? How long? I can only say that once there was a dark room and a man. Before that? I describe the boy who sat on the steps of the pretty house. Was that you? I hesitate. Then I mention my angel. I say that one day she will come to me again. Lift me on to her strong wings. Carry me back to the dark room. Save me.

They move me to another room, also white. Sometimes I am supposed to lie on the bed, sometimes I am supposed to sit in the chair, sometimes I am supposed to walk around a larger room where other people, dressed in the same white robes I wear, also walk. Eat this. Then go to sleep. Now wake up. I am obedient. I speak and they make dark lines upon white paper. They look at each other and exchange single words: shock, damage, trauma, amnesia. The more darkness they put upon the paper, the happier they are. I learn to please them; it is so easy to know what they want. Keep my eyes open and blink the lids. Look at people when they speak to me. Pull the corners of my mouth upwards. Don't mention my angel or my lover in the darkness. I please them, but they offer me no reward in return. No love.

One day I ask for a pair of blue shorts and a shirt with short white sleeves. They smile, giving me a pair of long blue pants. It's winter, they say, seeing my disappointment at the length of the cloth. I would like to live with my mother and father in the pretty house, I say. First they say that my mother and father can't be found. Then they say that my mother and father

are eagerly waiting for me to return to the pretty
house. Now they exchange different words: hope,
cure, miracle. They show me pictures of things I have
not seen before, and teach me the names for them.
One day I will learn to swim, to dance, to ride a
bicycle, they promise. I will walk beside the sea and
the sun will turn my skin brown. I will drive a blue
car to the pretty house where my wife and children
live. My name is Richard and I am fourteen years old
and I am as good as new. By the window I sit in the
chair and close my eyes. Heels click, click on the hard
shiny floor. Grow louder, fade away. They never
sound like his. A hand floats on my shoulder, a voice
wavers into my ear. It's good to cry, it says. One day
you'll forget, it promises.

The car isn't blue. The man and woman are not my
father and mother. This pretty house is not the one I
remember. I sense that these people are troubled
because I pay them and their rooms little attention.
Feel them watch me carefully, nervously. This is your
room, they say. I close the curtains, shut the door, lie
on the floor against the wall. A knock. When I do not
answer, the door opens. The woman's hand is so light
upon my head I cannot feel it. The man doesn't touch
me. Doesn't love me.

The woman always wants me to leave my room and
go out to play. You can go to the park or you can go
to the river. You're free. The winter sun is cold,
white. My eyes always hurt, I strain them looking for
blue cars. The loud noises and sharp air and vivid
world around me hurt, and I long for my lover's touch
to hurl me into darkness. I am forgetting what I yearn
to remember. I become dull with heavy food my
stomach is not used to, it makes me hungry for sharp

hunger. Have another helping, says the smiling woman.

I must go to school. In a small room I sit alone with a woman who says I can sit in a big, crowded room when I catch up. She teaches me this and that, sometimes I learn to please her. Then it's time for me to walk in the crowded hallways because a bell has rung. So many people. Several come up to me. You're Richard, they say; I wonder who told them my name. I answer their questions, I look into their eyes, I blink the lids of mine. They shrug, turn away. Their running shoes make no sound, they could be ghosts. Or maybe there is a squeak of rubber against tile. I think of mice scurrying in the dark, hunting roaches whose bodies they crunch with sharp, white teeth.

There is one boy who wears jeans of pale blue and a shirt with short white sleeves. I see his hungry eyes. Some other boys come by, his face changes. He smiles like them. They all pass down the bright hallway, marching in step to some beat I cannot hear. The boy's name is John, I learn.

The lockers I like. Everyone has their own, and they can be opened only by secret combinations. I watch them spinning the black wheels, hunting for certain private numbers. Then there's a click. A metal door opens, revealing a small dark space. Girls have posters of rock stars taped to the insides of their lockers. They take out small mirrors and pout at their reflections, puffing their lips and kissing red lipstick on them. Girls' lockers are as neat as dollhouses, but boys throw their books into a jumble of baseball gloves and running shoes and old lunches. After banging their lockers closed with dramatic gestures, boys always kick the door, making one more small dent.

[82]

My locker is number 267. I won't say the combi-
nation. I carry my books around with me or leave
them in the small classroom. The inside of my locker
is bare, except for the small figure of a toy soldier I
found in the park. Someone lost him or threw him
away. While the teacher draws white lines on the black
board, I see the soldier waiting in the small dark room.
He listens for my footsteps, but when only those of
others pass he doesn't cry. It's all right to cry, the
woman says to me. I am sitting on the front steps of
the pretty house. My arms are wrapped around my
legs, my head is resting on my knees. Watching cars
pass up and down the street.

My angel will never come for me, I know. She
thinks I do not need her any more, because I am in
light. Sometimes she flies with white clouds through
the sky, her long robes flapping. She sees me walking
below and waves her wand in greeting. The clouds
break, scatter, dissolve. My angel has gone to a boy
who waits dark days in a bare room. My fickle friend.

My skin is white, smooth, unmarked. A good healer,
the doctor says. There was never any lover, my blank
skin mocks. I dig the point of the knife into a secret
place on my body. Watch the blood rise to the surface
of the flesh. It feels warm and tastes salty. I write a
scarlet word on my arm. Love. Lick it up, swallow it
away. The small wound burns like fire, but one that
dies down too quickly. Too soon it becomes a pale
warmth, equal in strength to the spring sun. Summer
will come soon, the woman says. Then the sun will be
hot. Then it will burn me and then he will brand me.

I say some boys and girls have invited me to the
park down by the river that evening. We are going to
roast marshmallows and hot dogs over a fire, then
drink Cokes with them. Later, when the fire has

[83]

burned into hot, glowing coals, we will sing songs around it.

The man and woman are pleased. They smile and ask if I have enough money. I dress in blue jeans, white T-shirt, sneakers. I walk past the empty park by the river, through the streets lined with pretty houses and into the city. Many cars pass up and down the big, wide streets. On a corner I stand and watch for blue cars containing only one man. Count cars until I pass number 267. When the fire inside me has burned into hot glowing coals and my blood is singing, a blue car pulls up to the curb. The driver reaches over and opens the door for me. I get inside. As we move down the street, I stare straight ahead, not wanting to see his face. His sad, old eyes. He wants to know my name and age and place of birth. Out of the corner of my eye I see him glancing at me. He is trying to discover if I resemble a boy who sat on the front steps of a house, waiting. A boy who was himself.

Turn off the light, I say. Then the room is dark. He pulls me toward the bed. The floor, I say. He strokes my arm. Soft, he says. His touch is light as air, with my angel's wings I am falling through miles of empty sky. Hit me, I say. Feel him freeze. Feel myself fall upon the ground with a force that jars me, breaks me. Don't speak, I say. Harder, I say. More, I say.

It is very late when I return to the pretty house. The lights are on because the man and woman are waiting up for me. I tripped and fell on to cement, I answer their questioning looks at my bruised arms and face. The man says he drove past the park, but saw no fire or anyone singing around it. It was too cold, so we listened to records in John's basement, I say. In my room and behind my closed door, I lie on the floor against the wall. Darkness. Muffled sounds come through the wall. For a long time the man and woman murmur words I cannot hear. I feel my sore body. The tingling touch of love is with me through the night. Alive again.

I bury the money the men give me in the sand down by the river. Beneath a black ring of charred wood, ash.

At school the teacher no longer speaks so often of the day when I'll catch up. I no longer try to please her, or the man and woman. Save myself for the ones who offer right rewards. One morning I see that John has left his locker open. Quickly, I take the toy soldier from my locker and put it into his. That afternoon I see a crowd of boys and girls gathered in front of John's open locker. They fall silent as I walk past. John lives in a house on Jasmine Street, five blocks from the house where I stay. I walk by it on my way into the city, but John is never sitting on the front steps.

I search for him once or twice a week, when I feel the mark of the last hand leave me. Now the man and woman do not ask me where I am going at night. They look at each other when I leave the house in T-shirt and jeans. In the city I discover certain corners where cars will more likely stop for me. I learn that if I do not ask for at least fifty dollars, the men are disappointed and do not take me to their dark rooms. I tell them this or that story; it's so easy to know what they need to hear. My name is John, I say. No, that's my name, they laugh. I might go into a red or black car, if no blue ones stop for me and if my need is strong. Maybe there are two men in the car, instead of one. Sometimes I meet men whose love is not strong and who do not want to love me hard. Their eyes become puzzled or frightened, they hand me some money and ask me to leave. Others like to use their hands heavily and those ones seek me at the corner again. No thank you, I say when they find me a second time. I do not want to learn their faces well, and a single time is all it takes to teach me they are not him. None of them love me strongly enough. I am searching for the only man who can.

One night a car stops. I get inside, look straight ahead as usual. Richard, he says. I turn and see the man who lives in the pretty house. What are you doing? he asks. I was too tired to walk back home, so I was waiting for a ride, I say. He drives in silence. His hands grip the steering wheel tightly, his face is hard and angry. For the first time I think he might be able to love me. At the house the man and woman say they want me to stay home and not go out alone after dark. That night I lie in my dark room and wait for the man to come to me. I have not been loved in a week, my skin holds no tender memory of a touch. The man does not open my door. In the morning I walk towards school, past it, and into the city. The man and woman will not look for me, I know.

I live in a hotel. The hallways are dim, because one of the other prostitutes or drug addicts always steals the light bulb. I walk down the dark hall, passing closed doors on either side of me. They are scratched and marked, but without numbers. I hear the crying boys behind the doors fall silent at the approach of my step. How they hold their breath, then sigh in disappointment when I do not turn a key in their locks. My own room contains a bed, a chair, a small table, a sink. I lie on the floor, listening to roaches scurry into and out of the corners. The curtains are always closed, and I have taped thick black paper over the glass. I am visited daily, and sometimes my door is opened as many as five times in one night. My skin is never empty of traces of love. I glow with warmth. Tomorrow or the next day my only true love will come to me. One or another of the men will be him. I will not need to see his face, because my skin's perfect memory will recognize him at once. He will love me hard and finally, so I will never crave his touch again. In pure darkness I lie and await the approach of his footsteps down the hall. They will march to the rhythm of my hopeful heart.

RIGHT HAND
MAN

Laura Kalpakian

It's one of those afternoons, cold and so damn dull you can only shit and shiver, and we're all four of us hunkering in a square of sunlight in front of Ernton's filling station, flicking our smoking butts out towards the pumps. No one cares how close they roll either. Ernton would care. Plenty. But Ernton ain't here. He's at the funeral of his wife's aunt, holding the wife's hand, moaning in the Methodist graveyard, laying on the Methodist smarm, says Eddie. Eddie can say that because he's a Methodist, even though he swears he ain't been in the church since before the Great War begun. Much less ended. We all wish he hadn't said that last. That's the whole trouble, see? We were all too young for the war and now it's over and the soldiers come home with the uniforms and their canes and crutches, arms in slings and the girls swoon into little honey puddles at their feet. Who'd want an eyepatched cripple when she could have a whole man? That's what we want to know.

Duke quick wipes his nose with his oil rag and says, 'So, how much you think Ernton'll get from the aunt?'

'You mean the wife. It was the wife's aunt croaked,' says Lew.

Duke gives Lew a look like he don't have buckshot for brains (and poor Lew, he don't) and Duke says slow and patient, so Lew can take it all in, 'When-the-wife-gets-money-the-man-gets-money.' He rolls a quick fag and licks it. 'Hells bells, Ernton don't even need it. He's got the only two filling stations in St

Elmo and now that Stetler's selling Fords downtown, don't tell me Ernton ain't raking in the straw. And plenty of it.'

'Too bad Ernton don't love you like a son, Duke,' I say with a little snicker and the others laugh too because Ernton's such a cluck he named his son Richard and his daughter Frances and so they got a Dick and a Fanny all in the same family. The same rich family. I flick the last of my butt and it rolls in smoking, real close to the first pump. Don't no one go after it. Just then a gas buggy rumbles up and Duke hauls out his oil rag and jaws with the driver while he puts the stick down the tank, brings it out, reads it, same time he's stepping neatly on my still-smoking fag. Clarence Hershey, he says hey boys to all of us, but who's going to pass the time of day with a man who's got grease stuck to his hands and overalls and his hair stuck out all over his head? But Duke, he's got to listen to old Clarence's old Whizz Bang jokes and laugh. I guess that's part of Duke's job too, same as pumping gas. Finally Clarence's flivver is out of there and Duke comes back, squats in the sunshine with us and says pretty soon everyone in this whole town is going to have a car.

'Everyone 'cept us,' sulks Lew.

'It's cold,' I say, buttoning up my coat. 'We live in the goddamned desert and we're cold.'

'It's the wind!' says Lew, his big round face shining.

'Shut up, Lew,' says Eddie.

It is the wind though. January, that cold snaking wind winds up from the desert and down through Jesuit Pass, and way out here at Ernton's filling station on the eastern road, well out of town, there's nothing to stand 'tween you and that wind. Though we oughta be glad it's blowing from that direction or we'd get the

[92]

smell from the city dump half a mile away. In summer
that dump-smell's a killer. Duke always says he works
in No Man's Land and the trenches couldn't have
smelled no worse than the St Elmo dump. Ernton's
other filling station, the one in town, his son Dick gets
to work that one and Dick gets tips when he steps
lively. All Duke gets is yahoos like the one that just
come through. Well, you could say Duke was lucky to
have the work and you'd be right. All the rest of us
('cept for Lew who didn't make it that far), we all
went to St Elmo High and I wanted to quit and join
the Army, soon as I knew America was in the fight
against the Hun. But, oh no, my old lady says no, so
I graduate and then she tells me she needs me to fix
the roof before I join up because who knows if I'll
come back from Over There. She cries. I miss the war
(because it's over by the time I fix the roof) and I still
can't find no work fit for a white man and what work
there is goes to demobbed soldiers. They get the girls
and the work.

Duke gets up off his haunches and looks to where
the sky is getting gray and faint in the east and he
says, 'The aunt's funeral will be over pretty soon and
Ernton'll be back out here to close up. He still don't
trust me to close the till, afraid I'll nick him.'

'He'd deserve it,' says Eddie.

'So I better crack on the delivery truck Mason
Douglass brung in this morning. It's his mother's
truck for the Pilgrim Restaurant and he lets me know
she needs it in a jiffy and I'd better look smart about
it. Lousy bastard.'

'Didn't he just get back from . . .' asks Eddie.

'Didn't he?' snarls Duke. 'The mademoiselle from
Armentiers, parly voo.' Duke peels a piece of tobacco

[93]

from his tongue. 'That fat Mason Douglass was prick-proud all right and I had to listen to all of it. And then, if it ain't bad enough hearing about the past, he starts telling me about the future, about how he's blowing this burg soon as opportunity knocks.'

'Knocks his cock,' I say.

Hands cupped against the wind, Duke lights his fag. 'The thought of that truck don't make me want to get up and sing "Oh say can you see". Maybe I'll just leave it go till tomorrow.'

'Yeah, but Duke . . .' Lew's jaw goes slack and worried-looking. 'When Ernton comes back to close up, he'll know you ain't touched the Pilgrim truck and he's gonna peel your dick right down to the bone.'

I'm ready to laugh because I know Duke's going to say something about dicks, more especially Lew's and I got my papers and tobacco out, rolling another, but when Duke don't say nothing funny, I look up at him and his face has gone sort of greeny-white, the color of pigeon shit and he's looking out beyond the pumps. I look and I see too: coming out of the dusk wrapped in that chalky blue and milky pink comes something staggering, stumbling gray hair, gray face and blue gray lips, right hand wrapped round the left wrist, holding out the left hand or what's left of the left because hanging down are bloody strings and bloody stumps and staggering at us, arm out, beseeching. No one moves. Lew starts to cry.

'*Help*,' lurching towards us, dripping blood. '*Help*.'

We all of us stand up together, slow, not scrambling to our feet, but slow and wishing we *was* Methodists or Mormons or mackerel snappers or even Chinks and praying this ain't bloody death come for us at Ernton's filling station. 'It's Mr Forrest,' whispers Eddie.

[94]

'He'd be in town, running the newspaper. He wouldn't be out here.'

'He would if he was dead,' I say, quiet like, 'if he was dead, he could be anywhere he wanted. He would be here. He would look like that.' Good clothes, pressed shirt and pants, collar and tie in place, but the hands nearly red to the elbow. Flapping untied at the thigh there hangs a mutilated holster.

'Help me, boys. Help me. Help me before I die of the pain.' So he wasn't dead, but slumped now against a pump. His face was gray as his hair, though Jake Forrest ain't that old. Forty maybe, but out here in No Man's Land he looks like death itself. He brings his blue eyes up to rest on us and says, 'I've bitched it, boys. I've done it this time.'

I hotfoot in and get clean rags. (Duke had his oil rag out, but thought better of it.) We start to wrap the left hand while Mr Forrest keeps pressure on the wrist, but it's hard because the ends of the two middle fingers are still hanging by long bloody threads. Right then, one drops, the bloody thread spindles and the stump drops into Mr Forrest's lap and with another clean rag (and a quick breath) I pick it up, wrap it and put it in my coat pocket.

'Where's your car, Mr Forrest?' Duke shouts like he's deaf.

Mr Forrest sputters out somehow that the car wouldn't start or crank over or something. He scratches up the words, but we get the meaning. He left the car. At the dump.

'The dump's half a mile from here,' says Eddie.

'Longest half mile of my life. Get me to the doc, boys.' He grinds his teeth so hard we can hear them breaking down. 'Any doc. I got to save my fingers. I'm a printer. I got to have my fingers.'

[95]

Well his fingers was long past saving, but didn't none of us say so. Along with the blood you could see little white dangling nerves and white bone sticking up jagged. The top knuckle of his ring finger was clean shot away and gone altogether, but his wedding ring clung there, twinkling wet and red.

'I'll run to the dump and get his car,' says Eddie.

'No time,' I say. 'He'll bleed to death. We need to . . .'

'No telephone here,' says Duke.

'There's the truck. The Pilgrim delivery truck.'

'No,' says Duke. 'Ernton would flay me alive. He'd have my hide on a . . .'

Mr Forrest starts shivering and his breath comes in long streaks, like the sound of something being ripped out of his chest. Duke looks once at me and we nod. What else can we do? We pick Mr Forrest up and carry him out to the garage. Duke tells Lew to stay there and mind Ernton's filling station, but Lew don't hear or heed and he climbs in the back of the Pilgrim delivery van. Three of us lift Mr Forrest up. We're surprised how heavy he is because he's only a fair-sized man, not as big as Duke or tall as me. He says he's fine, but he falls over, head in Lew's lap. Eddie jumps in the back too.

We got to ride like hell and we know it.

Duke gets in behind the wheel and tells me to give her a crank up and I do, but the truck don't start. Again and again. Duke calls that truck a motherless, fatherless dog of a piece of flyspecked shit.

'Hurry,' Eddie cries from the back.

Duke gets out and I get in behind the wheel. Duke gives that truck a kick. I mean right where it hurts. Duke is big and he is smart and he can fix anything that don't bite back, but I know (and so does he) that

[96]

when Ernton comes to close up and finds the truck
and Duke gone, it won't matter if Duke ferried Adam
and Eve back to the Garden. Ernton'll fire him sure
and that'll be tough on Duke because his old man
don't work regular, though he drinks regular and
Duke's got a mother and three younger brothers, and
a mule tethered out in their front yard. In fact, Duke
was just last week cursing Jake Forrest because the
Enterprise-Gazette was having a paper rage about
cleaning up St Elmo and going after people who kept
illegal livestock inside the city limits and picking on
Duke's family mule in particular, saying it (and they)
was a disgrace. Duke was ragging all over Mr Forrest,
then. Here he is now, saving his life. That Duke is a
good man.

Truck starts right then, she don't purr, but knows
to start and I move over and Duke jumps in and drives
us west, back into town which ain't that far, but feels
far. We rattle and shake all over the roads since
nothing is paved out here and the dust we make
catches up with the smoke coming from the back of
the truck and it's so powerful up there in front, I
wonder if they're dying in the back. If they're all three
dying and not just Mr Forrest.

We drive into the dusk which has got itself down to
a hard, blue line in the west, like it does in winter and
there's a single star hanging there. I kick myself and
say inside, *dammit, Emmett, there's a man bleeding to
death in the back*, but every time I look up to that fool
goddamned star, comes rolling back through my head
that verse that Helen McComb wrote me in Geog-
raphy that day:

For Emmett Wells:
  When evening drops her curtain down

[97]

And pins it with a star,
Remember that you have a friend
Though you may travel far.

And I seize up, just like I did that day she sent the note back to me, got it passed under desks, right under the teacher's nose as he stood there with his pointer going over the war in Europe. What did I care about the Western Front? I read Helen McComb's poem and I get this queer, deep ache, right down there where you live and my face got hot and my own pointer spronged up and it wasn't aiming for no map of France either. I stare over at Helen and saw only the back of her golden head till she turned around, all but rested her chin on her shoulder and give me a look. Not quite a smile. It was all in her blue eyes, that look, and suddenly I knew I was close to her – my body even – could smell the soap and talc on her arms and the lavender-water at her throat, could touch the buttons down her blouse, ease them loose, free them, free her, free us both, even though my real body was stuck there in that pint-sized desk where my knees scrape. When she give me that look, her eyes were blue and level, open as the sea and I knew she knew too, how it was my hand touched her golden hair, her shoulder, what it felt like, what it would feel like, what it will feel like, if I can only get a job and some money and marry her.

'There it is! The lights are on!' cried Duke, 'Doctor's in. Damn! Thank you, God! Thank you.' He pulls the Pilgrim delivery van in behind Dr Tipton's Ford. He turns it off and says, 'Trouble's in the pistons.' (Duke's smart like that.)

We're out of the cab and round the back and the

[98]

doors fly open and there's Lew and Eddie and Mr Forrest. 'I th-think he's d-dead,' says Lew.

Maybe he was. His grip had slacked on the left wrist (Eddie's holding it now) and there was blood on the floor and blood on Lew and Eddie and they are looking pretty gray too. We tug Mr Forrest's legs and pull him out and he ain't dead yet because he twitches and winces all over. We get him to the back door there which is already open, the light shining up behind Lucius Tipton, lighting his white, wiry hair as he fills the doorway, his gray eyes taking everything in. He says for us to follow.

Duke and me together, we make a sling of ourselves and we carry Mr Forrest into Doctor's surgery where doctor flips on the electric light and then he's washing his hands in the sink and – whew! The smell of some powerful antiseptic he pours over his hands while he's asking us what happened.

We don't have any damned idea whatever and we say so. Doctor don't look like he believes us, but he takes Mr Forrest's left wrist from Eddie and binds it fast with something and we all start to shuffle out the door, but right then, Mr Forrest reaches out with his right hand and he grabs hold my wrist, clutches like he is trying to keep *me* from bleeding to death. His lips curl back from his clenched-tight teeth, his eye-balls roll into his head and Mr Forrest says to me: 'Don't let him cut my fingers off.'

I look over at Dr Tipton and I say, 'Tell him yourself, Mr Forrest. Tell him. Doctor's right here.'

'It's me, Jake,' says Doctor.

But Mr Forrest clutches me all the tighter and says again, fierce, 'Don't let him cut off my fingers. I need my fingers. I have to have . . .'

[99]

'Jake,' says Doctor, 'I'll do what I can, but I got to tell you now, Jake, it looks bad. It looks real bad.'

Then I remember the wrapped-up fingertip in my coat pocket. With my other hand, I find it. The rag is all bloodied up and soaked through. Doctor takes it. I try to get my wrist from Mr Forrest's grip, but he don't let go. Won't. My fingers tingle.

Doctor tells the others to go into the study and in the bottom desk drawer they'll find a bottle of Burning Bush and they all look like they could use a drink. They close the door. Doctor's gray eyes come up and meet mine. 'It looks like you been drafted for this one, Emmett. You ready?'

'I'm ready, sir.'

But I wasn't. I done what he told me to do, everything he said and I didn't vomit or pass out, and it wasn't even the blood and Doctor's needle stitching in and out of flesh that got me. It was the screams. Guards at the gates of hell could not have stood to hear such screams. The snort of chloroform was merciful for Mr Forrest, but it did not do me a damn bit of good.

When it was over, I had to go outside and have the dry heaves, fight off the shakes and chills, walking around out back, smoking, kicking clods, flapping my arms at my sides and hooting a few times. Dr Tipton saved Jake's fingers, or saved what was left of them. What I mean is, he sewed the one still hanging down and he even sewed up the one I gave him from my pocket. The top of the ring finger was gone for good and the mended ones would never look or work right. They were whole, but broken looking. It was some job and even Dr Tipton said it woulda been so much easier just to cut them off and be done with it.

Finally I come back inside, stop at the kitchen pump, put my face under the water. I can hear their voices from the study as I dry off and go in there. Doctor's behind the desk and Mr Forrest, I am surprised to see, is propped up on the couch, white bandages glowing in the electric light, his left hand splinted and his arm in a sling. The sleeves of his coat and shirt have been cut away and you can see he has a small tattoo. A pale rose and anchor. The pain must be a killer, but you got to admire Mr Forrest, he's keeping it all in his clenched jaw. Lew looks worse than he does. In fact, they all look pretty grim, except for Blanche, Doctor's skeleton, hanging there behind his chair and she's grinning like she just heard the one about the traveling salesman.

Dr Tipton has a glass all ready for me, pours me some Burning Bush (and don't have to ask!) and then he says to Mr Forrest that he hates to have to ask again, but he must. 'I didn't say – were you alone, Jake. I asked what happened.'

Jake Forrest takes a little sip of Burning Bush like he don't really need it. His right hand trembles and he slowly lowers it back on the arm of the couch. He says, well he was out at the city dump shooting rats. Target practice on the rats. And funniest damn thing, he forgot to tie his holster to his leg (and he points to the holster still buckled round his hips and shot to hell). 'And I quick drew and the gun went off still stuck in the holster and since it wasn't tied, it twisted and I had my hand out and . . .' He raises his right hand again, sips slow on the Burning Bush.

'Careless, Jake,' says Doctor. 'You were careless.'

'That's the worst of it. I did it carelessly.'

[101]

'You're an experienced man with a gun. How could you forget something like that?'

The pain must be eating Mr Forrest alive by now, but he answers the question. 'I didn't know how important it was. I bitched it bad all right. Careless.'

'Well, Jake, you probably wrote more words about this town in the *Enterprise-Gazette* than any living mortal, so I don't need to tell you what the law is. When there's firearms involved – accident or not – the doctor's got to tell the sheriff. I'm sure he won't take it no further than that, but he's got to be told.'

'Well, sure I know that, Lucius. Everyone knows that,' says Jake like Doctor has asked after the tune of the 'Battle Hymn of the Republic.' 'Why every man in St Elmo . . .' he looks at each of us, 'knows that.' He holds up his mummified left hand and I can almost see the pain throbbing in front of my eyes, beating through his hand, but it don't show on his face. Mr Forrest grins. I never seen anything braver. He grins and he says, 'Gentlemen, you see before you, walking testimony to the kind of accident you do not want to have. Careless. That's the kind of man Jake Forrest is.' He laughs. Lew laughs. Only Lew sounds like the mule in Duke's front yard. HaWHaWHaW.

Doctor don't laugh. He pours himself another shot of the Burning Bush and digs around the desk till he finds a cigar and a safety match. He don't light the cigar. He's thinking on lighting it. He's thinking. He shakes his head. 'Jake, I can't . . .'

'Listen,' Jake says fast, 'No one else was involved. It was an accident. A damned, stupid accident. I forgot to tie the damned holster down, that's all. It was a target practice accident.' He takes another drink and you can see him fighting pain back into a corner, dueling with it. 'Can't we just forget it?' The blood is

starting to beat back into his face and his blue eyes are
focusing hard.

Dr Tipton, he thumbles around with the cigar and
the unlit match. He finally strikes that match and then
another and another, but he don't ever light the cigar,
though he keeps his eyes there. He don't look at us.

But Jake Forrest does. The pain is killing him off,
but he looks at us, each one. And I think: *Yes, of
course*. And it's like my mind can see the banner runs
at the top of every issue of the *Enterprise-Gazette*:

A NEWSPAPER CAN HAVE NO SECRETS FROM THE
READERS IT SERVES.

In fact it was that line he used when he gave one of
the speeches at my graduation. He said, in print as in
life, that was his motto. It made your blood quicken,
his talking about growing up and keeping yourself
clean and proud so you could serve your family, your
native St Elmo, the great state of California and this
great nation America too. That's the kind of man Jake
Forrest is. He lives the most public life in the county,
though he don't hold public office and never has.
There's no one who don't know – or know of – him.
Seems he has time for everyone. He can talk with
working men who wear boots and braces, with growers
in overalls and he knows the citrus and alfalfa crop,
understands railroads and irrigation. He charms the
old ladies who get their health asked after and dazzles
the young matrons who get listened to (like they never
do at home – you can bet). Schoolchildren who
graduate at the top of their classes, they get their
names in a special column in the newspaper and a
silver dollar if they come by the front counter of the
Enterprise-Gazette, which believes in education and

[103]

right there at the front counter you can see why: Mr
Forrest's framed degree from Central Methodist College is hanging up. Jake Forrest is the only man who
can walk from the railyard roundhouse, down where
old St Elmo once washed away, all the way up to New
Town, and know everyone in between, walk too into
the Pilgrim Restaurant, sit down and have the manners
to eat with the best of them. He ain't rich, but
everyone courts him up anyway and anyone who hates
him is afraid to say so. (Usually. Duke's old man said
so after the mule business, all right, but he didn't *do*
nothing.) There's been a few though, try to get after
Mr Forrest, but no one can say the *Enterprise-Gazette*
plays favorites because it don't. It's always throttling
on about making St Elmo safe for democracy, about
water rights and community service, sanctity of the
public trust and the civil rights of Chinks. Mr Forrest
is in the Methodist pew every Sunday alongside his
wife and daughters and you need only ask Jake Forrest
for a favor to find that he is ever-obliging. People
always say, *That's the kind of man Jake Forrest is.*

You got to admire a man who's good as his word
and no hypocrite. Mr Forrest don't try to hide it that
he's also the kind of man plays poker with the big boys
two or three nights a week at the Alexandria. (And
maybe that's why the Alexandria's the only saloon not
been attacked by the Women's Christian Temperance
Union.) Jake Forrest's been known to drop a hundred
dollars there on a pair of black queens. (Imagine, that
kind of money running on a simple pair.) When he
loses, he folds up his hand and leaves without a word.
But when he wins, why everyone from the dealer right
down to Lew's old man (who cleans spittoons at the
Alexandria), Jake Forrest strews money on them like
they all done him a personal favor just by drawing

breath. Everyone likes to see him win. And me, right now, I'd like to see him win. I know (like humming the tune when you only hear the song-words spoke) that it ain't the dump, or the gun, or the untied holster, or what's left of the left hand. He bitched something else. He has a secret from the readers he serves and it's like I can see the words before he says them. Smell the words and greenbacks. Say it, Mr Forrest. Say: *I'll make it worth your while*.

Then I look over at Lucius Tipton and I know Jake Forrest would be a damned fool to say those words to Dr Tipton. There couldn't be two more different men. Lucius Tipton lives a real private life. Real private. He's kept secrets for folks who live on Silk Stocking Row, just like he's kept them for Chinks who smoke opium in the cribs out back of their laundries. But you couldn't buy his silence. If it wasn't a gift, it wouldn't be at all. But I am not Lucius Tipton. I am Emmett Wells and I think: *Say it, you can buy my silence if you'll only just say it*. And I look to the others ('cept for Lew. He don't know what's happening) and I know they're thinking too. *Make it worth my while*.

So, I can see the words and smell them, but I don't hear nothing except the tick of the clock and the snap of Doctor's match when he (finally) lights that goddamned cigar and the squeal of his chair and the clatter of Blanche's bones when he accidentally bumps into her. 'Jake, it can't work this way. Even if I want it to. Even if you want it to. Every soul in this town – including the sheriff – is going to come up to you and say, what did you do to your hand? Everyone's going to ask after that left hand, Jake, and wonder how it was these men brought you into town from way out there at Ernton's and . . .'

[105]

'Then we'll have to think of some other story.'

'Why don't we tell the sheriff enough so he don't feel obliged to *ask* for more? We could . . .'

'No. It can't be that way. It can't. I would . . .' Jake finishes off his Burning Bush, studies the empty glass in his right hand. 'There is a woman involved. A lady who . . .' he swallows hard, so hard we hear it. 'I was at the dump. Alone. Shooting. It was not target practice. I didn't care what I hit or hurt. I just wanted something else destroyed. Something besides me. It was the old destruction,' Jake looks at Lucius Tipton alone. 'You know what I mean. It was the old destruction incumbent on love.' His face grows gray and pale again. He tries to shrug, but the pain won't allow it. He rests his eyes on Blanche for a minute and I think he's going to cry, but instead, he lifts his empty glass and in doing that, he seems to pull another trigger. BANG! In front of my eyes, Jake Forrest puts on cheer and charm like they was hat, coat and collar stud, all snapping into place. He laughs. 'Well boys, you can't change the past, can you?'

Dr Tipton says: 'You get one chance at the past. And that's when it's still the present. That's the only chance you ever get to change it.'

Eddie rolls a fag and rolls me one too. Mr Forrest don't smoke, but Duke and Lew are smoking and with Doctor's cigar smoke, we don't even have to see one another, till finally, Doctor waves his away, cuts a big swath through the smoke and says, 'Well men, killing rats in the St Elmo city dump, that's a public service by my standard. I can't go calling the sheriff every time a citizen renders a public service. Why that would mean . . .' He puzzles over what it would mean.

'You'd have to call the sheriff when someone fell out

[106]

of a tree chasing a cat,' says Lew, his round empty face glowing.

'Good work, Lew.'

'Or a dog, or maybe a baby bird. Or a chicken. Chickens can get into trees. I seen one once.'

Well, then Eddie has to jump into it, how the four of us might just have sort of happened on Mr Forrest there with his hand hurt and needing a ride into town. Then Duke says he hates like hell to bring this up and he's glad Mr Forrest done us all a public service, but there's still the matter of the truck. 'Ernton's already closed up by now. He's found me gone and the truck gone. He'll have my hide and he won't buy no cock and bull story.'

'That's the Pilgrim's delivery van, isn't it?' asks Doctor and Duke nods and Doctor adds, 'Then don't worry about that. I can right that easy with Mrs Douglass and she'll right it with Ernton.'

Well, everyone stands up now like we're just out of Sunday School. Mr Forrest weaves a little. 'I'd be obliged for a ride home, men. I hope my wife has kept my supper warm.' We kind of crowd him to the door so he don't have to be exactly helped like some damn cripple. We go out to the delivery van (she starts, first crank) Lew and Eddie get in the back, me and Duke with Mr Forrest between us in the cab. Mr Forrest holds out his right hand for me to shake and his old, rich voice rolls out, just like it did on graduation day. 'Thank you, Emmett. Thank you for letting me hold on to you. It was a real service.'

'It's nothing,' I say. 'I guess I am your right hand man.'

It's full dark now and that single evening star that made me think of Helen McComb is lost in a hundred thousand stars all looking like each other, spilled across the cold black sky. Duke drives without even asking where Mr Forrest lives because everyone knows where he lives. Everyone in this burg knows everything. Hell, in St Elmo you know which dogs are summer homes to which fleas. But I would give my own right arm to know who was the woman, once the present, now the past, the reason that a man like Jake Forrest is out at the city dump trying to destroy something besides his own self.

Just then we pull slowly behind a man in uniform walking with his arm around a girl and Duke snorts out, 'Another goddamn returning hero.'

'Yes,' says Mr Forrest, like we might not know this, 'The war is over.'

I don't know the soldier, but my heart comes up and beats in my throat because I know that golden hair, those hips and shoulders. I know or would have known them and I push the window down quick and look out into the cold to see *When evening drops her curtain down* who Helen McComb is with *and pins it with a star*. 'Can you beat that?' My breath hard and hurtful in my chest. 'Mason Douglass. Mason Damn Douglass.'

'Hope he don't notice his mother's truck,' Duke mutters, speeding up.

'He won't.' He won't notice anything but what Helen McComb must feel like, close up, near his body, so close he can smell the soap and talc and lavender-water on her.

Engine still thumping, we stop in front of Mr Forrest's house, the windows spilling yellow light on the porch and the porch swing, which they had not yet took down, even if it was January, rocking in the cold, a steady squeal like the ghosts of summer lovers. You could hear one of his daughters playing piano.

[108]

Trying to. I jump out and I ask Mr Forrest if he wants some help up the porch steps.

He says he is fine as he is. And, he seems to be – the old Jake Forrest back in place, his smile promising you Principles and Interest in whatever you was about to say. He even gives us a kind of salute. 'Goodnight, men.' Then he walks slowly up the stairs. He don't look back.

It turned out Dr Tipton couldn't right it about the delivery truck, even though Mrs Douglass did just as he asked. She wrote a note to Mr Ernton to say how very pleased she was that Duke had driven her truck into town to try to find out what was wrong with it and Duke was a fine, responsible, clever young man and Mr Ernton was lucky to have him working and wasn't it even more lucky Duke happened to be driving past the *Enterprise-Gazette* when Mr Forrest had his accident and that Mr Ernton should not give a thought to the blood on the floor as she would have it painted over.

Ernton still sacked Duke, turned round and hired one of 'our boys come back from over there.'

Dog vomit. That's what Duke called Ernton. But he stayed home after that, sulking, stuck with his drunk father and the mule tethered in the front yard.

For me, I might go out afternoons with Lew and Eddie, or maybe look for work, but mornings I'd hang around till the mail come. (Even though my mother give me this sneer she's been practising for nineteen years that I *know* of.) I hang around the mailbox hoping Mr Forrest would make it worth my while, reward me for having been his right hand man, buy my silence. But after a few weeks, it looks like I have

[109]

given my silence for free because everyone else buys the story how he'd smashed his hand up in the press, an awful accident right there in the pressroom of the *Enterprise-Gazette*. Oh, I think Lew mighta said something else, but no one pays him any mind because Lew means well, but he don't have biscuits for brains.

Then – February – Duke turns up behind the counter at the *Enterprise-Gazette*. He says Mr Forrest really needs someone who has experience setting type because his hand is so busted up now and won't ever be the same, but he hires Duke anyway. Duke's fast and mechanical. Days, Duke's on the counter, nights he's learning the presses. And then, why look here, Lew's delivering papers along with boys half his age. He's working, ain't he? And if you give Lew a set task and tell him how, he's a good man for it. And well, next thing you know, Eddie's up at dawn too, working a full day, hauling, loading, driving, supervising Lew and the others. Eddie's doing real good. He's still living with his mother, but he is busy days and I am not.

So, one of them un-busy days, I'm looking for work or something like it and I find I'm way the hell out by Ernton's and pass by the filling station where the new man is jawing a yahoo. I keep walking on the road that leads to the city dump and walk the quarter mile on up. The smell – whew! How many cat and kitten corpses are rotting out here? I walk round the edges of the dump, paper blowing past me, kicking a few cans and bottles, piles of dusty rags, keeping my eyes peeled for rats because Mr Forrest couldn't have killed them all. And looking too for his pistol which must still be here somewhere, but not on the edges, more likely somewheres in the middle and the muddle of the dump where I stumble over buggy wheels and wagon tongues and singletrees because everyone's got cars now, and kick candlesticks and headless lanterns because the whole town's electrified. Don't no one need this junk. Sun squints off broken glass and toasts up rusted cans and broken scales, a toothless rake, a busted bucket. A stove up-ended looks to be a fat lady kicking her feet, iron skirt over her head. The sun shines off a broken bedstead and dries up even the kill-death stench. The flies wink at me and rub their legs and chuckle over all these things that have been thrown out of people's lives. Like me.

I'm ankle, sometimes knee-deep in this trash while I wonder about Mr Forrest's ring finger. Lost the finger. Saved the ring. That's the kind of man Jake Forrest is. Everyone likes to see him win, but for a man whose life is open and shut, public as a clothes-pin, you long to know who was the woman before that present became past and what it was he bitched so bad. His left hand will always be crooked and broken and cut off, and whatever he bitched, now he'll never forget. Me, my hands are fine and I'll never forget *Remember that you have a friend*. Hell, my hands are big and strong and my fingers aren't wrecked. My fingers could have laced through Helen McComb's golden hair and cupped her chin and brought her lips to mine. My hands are strong enough to hold Helen McComb's bare shoulders, that's how strong my hands are, strong enough to pull her up against me tight, and hold her there forever. My hands are so god-damned strong I can fling this goddamned topless food mill so it strikes an old bureau, hits, splinters the bureau and the bottles and they break and splinter too – shatter, splatter, sing through the air, burst, empty cans ricochet. The old destruction comes on me *Though you may travel far* because I'm not going

[111]

anywhere, am I? With my strong hands I heft a busted
up sewing machine, cabinet and all, high over my
head, throw, heave it and it bounced twice, wood
cracked open on a broken soapstone drainboard and
the ash-sifter I hurl, it hits a rusted washtub full of
paper and rags and when I kick that over, the paper
and rags all fly before I trip on a skillet with a hole in
it, curse it, throw that and a bottomless kettle and all
the crockery I can get my hands on, throw them too,
throw whatever was warped, whatever was worthless,
like this dirty goddamn clock lying on its wooden side,
its hand sprung off, but its gizzards don't splinter
when I kick it. *All right. All right* and kick again. My
boot goes through this time, but its dirty goddamn
face is still grinning at me and I pick it up and throw,
not aiming or caring what I hit or hurt, just wanting it
destroyed, but it bounces off an unstuffed mattress,
goddamnit and don't break. Paper flying from my feet,
find that goddamn clock and this time my boot catches
its handless face and splits it off and it goes sailing,
high, falls, lands in a goddamned baby carriage.
Damned if it don't! I laugh out loud. Laugh. Because
that's what Mr Forrest did, isn't it? You don't catch
Mr Forrest crying. He shot his fingers off and
screamed all right, but he didn't cry. And when it was
over, he laughed. I heard him. I was there.

By mid-May I was working the front desk at the
Enterprise-Gazette. Duke had took over the pressroom, so I am on the counter days. Nights, Duke's
teaching me to set type. I'm not smart or quick as
Duke, but I am doing all right. I am working anyway.
It's been worth my while. And, though no one ever
mentions it, I notice how Mr Forrest's learned to keep
his left hand half-hid and never – ever – again says

[112]

he'd bitched anything. So, maybe even with the busted up fingers, he forgot after all. I didn't. You only get one chance at the past and that's when it's still the present. Helen McComb married someone else.

SOUTH DUBLIN

Isidoro Blaisten

Translated from the Spanish by
Norman Thomas di Giovanni and Susan Ashe

'The women we want, the things we want for ourselves – in the end, alas, we get them.'

Adolfo Bioy-Casares, *Guirnalda con amores*

I did it! I won! I cleaned up in the last round, and the whole jackpot was mine! Every Thursday for a whole year I'd been answering questions about 'The Life and Work of James Joyce.' I won, and my golden dream came true. My golden dream was to walk out on my family, run away to Ireland, buy myself a castle, sit in front of an open fire reading *Ulysses* while two Irish wolfhounds licked my boots, get stinking drunk once a month at the local pub, have a punch up *à la* Hemingway when he went out drinking with the Master, and nurse along my schedule of a different young girl for every night of the year.

That's why on Friday, the twenty-fourth of September, 1975, while Maruja and little Molly were still fast asleep after my night of blazing glory, I slipped silently out of the house, a copy of *Ulysses* under my arm, made a beeline for the biggest travel agent in town, and changed my prize cheque into pounds sterling. I still remember the fuss that the staff made of me – even the manager wanted to shake my hand. He sent someone for coffee and gave me his heartiest congratulations.

At eleven that morning I was aboard a British Caledonian plane, and by a most amazing coincidence

[117]

the flight number was 768 – the exact total of the pages in *Ulysses*.

I left no goodbye letter. Only a little note pinned with a safety pin to the party frock Maruja had bought especially for that Thursday. In the message, I had copied a paragraph of the Master's which ran:

> – That may be too, Stephen said. There is a saying of Goethe's which Mr Magee likes to quote. Beware of what you wish for in youth because you will get it in middle life. *Ulysses*, page 194.

But the high point of this whole space-time relationship was the evening of Thursday, the twenty-third of September, 1975. That night, Studio B of 'Channel 15, Buenos Aires – TV for all the family' was bursting at the seams when, overcome with excitement, J. J. Damico the quizmaster addressed me, saying, 'Mr Esteban Dedales, you have reached the final question of the night and the final question of the series, which you've been answering up to now on your chosen subject, The Life and Work of James Joyce. All right, Mr Esteban Dedales, for one thousand million pesos . . .' J. J. paused a long pause, and a hush worthy of an interior monologue fell over the studio audience. '. . . for one thousand million pesos. You have sixty seconds in which to think before you answer. If your answer's right, you will have earned one thousand million pesos, entirely tax-free. If you do not answer the question correctly, the sum will be added to the Oriol jackpot – *Oriol, the smile the whole nation smiles*.'

J. J. Damico was so excited he could barely pick up the envelope with the question. The tray, held by

[118]

Haydée, the programme's girl Friday – quite a number she was! – trembled in her hands.

I say that J. J. was keyed up with excitement, and no wonder. Me, I'm not easily moved to tears, but even I felt my eyes misting over. The fact is that, after a whole year of seeing each other every Thursday, J. J. and I had become fast friends. And it wasn't only those vermouths we'd knocked back every Saturday lunch-time at the old London Bar in Flores; there was a sort of stream of consciousness between us.

Now that I'm here all these thousands of miles away in Ireland, living out my wildest fantasy, I really miss him, and in my letter I shall tell him so. J. J. Damico is one hell of a lad! I hope this letter will stir him to pay us a visit and to tuck into some of Patricia's Irish stew. Seeing him again is going to be one of the all-time great pleasures.

But to go back to the unforgettable night. J. J. took the slip of paper out of the envelope, and the whole audience held its breath. He was so nervous he could barely read the words. I saw that Maruja was about an inch away from fainting. Finally, J. J. said, 'Mr Esteban Dedales, for the sum of one thousand million pesos, this is your jackpot question: The entire action of Joyce's novel *Ulysses* unfolds in one day – one day in the life of the book's hero, Leopold Bloom. All right, then, Oriol for gleaming teeth asks you to tell us with absolute precision . . . on what day and in what year does the action of *Ulysses* take place?'

Again the auditorium was plunged in silence. But the question was easy. The fact of the matter was that the panel had run out of hard ones. 'The action of *Ulysses* takes place on the sixteenth of June, 1904.' I was going to expand on that, but they wouldn't let me. While the treasurer rushed forward to hand me the

[119]

cheque, the audience went berserk, clapping and cheering, the studio became bedlam, and the girls from the bank where I worked pressed in to hand me flowers. In the shambles, I remember that two cameras were knocked over, demolishing the lens of one. I was touched to see my boss, Henríquez, carrying his younger son Alejandrito. Aloft on his father's shoulders, the boy had hold of the mike boom with one hand and with the other was waving a pennant showing a picture of the bank's central office. Photographers asked me to kiss my primary-school teacher, and a whole set of ads had to be put on the air while order was restored so that the sponsors' head of public relations, Dr León Olguín, could say a few words.

Now, at midnight, sitting here at this walnut table, warming my boots before a coal fire – Cardiff Coke, of which, thanks to Patricia, I'm a shareholder – while Patricia and Patricia's mother and father are peacefully asleep in the east wing, all alone in the library of my Irish castle writing to J. J., I think back. I think back and reflect that Maruja was to blame for the whole thing. Thinking about Maruja, by association I think about my daughter Molly, and I miss her a lot.

Maruja. Occasionally I remember her making popcorn and I think that the only really good thing about that woman was her sense of organization. A first-rate manager, Maruja, that's for sure, but in every other respect she soured my life. And yet, by another odd analogy, she was the one who actually pushed me into all this.

With her eminently practical sense, one holiday Thursday late in August, 1974, while we were eating dinner in front of the television, she said, 'Why don't you go on, Esteban? With all you know. If I were in

[120]

your shoes I'd be there like a shot. Look at that! Look at the winners' faces!'

'They're ugly,' Molly said.

I said no, I was too shy and I'd forget everything the minute the camera pointed at me. The whole business of making a spectacle of yourself was just a cheap circus, and you had to be a show-off to do it, a bit full of yourself, a clown, a poor clod without a shred of dignity, and what would my friends at the bank think if they saw me.

'Oh, dignity, pignity,' Maruja said. 'You've been reading him for eight years – since the day Molly was born – and you know him inside out. You've no spunk, that's your problem. You don't know what you want.'

'Go on, Daddy, please do it,' said Molly.

One afternoon as I left work I decided I'd give it a try. It was the middle of September. I went to the television studios, chose a topic, and put down my name.

'Esteban Dedales, Argentine, from Flores, forty-four years old, junior accountant at the Almagro Branch of the Banco Albanés, married with one child, answering questions about the Life and Work of James Joyce,' said J. J. on that first Thursday I went before the cameras.

Now, two years later, thinking back on that night, I have to smile. I was so nervous my knees were moving all by themselves. The staring faces of the three members of the panel suddenly reminded me of the three teachers in my last year at school when I was doing literature and had to resit my orals. Note the analogy – literature, no less. Just goes to show, doesn't it?

The first series of questions was easy. What year was *Dubliners* written, what happened to its first

[121]

printing, and what was the date of its subsequent publication? I answered straightaway, almost anticipating the questions.

To tell the truth, now that I think about it, the feeling I felt that night I never felt again – not once in any of the next fifty-two programmes. Before those three questions, while J. J. was unfolding the slip of paper, I had experienced a sort of emptiness in the pit of my stomach. But then, the moment I began to answer, I saw the Master in his photograph raise his eyes and stare at me. It only happened that one Thursday. After that he never stared at me again.

That became the greatest year of my life. People greeted me in the streets and even asked for my autograph. Neighbours sent Maruja joints of suckling kid, puddings, and greetings for me. They'd phone on the day of the programme just to wish me luck.

I was interviewed in the *TV Times*, in *Radio World*, and in *The Tatler*. The Irish-Argentine Institute of Culture phoned to invite me to a cocktail party on the seventeenth of March. We got Maruja's father, don Leopoldo, to babysit for us. Handing me the scroll of honour, together with the Institute's banner, Dr Patrick O'Brien, the Irish cultural attaché, said that whatever the outcome of the contest, my participation was already a solid contribution to the drawing together of our two peoples. I remember when I noticed on the banner that the Irish coat of arms had a harp on it, I felt shaken to the quick.

Incredibly, even my cousins, Dedales Cucumber Farms, who never thought twice about me, phoned Maruja to say, 'Why is it we never see each other? We're kin, after all. You must come round one evening. What's this about hardly knowing us?' No comment.

I have no idea how don Leopoldo found my old schoolteacher, but one night she was brought to the programme. To be honest, I didn't recognize her. The old dear cried, and I patted her head. Absolutely radiant, Maruja went out and bought all new furniture. Molly was the toast of her school, and the headmistress wrote something very nice in her exercise book.

I need hardly mention the bank. Henríquez, a big man and every inch a manager, turned up each Thursday to cheer for me, and he always brought little Alejandro with him. At the bank, the girls and the blokes and all their birds formed a committee that got together on Wednesdays round the corner at the Trianon. The week before they'd go to the National Library, fill in filing cards, and try to anticipate tricky questions. They wanted to talk to Borges, but I put my foot down. Nor did I need the cards. I knew all there was to know. And Fridays at the bank! Fridays were the apotheosis. The minute I walked in everyone stopped working. Even our customers forgot their deposits and queued up at the counter just to congratulate me and pass on information. Everybody was a Joyce freak. After four o'clock, Henríquez sent out for sandwiches and ice-cold cider from the Trianon, and we all drank a toast.

As the programme moved on week after week the tension mounted in proportion. The jackpot got bigger and bigger, the questions harder and harder. I went along eliminating contestants and climbed the ladder to the finals. But the closer I came to that last question – the one that would make me rich for the rest of my life – the more I felt I could no longer live in Buenos Aires. I'd go live in Ireland. I pictured myself in my castle, sitting by the fire, eating Irish stew, and reading

Ulysses while the most sensitive of my 365 young girls played the harp for me and sang old Gaelic songs. Or else I saw myself in certain fog-shrouded districts of Dublin, crisscrossing the streets round about the textile mills, or (before climbing back on to my white horse) on long rambles among the very spots which had been, on that one day in 1904, the scene of don Leopold Bloom's many comings and goings.

I spent all my time thinking about Ireland, making my plans. Once there, I knew what I'd have to do. First and foremost, I'd stroll through the clusters of hovels that ringed the city centre and rescue 365 young girls who verged on the tubercular and also knew how to play the harp.

My idea was to lodge them in special rooms, in a south-facing wing of the castle – in pairs, so's to keep them from pining. There'd be no problems with their mothers: I'd shell out my good guineas, and that would be that. Their nubile daughters would come and live an honest life with me. There'd be no worry about their going astray, or becoming streetwalkers, or – as in *Ulysses* – ending up in Bella Cohen's brothel. In my castle they'd live a trauma-free existence. Each would have a turn, one night a year, sleeping with me. I discussed this obsession of mine at length with J. J. Damico. He claimed it was my way of not forming ties.

'Maybe,' I said, 'but don't forget, J. J., this thing obeys its own inner logic. If the lass works out, I'm going to remember that night for the rest of my life. If she doesn't, the next night I'll try with another one, and that's all there is to it.'

'Yes,' J. J. said, 'but don't you see your hang-up, your fixation? You only think about the nights. What about the daytime? Don't the days exist for you?'

Well, there it is, lunch-times sipping vermouth in the old London, Saturdays that will never happen again, conversations that no longer exist. . . . Round here no one even drinks vermouth. I'm going to ask J. J. to surprise me with a bottle or two when he comes.

But getting back to the subject, what I found most seductive was the space-time relationship. My plan, you see, was to change the girls' names. So as to tell them apart, I'd call each one after a different saint according to the calendar. If one's turn fell on San Eufrasio's day I'd change the 'o' to an 'a' and call her Eufrasia. If another's fell on San Evaristo's day, I'd call her Evarista, and so on.

Those were my plans. Meanwhile, every Thursday I sailed merrily on my way to the final, answering each question J. J. drew out of the envelope with 'staggering erudition', as the interview with me in the *TV Times* said.

But to tell the truth, I never completely understood *Ulysses*. What I mean is, there are parts of it I don't understand – I mean, well, I barely understood a word of it. But I hung in there for all I was worth. Because the first time I laid eyes on the book, my intuition told me it was very important and was going to change the course of my life. I clung fast, and my sixth sense didn't fail me. I'd been reading the book for eight years – from the time Molly was born – and I felt more and more that the Master, by now blind, his faith lost, was nonetheless sending me secret, spiritual smoke signals so that I wouldn't cave in. Not an iota of doubt about it. In the last few programmes of the series, when the thousand million began to take on a certain reality, I felt *Ulysses* had not been written in vain.

Then I understood why for eight long years every

time Maruja saw me pick up *Ulysses* or heard me make the slightest remark about it, she'd say, 'You dummy. You haven't a clue what any of it means.'

Sure, I used to think to myself, because I'm not on my own turf, because I haven't got a castle in Ireland, because I'm going off my head working in a bank, and because in you, Maruja – face to face with the dazzling spectacle of my supreme doggedness – there beats a hidden envy.

'I'm up to here with you and that four-eyed Irishman,' Maruja would say, holding an index finger across her throat. But, in spite of herself, Maruja was enthralled and couldn't help sneaking looks at the photograph of Joyce I'd cut out of an old copy of the *Revista de Occidente* I'd bought by chance at a second-hand bookstall in the subway by the Obelisco and had had sealed in plastic at Peloso's – in the days when you could get things sealed in plastic at Peloso's – and that I kept inside the back cover of a copy of *Exiles*. It's that famous photo of the Master peering down through a magnifying glass.

I never answered back, because I'd retreated into a sort of interior monologue. A series of analogies was shaping my destiny, and I refused to turn my back on that. First off, there was my name. Esteban Dedales. From that to Stephen Dedalus (one of the two main characters in *Ulysses*) is but a tiny step. Maruja's grandfather (who died a short time ago) was called Leopoldo Bulnes, and Maruja's father, Leopoldo Bulnes, Jr. That's pretty close to Leopold Bloom. Maruja's called Maruja and she's in *Ulysses*. When Molly was born (that whole last interior monologue in *Ulysses* is Molly Bloom's) we named her Molly without thinking twice.

Something else. John Henry Menton is a character

in *Ulysses*, and Henríquez, my boss at the bank, is called Juan Matías Henríquez. As far as J. J.'s concerned – like it or lump it – one whole chapter of *Ulysses*, the one where poor Bloom is humiliated and reviled, has a character named J. J. in it, and you'll notice that the Master writes it J. J., just as I do. Anyway, there must be dozens of other analogies I'm not even aware of. J. J. Damico and I delved deeply into all this during those unforgettable lunch-times of ours at the London.

Why is it that one values things more from afar? Tonight, here in Ireland, writing to J. J. from my castle, which is called 'South Dublin' in homage to South Buenos Aires and to all my other old haunts and obsessions, which I shall never forget – just as I shall never forget my daughter, who must be quite big now – I think J. J. was right when he told me, 'Don't you see, Esteban, sensuality is a product of absence.'

And he was right, because I sent all the nubiles back to their respective mothers, and this year, on the seventeenth of March, St Patrick's Day (I couldn't go wrong), I got married.

I married Patricia Boyle O'Connor Fitzmaurice Farrell. And here's the oddest omen of all: As Patricia was born on her saint's day, the seventeenth of March, she was the only girl whose name I didn't have to change.

There's something else, too. I'll never forget that night as long as I live. And not because I found any great difference – anything you can put a finger on – between Patricia and the seventy-seven or seventy-eight other young girls I got to sleep with. (By the way, non-consumptive virgins are a pitiful lot.) Anyway, for all sorts of reasons, J. J. would know exactly what I'm talking about. They stare like baby lambs, they don't know what's happening to them, they remember their first doll, one or two burst into tears thinking of some squirt of a boy friend from Rosslare – oh, well, that's the way it goes. It could be that my own conscience was having hyperactive pangs. I realize this. But more than anything there was the photo of the Master looking at me through his magnifying glass. The fact is that between Patricia and Telésfora, or between Patricia and Pabla Navarra or Emetria – to name but a few – I found no earthshaking difference. No, no difference at all, and, now that I remember it (what a wonderful thing is the unconscious!), that picture of the Master came into my mind every night. For all his advanced ideas, his wealth of language, his deliberate coarseness, at heart he was still a good Irish Catholic, and – modesty apart – my family too has a Celtic strain. That's why when I say it was different with Patricia what I'm talking about is that unforgettable detail that reveals her completely – to say nothing of her sense of organization, her practical bent, and what an excellent manager she is.

Just listen to this: on the seventeenth of March I'm lying in bed consulting my diary to see whose turn it is when I look up and there's Patricia in her nightdress, hands behind her back as if she's hiding something.

'Come here, lass,' I say to her in Gaelic. A Gaelic still more or less patchy, since I'd only recently begun lessons in it with Keogh Kilkenny.

Not a peep out of Patricia. She just stands there on the carpet, smiling.

'What's the matter, lass?' I say.

Then Patricia steps forward and shows me what she's got. She hands me *Ulysses*.

I believe I have on a special shelf over the fireplace

[128]

every single edition of *Ulysses* in English. I even own the Shakespeare and Company Paris edition. It was the first thing I acquired the moment I got off the plane in London – before setting foot in Ireland, before buying 'South Dublin', before anything else. I bought up every edition of *Ulysses* I could find – including first editions, rare editions, and limited editions. I did it out of the sense of gratitude I felt towards the Master. But when I saw in Patricia's hands my *Ulysses*, the Argentine translation by Salas Subirat, published by Santiago Rueda, for me the only edition of the book in Spanish; when I saw in her hands my beloved old dog-eared, underlined translation of *Ulysses* that I brought as my only luggage from my beloved Buenos Aires – I'm looking at it on this table right now – I wept. Me, a bloke not easily given to tears – I wept like a woman.

But that's by no means all. The next morning, as soon as I came down to my library, where I'm writing now, I found out something else about Patricia – an incredible detail which decided me to marry her. On the mantelpiece, beside the portrait of Parnell put there by Mrs Conway, was a photograph of our national hero of the tango, Carlos Gardel.

All right, I confess that on glimpsing Gardel's picture in a castle lost out on the Irish moors, alongside the portrait of one of Ireland's greatest political figures, I felt shaken to the core. I won't say I wept, no, but I came close to dropping the copy of *Ulysses* I was putting back on the shelf.

How on earth could she have turned up a picture of Gardel around here, where you can't even find vermouth? I remember standing there, utterly amazed, deep in an interior monologue, eagerly searching the space-time relationship to discover whether or not this

[129]

was the crucial moment of my life, when suddenly behind me I heard Patricia's voice.

I turned, overcome with emotion, and hugged her. I wanted to talk to her about the photograph and about what Gardel meant to me, but, before I could, Patricia, who had a receipt and a pencil and sheet of paper in one hand and a plan of the castle in the other, in her sweet Gaelic lilt told me eight things:

1. I have sent those poor girls home. Their dear mothers must have been missing them.

2. After all, what were they bringing in? Nothing but added expense.

3. Look here, Esteban. There's always a grass somewhere about. The boys from the IRA wouldn't have liked this at all.

4. This castle uses a terrible lot of electricity.

5. Mrs Conway is another useless expense.

6. Here is the receipt. Antiques, holidays, staff wages, Christmas bonus. Sign it.

7. As a teacher of Gaelic, Keogh Kilkenny is a dud.

8. You've got me here; why do you need him?

As a matter of fact, Mrs Conway was pretty useless. Her Irish stew was enough to turn your stomach. The poor old dear was quite stupid as well, but she was the only house-keeper I could find in all Ireland with that surname. There were wonderful little old ladies in Dublin, but they were all O'Connors, O'Rourkes, and O'Donnells – yet not a single Conway among them. And she had to be a Conway, because Conway was the name of the Master's governess when he was a young lad.

Patricia got rid of Keogh Kilkenny too, which

caused me no little pain. He was a bit like J. J. Damico. He taught me the language of the gutter so that I could needle the pub regulars in preparation for my monthly punch-ups, and he brought me capes from Belfast, and he went out of his way to find me a harp, and he got me a beautiful white horse and the two dogs to lick my boots, and although Mulligan and O'Rourke turned into two of the stupidest bloody dogs I ever saw that wasn't Keogh Kilkenny's fault. I shall always remember him as an exceptionally beautiful person. Oh, well, that's the way it goes.

Patricia cooks like an angel and almost as well as Maruja. But two months after taking over the reins of the castle she put an end to my monthly brawls. Just like that. She raised all the castle drawbridges and refused to let me in. The whole thing was over a torn cape. Because if I came back from the pub with a black eye or a split head, Patricia said nothing. But whenever I came back with my cape in tatters, she turned into a veritable basilisk. The capes I wore were things of beauty – black cloth woven in Belfast, bought especially for me by Keogh Kilkenny.

That October dawn Patricia saw me coming at the gallop. She was watching through a spyglass from one of the castle's little turret windows. My cape was in tatters. It was the third cape in a row to come back in shreds, for I had shouted poofter in Gaelic at Alf Lenehan, the foreman of the spinning mill, a great bear of a man who stood about six foot six. It was a brawl worthy of an anthology. All it lacked was Hemingway. Patricia went and pulled up the seven drawbridges and left me locked out until after the sun came up. I nearly froze to death. I spent the time staring at my boots and shivering, while the mist lifted and poor Beckett, perishing with hunger, went round

[131]

and round in circles over the moor looking for a miserable tuft of grass to nibble on.

In the end, towards ten o'clock, Patricia, a lot calmer by then, let us in. She led me into the library and on this very writing-table showed me with pencil and paper that the column headed 'Monthly Pub Brawls' recorded a loss. First-rate manager, Patricia.

That same afternoon Patricia sold Beckett. She sold him to Lieutenant Nosey Flynn from the barracks of the Irish Fusiliers. Beckett was a gorgeous grey, a pure-blood Irish stallion who could gallop into a pub as if he were human. I'd named him Beckett because Beckett was the Master's secretary from 1922 to 1929. I wonder what name Lieutenant Nosey Flynn will have given him now.

Patricia sold the harp as well. She placed an ad in the *Irish Times*, and the very next day a van came for it. As the instrument was very large, they had to take it out by 'Puente Alsina', my drawbridge Number Five. That's another strange analogy with my life. All things considered, it was a lot of harp for me. Then, too, none of the nubiles had had enough sensibility to play it.

In November, Patricia went to a stockbroker. She bought shares in Cardiff Coke and exchanged the two dogs for fourteen sacks of winter wheat. To be honest, the dogs were a failure. There was no way they would lick my boots. Keogh Kilkenny and I tried everything: we gave them their meals on pieces of leather from the same hide that the boots were made of, we even smeared the boots with a special food for Irish wolfhounds who had no appetite. Keogh Kilkenny got it somewhere in Ulster. No luck. Keogh Kilkenny ended up finding them a trainer from Iceland, not

Ireland. An Icelander, born and bred in Reykjavik, used to handling dogs as a boy – but nothing worked.

The worst of it was that food for dogs off their food smelled terrible, and my boots had a frankly pestilential pong. Mulligan and O'Rourke, the two stupid hounds, turned tail and ran every time they clapped eyes on me. They weren't the only ones. It was a habit of mine to enter the pub at full gallop. I enjoyed it. There was something romantic about it. Mounted on Beckett, I'd leave the castle by drawbridge Number Seven, which I named after the tango 'Almagro de mi vida', and ride over the moor to the pub as fast as Beckett could go, singing, 'My beloved Buenos Aires, the day I see you again. . . .' I fondly imagined that the mill hands and the poor drunks recognized me at some seven hundred yards by my immortal tango verses, but it wasn't my verses it was my pong.

Patricia brought her father and mother to live with us. They are in the east wing, on the esplanade overlooking 'Corrientes and Esmeralda'.

'Corrientes and Esmeralda' is drawbridge Number One. The seven drawbridges (a curious number, as Joyce points out), are all named after old tangos, some of which were also old Buenos Aires haunts. Number one is called 'Corrientes and Esmeralda'; number two, 'San Juan and Boedo'; number three, 'Pepirí'; four, 'Cafferata'; five, 'Puente Alsina' (it's the biggest); six, 'Honeysuckle Blossom' (on which, oddly enough, a rhododendron has sprouted); and seven, 'Almagro de mi vida' – my unforgettable Almagro.

That's it. Now, in the silence of this night, while writing to J. J., I hear the Cardiff coke crackling in the grate, and it reminds me of Maruja making popcorn.

You're going to eat an Irish stew that's out of this

[133]

world, I'm going to say in my letter to J. J. Patricia
cooks almost as well as Maruja. And I'll put in the bit
about his bringing a few bottles of Cinzano too,
because round here you simply can't find the stuff. I'll
just finish this letter now and settle down yes to read
the Master.

THE SERPENT
SHE LOVED

Janice Elliott

'One has been misunderstood.'

'Oh yes, my dear.'

The serpent she loved rearranged himself in the wicker pram he had come to prefer to the basket. From here, as she wheeled him or sat by his side in the autumn sun, he could observe her as she talked – her little teeth, dry, cool skin, amber eyes; her smile for him, her frown for Revelation. While as for Moses – that monstrous misleader!

'Hush, what have I taught you? Consider Milton. In five minutes a proper reading could correct all misunderstandings. I was sleeping when Satan entered.' His voice was sibilant but she had learned to understand it with remarkable facility after her first surprise, walking in the garden. Thus, each had adapted to the other, although at times the snake was concerned for her sacrifices that brought him such advantage. What was the price to him of minor inconveniences when he could ride high in his pram on a level above the beasts of the field? She must live far from her own kind and, in encounters, dissemble. When she could catch none she had had to shop for mice. An exhausting procedure since she could hardly visit the same pet shop twice. It was the serpent, observing how weary she was from this eccentric marketing, who had conceived the idea of breeding his daily dinner.

'A cage in the attic? Why not?'

'You are so clever.'

[137]

The snake smiled. 'They don't call me subtil for nothing.'

'Would you like to go to the end of the spit, to the sea?'

The snake liked the sound of the sea. Not the crash or roar but the shush, the suckling at this flat land on the ebb tide, the bubbling of the mud, the gravelly retreat. The sky was low and wide, the light yellow. At a certain hour of day the sussuration of the reeds ceased and unseen birds no longer called. This was a stillness in which anyone who looked out from the cluster of tarred cottages on the other side of the estuary saw the small cloaked figure of the crazy girl with the empty pram. After the first sighting they were not curious. They could see great distances in this country but their eyes turned inward, blankly. The shuttered windows were blind.

'Should we go back? It's getting late.'

'Hush. Listen. I was Leviathan, you know.'

'I have slept in the bosom of Cleopatra. In Egypt I was properly respected.'

'You told me before. Eat your frog.'

'I am tired.'

'I'll build up the fire. You're just cold.'

'Is winter coming?'

'Oh no, not nearly!'

She watched the firelight on his beautiful scales. She was not repelled by this throat engorged with frog. Indeed, as she had come to know him and grown acquainted with his habits she had found herself embarrassed by her own clumsy eating. How economical to begin digestion already in the mouth, how neat the arrangement by which (so he had explained)

[138]

the windpipe simply shifted forward to permit breathing while the saliva (a word he preferred to 'venom') got to work.

By comparison how gross her own method appeared! The boiling or browning of flesh that had already been slaughtered on her behalf in ways she preferred not to contemplate. The knife and fork, the cutting up, the inelegant chewing in a carious mouth she had begun to see as a most unpleasing orifice. And then the detritus, the plates to be scraped and washed.

When she was first struck by the inelegance of human eating, she took her meals quickly in the kitchen out of sight of her fastidious friend. Lately and secretly she had been experimenting and tonight for the first time in his presence popped a small piece of raw liver into her mouth, held it there, closed her eyes and forced herself to swallow.

'Please don't watch.' As a tree-snake his eyesight was good.

'You wouldn't prefer a frog?'

'That's very kind but I'm not sure I can manage at all.'

'Possibly you are not carnivorous.'

'I do prefer vegetables.'

He had a quick tongue. She had her pride. So it was only when she believed him to be sleeping on the climbing frame she had set up by her chair that she allowed herself to dwell on her failure.

'Why are your eyes wet?'

'I thought you were asleep.'

'Are you about to shed your skin?'

'Oh, snake, how I wish I could! I am weeping because I would be as you in all ways.'

His tail embraced her neck as he lay coiled in her lap.

[139]

'Hush! Each to his own nature. It is my snakeness you love, your womanliness I cherish.'

'But God,' she said, ashamed.

'Was wrongly reported. See – there is no emnity between us. Serpent and woman have always been compatible. Children, you will have observed, have no fear of snakes until they are taught to fear. In lands where Moses holds no sway, we are cherished. There I am known as Ejo. Call me that, if you like.'

'My name is Eva.'

'A remarkable coincidence, though I daresay it means nothing. It is cool between your breasts. May I lie there?'

'Please do!'

Winter – and her fear of it for Ejo – for a time withdrew and the flat eel-country woke up one morning and found itself turned to gold. Even the mud of the saltings was gilded and pools blinked at a blue-eyed sky.

From a great distance a figure was approaching.

The earth was warm enough from its hoarded summer for the girl and the serpent to play in the orchard.

On their bellies they wriggled and raced through the crisply toasted leaves. Ejo won, of course. However hard she worked her elbows and her knees Eva arrived at the king of trees – the richest Worcester of the reddest fruit – to find him already hiding among the fallen waspy apples or coiled on a branch.

'Snake!' she cried, laughed and flung off her clothes.

Now she was almost like him. On glass she would have been helpless as he but on the uneven earth her nakedness together with her greater reach would have made her the winner but for her fear of wasps. Her breasts, her thighs, the little mound of Venus versus his sidewinding (learned long ago from the viper in the desert) very nearly cut the odds to equal. Though her movements were those of an awkward swimmer and she was dreadfully scratched by brambles.

'I have seen something like that before,' said the snake. 'The reptile from the primeval waters taking its first walk on land. I advised against it.'

'I used to have legs,' said the snake, 'but I gave them up. Pointless appendages.'

'You are perfect as you are,' she breathed and together they rested in the garden and played. His particular gift was self-concealment and more than once she feared that she had lost him forever; then a mossy branch gave the sibilant hiss she had come to know as laughter.

In those days of Indian summer Eva cast off shame with her clothes and walked naked in the orchard. Ejo caught his own frogs from the pool. In winter, they agreed, the bath would be converted to a tank.

Once, she imagined she had caught a glimpse of two figures halfway along the causeway through the flats. But the light in these parts was hallucinatory. On a hot summer day she had seen a ship in the sky. A man waving might be one of the few sparse trees. Or a crow.

'I am so happy,' she said by the fire at night, munching an apple.

'Happy as Eve,' said the serpent, coiled around her waist, the sweetest belt she had ever known.

'But surely Eve – ?'

'Another calumny. Adam was the fool, not to be grateful. For form's sake I acknowledge Satan but the truth is, it was mostly my work. And Eve's. Without that first apple you would not be happy now.'

'But the Fall?'

'A wicked rumour perpetuated by those with a vested interest in guilt. How could their first innocence have been bliss, since in ignorance one does not know that one is blissful? After Eden they had a few bad patches but nothing's for free.'

'So the whole story – ?'

'Propaganda. Blatant discrimination against serpents and women. God made Eve first, anyway. Adam was an afterthought, the brainstorm of a tired creator. A pretty slapdash one too, as your liberation movement has finally grasped. I mean, who in his right mind would wear his genitals outside?' The snake quivered with distaste in his own delicious way – a contraction of every muscle from tail to handsome head that shone sometimes green, sometimes brown, by firelight pure gold. 'You don't. I don't.'

'Ejo? You are not by any chance gay?'

'Certainly not! I believe we must propagate as best we can. Though an ideal future would lie in androgynous parthogenesis. Who wants that idiot's seed anyway?'

'I think there is some work in that direction,' Eva mused. 'Though I understand the primitive system is quite pleasurable.'

'You want pleasure? Just let me get this mouse down and I'll show you.'

How gently the blunt nose searched, teasing, probing, loving, the tail at work too until Eva sang with joy all through that night; and at last before the dead fire they lay so twined it was hard to tell which was serpent and which woman. Were it not for the

[142]

limitations of their species Ejo-Eva would have been born, serpent-woman.

Perhaps she sang too loud or in this eel country the men who gathered with their tarred brands around the cottage could snuff out a snake. By the morning winter was back and they crouched hunchbacked, crippled trees that have always grown as they are because gravity is heavier here and the sky presses and between the two sleet is carried on a wicked wind.

Ejo said: 'I shall need a hibernaculum.' But his voice was faint and his eyes were milky.

Eva stoked the fire and bolted the door. His poor skin was dull, all shine gone, and it seemed to her that he must be dying.

'There! See – the fire.'

'I am blind.'

The skin was splitting at the edges of Ejo's lips.

In the evening they lit their brands.

'Why do they hate us?' she said.

'Because we are sisters. The greatest offence against man is not the serpent but the friendship of women. It was the same in the Garden.'

'Ejo?'

'A goddess. Just a name among many. I've been worshipped as often as I've been bad-mouthed.'

'Hush. You must rest.'

The crazy girl pulled on her boots and her cloak, wrapped her serpent in a shawl, laid it tenderly in the wicker pram and the two made their escape through the wicket gate at the eastern end of the garden.

Ejo sloughed her skin.

Eva moved to the city.

[143]

They live happily now in the parlour behind the pet-shop at a temperature thermostatically controlled not to rise above 40 degrees centigrade. They give no trouble to anyone and no one bothers them.

THE HAIR

Joyce Carol Oates

The couples fell in love but not at the same time, and not evenly.

There was perceived to be, from the start, an imbalance of power. The less dominant couple, the Carsons, feared social disadvantage. They feared being hopeful of a friendship that would dissolve before consummation. They feared seeming eager.

Said Charlotte Carson, hanging up the phone, 'The Riegels have invited us for dinner on New Year's,' her voice level, revealing none of the childlike exultation she felt, nor did she look up to see the expression on her husband's face as he murmured, 'Who? The Riegels?' pausing before adding, '. . . That's very nice of them.'

Once or twice, the Carsons had invited the Riegels to their home but for one or another reason the Riegels had declined the invitation.

New Year's Eve went very well indeed and shortly thereafter – though not too shortly – Charlotte Carson telephoned to invited the Riegels back.

The friendship between the couples blossomed. In a relatively small community like the one in which the couples lived, such a new, quick, galloping sort of alliance cannot go unnoticed.

So it was noted by mutual friends who felt some surprise, and perhaps some envy. For the Riegels were a golden couple, newcomers to the area who, not employed locally, had about them the glamor of temporary visitors.

[147]

In high school, Charlotte Carson thought with a stab of satisfaction, the Riegels would have snubbed me.

Old friends and acquaintances of the Carsons began to observe that Charlotte and Barry were often busy on Saturday evenings, their calendar seemingly marked for weeks in advance. And when a date did not appear to be explicitly set Charlotte would so clearly – insultingly – hesitate, not wanting to surrender a prime weekend evening only to discover belatedly that the Riegels would call them at the last minute and ask them over. Charlotte Carson, gentlest, most tactful of women, in her mid-thirties shy at times as a schoolgirl of another era, was forced repeatedly to say 'I'm sorry . . . I'm afraid we can't.' And insincerely.

Paul Riegel, whose name everyone knew, was in his early forties: he was a travel writer, he had adventures of a public sort. He published articles and books, he was often to be seen on television, he was tall, handsome, tanned, gregarious, his graying hair springing at the sides of his head and retreating rather wistfully at the crown. 'Your husband seems to bear the gift of happiness,' Charlotte Carson told Ceci Riegel. Charlotte sometimes spoke too emotionally and wondered now if she had too clearly exposed her heart. But Ceci simply smiled one of her mysterious smiles. 'Yes. He tries.'

In any social gathering the Riegels were likely to be, without visible effort, the cynosure of attention. When Paul Riegel strode into a crowded room wearing one of his bright ties, or his familiar sports-coat-sports-shirt-open-collar with well-laundered jeans, people looked immediately to him and smiled. There's Paul Riegel! He bore his minor celebrity with grace and even a kind of aristocratic humility, shrugging off questions in pursuit of the public side of his life. If, from time to time, having had a few drinks, he told wildly amusing exaggerated tales, even, riskily, outrageous ethnic or dialect jokes, he told them with such zest and childlike self-delight his listeners were convulsed with laughter.

Never, or almost never, did he forget names.

And his wife Ceci – petite, ash-blonde, impeccably dressed, with a delicate classically proportioned face like an old-fashioned cameo – was surely his ideal mate. She was inclined at times to be fey but she was really very smart. She had a lovely whitely glistening smile as dazzling as her husband's and as seemingly sincere. For years she had been an interior designer in New York city and since moving to the country was a consultant to her former firm; it was rumored that her family 'had money' and that she had either inherited a small fortune or spurned a small fortune at about the time of her marriage to Paul Riegel.

It was rumored too that the Riegels ran through people quickly, used up friends. That they had affairs.

Or perhaps it was only Paul who had affairs.

Or Ceci.

Imperceptibly, it seemed, the Carsons and the Riegels passed from being friendly acquaintances who saw each other once or twice a month to being friends who saw each other each week, or more. There were formal dinners, and there were cocktail parties, and there were Sunday brunches – the social staples of suburban life. There were newly acquired favorite restaurants to patronise and, under Ceci's guidance, outings to New York City to see plays, ballet, opera. There were even picnics from which bicycle rides and canoe excursions were launched – not without comical misadventures. In August when the Riegels rented a house on Nantucket Island they invited the Carsons to visit; when the Riegels had house guests the Carsons were almost always invited to meet them; soon the men were playing squash together on a regular basis. (Paul won three games out of five, which seemed just right. But he did not win easily.) In time Charlotte Carson overcame her shyness about telephoning Ceci as if on the spur of the moment – 'Just to say hello!'

Ceci Riegel had no such scruples, nor did Paul, who thought nothing of telephoning friends – everywhere in the world: he knew so many people – at virtually any time of the day or night, simply to say hello.

The confidence born of never having been rejected.

Late one evening the Carsons were delighted to hear from Paul in Bangkok, of all places – where he was on assignment with a *Life* photographer.

Another time, sounding dazed and not quite himself, he telephoned them at 7:30 a.m. from John F. Kennedy Airport, newly arrived in the States and homesick for the sound of 'familiar' voices. He hadn't been able to get hold of Ceci, he complained, but they were next on his list.

Which was enormously flattering.

Sometimes when Paul was away on one of his extended trips Ceci was, as she said, morbidly lonely, so the three of them went out for Chinese food and a movie, or watched videos late into the night; or, impulsively, rather recklessly, Ceci got on the phone and invited a dozen friends over, and neighbors too, though always, first, Charlotte and Barry – 'Just to feel I *exist*.'

The couples were each childless.

Barry had not had a male friend whom he saw so regularly since college and the nature of his work – he was an executive with Bell Labs – seemed to preclude

[150]

camaraderie. Charlotte was his closest friend, but he rarely confided in her all that was in his heart: this wasn't his nature.

Unlike his friend Paul he preferred the ragged edges of gatherings not their quicksilver centers. He was big-boned with heavy lidded quizzical eyes, a shadowy beard like shot deep in the pores of his skin, wide nostrils, a handsome sensual mouth. He'd been an all-A student once and carried still that air of tension and precariousness strung tight as a bow. Did he take himself too seriously? Or not seriously enough? Wild moods swung in him, rarely surfacing. When his wife asked him why was he so quiet, what was he thinking, he replied smiling, 'Nothing important, honey,' though resenting the question, the intrusion. The implied assertion *I have a right to your secrets*.

His heart pained him when Ceci Riegel greeted him with a hearty little spasm of an embrace and a perfumy kiss alongside his cheek but he was not the kind of man to fall sentimentally in love with a friend's wife. Nor was he the kind of man, aged forty and wondering when his life would begin, to fall in love with his friend.

The men played squash daily when Paul was in town. Sometimes, afterward, they had lunch together, and a few beers, and talked about their families; their fathers, mainly. Barry drifted back to his office pale and shaken and that evening might complain vaguely to Charlotte that Paul Riegel came on a little too strong for him: 'As if it's always the squash court and he's always the star.'

Charlotte said quickly, 'He means well. And so does Ceci. But they're aggressive people.' She paused, wondering what she was saying. '. . . Not like us.'

When Barry and Paul played doubles with other

[151]

friends, other men, they nearly always won. Which pleased Barry more than he would have wished anyone to know.

And Paul's praise: it burned in his heart with a luminosity that endured for hours and days and all in secret.

The Carsons lived in a small mock-Georgian house in town, the Riegels lived in a glass, stone, and redwood house, custom-designed, three miles out in the country. The Carsons' house was one of many attractive houses of its kind in their quiet residential neighborhood and had no distinctive features except an aged enormous plane tree in the front which would probably have to be dismantled soon: 'It will break our hearts,' Charlotte said. The Carsons' house was fully exposed to the street; the Riegels' house was hidden from the narrow gravel road that ran past it by a seemingly untended meadow of juniper pines, weeping willows, grasses, wildflowers.

Early on in their friendship, a tall cool summer drink in hand, Barry Carson almost walked through a plate glass door at the Riegels': beyond it was the redwood deck, Ceci in a silk floral-printed dress with numberless pleats.

Ceci was happy and buoyant and confident always. For a petite woman – size five, it was more than once announced – she had a shapely body, breasts, hips, strong-calved legs. When she and Charlotte Carson played tennis Ceci was all over the court, laughing and exclaiming, while slow-moving premeditated Charlotte, poor Charlotte who felt, in her friend's company, ostrich-tall and ungainly, missed all but the easy shots. 'You need to be more aggressive, Char!' Paul Riegel called out. '. . . Need to be *murderous*!'

The late-night drive back to town from the Riegels'

[152]

along narrow twisty country roads: Paul behind the wheel sleepy with drink yet excited too, vaguely sweetly aching, Charlotte yawning and sighing, and there was the danger of white-tailed deer so plentiful in this part of the state leaping in front of the car, but they returned home safely, suddenly they were home, and, inside, one would observe that their house was so lacking in imagination, wasn't it? So exposed to the neighbors? 'Yes but you wanted this house.' 'No you were the one who wanted this house.' 'Not *this* house – but this was the most feasible.' Though sometimes one would observe that the Riegels' house had flaws: so much glass and it's drafty in the winter, so many queer elevated decks and flights of stairs, wall-less rooms, sparsely furnished rooms like designers' show-cases and the cool chaste neutral colors that Ceci evidently favored: 'It's beautiful, yes, but a bit sterile.'

In bed, exhausted, they would drift to sleep separately, wandering the corridors of an unknown building, opening one door after another in dread and fascination. Charlotte who should not have had more than two or three glasses of wine – but it was an anniversary of the Riegels': they'd uncorked bottles of champagne – slept fitfully, waking often dry-mouthed and frightened not knowing where she was. A flood of hypnagogic images raced in her brain, the faces of strangers never before glimpsed by her thrummed beneath her eyelids. In that state of consciousness that is neither sleep nor waking Charlotte had the volition to will, ah how passionately, how despairingly, that Paul Riegel would comfort her: slip his arm around her shoulders, nudge his jaw against her cheek, whisper in her ear as he'd done once or twice that evening in play but now in seriousness. Beside her someone

[153]

stirred and groaned in his sleep and kicked at the covers.

Paul Riegel entranced listeners with lurid tales of starving Cambodian refugees, starving Ethiopian children, starving Mexican beggars. His eyes shone with angry tears one moment and with mischief the next for he could not resist mocking his own sobriety. The laughter he aroused at such times had an air of bafflement, shock.

Ceci came to him to slip an arm through his as if to comfort or to quiet and there were times when, quite perceptibly, Paul shook off her arm, stepped away, stared down at her with a look as if he'd never seen the woman before.

When the Carsons did not see or hear from the Riegels for several days their loneliness was almost palpable: a thickness in the chest, a density of being, to which either might allude knowing the other would immediately understand. If the Riegels were actually away that made the separation oddly more bearable than if they were in fact here in their house amid the trees but not seeing the Carsons that weekend or mysteriously incommunicado with their telephone answering tape switched on. When Charlotte called, got the tape, heard the familiar static-y overture then Paul Riegel's cool almost hostile voice that did not identify itself but merely stated *No one is here right now, should you like to leave a message please wait for the sound of the bleep*, she felt a loss too profound to be named and often hung up in silence.

For it had happened as the Carsons feared – the Riegels were dominant. So fully in control.

For there was the terrible period, several months in all, when for no reason the Carsons could discover – and they discussed the subject endlessly, obsessively –

[154]

the Riegels seemed to have little time for them. Or saw them with batches of others in which their particular friendship could not be readily discerned. Paul was a man of quick enthusiasms, and Ceci was a woman of abrupt shifts of allegiance, thus there was logic of sorts to their cruelty in elevating for a while a new couple in the area who were both theoretical mathematicians, and a neighbor's house guest who'd known Paul in college and was now in the diplomatic service, and a cousin of Ceci's, a male model in his late twenties who was staying with the Riegels for weeks and weeks and weeks taking up every spare minute of their time it seemed, so when Charlotte baffled and hurt called, Ceci murmured in an undertone, 'I can't talk now, can I call you back in the morning?' and failed to call for days, days, days.

One night when Charlotte would have thought Barry was asleep he shocked her by saying, 'I never liked her much. Hot shit little Ceci.' She had never heard her husband utter such words before and did not know how to reply.

They went away on a trip. Three weeks in the Caribbean and only in the third week did Charlotte scribble a postcard for the Riegels – quick scribbled little note as if one of many.

One night she said, '*He's* the dangerous one. He always tried to get people to drink too much, to keep him company.'

They came back, and not long afterward Ceci called, and the friendship was resumed precisely as it had been. The same breathless pace, the same dazzling intensity, though now Paul had a new book coming out and there were parties in the city, book signings at book stores, an interview on a morning news program. The Carsons gave a party for him inviting virtually

[155]

everyone they knew locally and the party was a great success and in a corner of the house Paul Riegel hugged Charlotte Carson so hard she laughed, protesting her ribs would crack, but when she drew back to look at her friend's face she saw it was damp with tears.

Later, Paul told a joke about Reverend Jesse Jackson that was a masterpiece of mimicry though possibly in questionable taste. In the general hilarity no one noticed, or at least objected. In any case there were no blacks present.

The Riegels were childless but would not have defined their condition in those terms – as a lack, a loss, a negative. Before marrying they had discussed the subject of children thoroughly, Paul said, and came to the conclusion *no*.

The Carsons too were childless but would perhaps have defined their condition in those terms, in weak moods at least. Hearing Paul speak so indifferently of children the Carsons exchanged a glance almost of embarrassment.

Each hoped the other would not disclose any intimacy.

Ceci sipped at her drink and said, 'I'd have been willing.'

Paul said, '*I* wouldn't.'

There was a brief nervous pause. The couples were sitting on the Riegels' redwood deck in the gathering dusk.

Paul then astonished the Carsons by speaking in a bitter impassioned voice of families, children, parents, the 'politics' of intimacy. In any intimate group, he said, the struggle to be independent, to define oneself as an individual, is so fierce it creates terrible waves of tension; a field of psychic warfare. He'd endured it as a child and young adolescent in his parents' home and as an adult he didn't think he could bear to bring up a child – 'especially a son' – knowing of the doubleness and secrecy of the child's life.

'There is the group life which is presumably open and observable,' he said, '. . . and there is the secret inner real life no one can penetrate.' He spoke with such uncharacteristic vehemence that neither of the Carsons would have dared to challenge him or even to question him in the usual conversational vein.

Ceci sat silent, drink in hand, staring impassively out into the shadows.

After a while conversation resumed again and they spoke softly, laughed softly. The handsome white wrought iron furniture in which they were sitting took on an eerie solidity even as the human figures seemed to fade; losing outline and contour; blending into the night and into one another.

Charlotte Carson lifted her hand registering a small chill spasm of fear that she was dissolving but it was only a drunken notion, of course.

For days afterward Paul Riegel's disquieting words echoed in her head. She tasted something black and her heart beat in anger like a cheated child's. *Don't you love me then? Don't any of us love any of us*? To Barry she said, 'That was certainly an awkward moment wasn't it – when Paul started his monologue about family life, intimacy, all that. What did you make of it?'

Barry murmured something evasive and backed off.

The Carsons owned two beautiful Siamese cats, neutered male and neutered female, and the Riegels owned a skittish Irish setter named Poppy. When the Riegels came to visit Ceci always made a fuss over one or the other of the cats, insisting it sit in her lap,

[157]

sometimes even at the dinner table where she'd feed it on the sly. When the Carsons came to visit the damned dog as Barry spoke of it went into a frenzy of barking and greeted them at the front door as if it had never seen them before: 'Nice dog! Good dog! Sweet Poppy!' the Carsons would cry in unison.

The setter was rheumy-eyed and thick-bodied and arthritic. If every year of a dog's age is approximately seven years in human terms poor Poppy was almost eighty years old. She managed to shuffle to the front door to bark at visitors but then lacked the strength or motor coordination to reverse herself and return to the interior of the house so Paul had to carry her, one arm under her bony chest and forelegs, the other firmly under her hindquarters, an expression of vexed tenderness in his face.

Dryly he said, 'I hope someone will do as much for me someday.'

One rainy May afternoon when Paul was in Berlin and Barry was in Virginia visiting his family Ceci impulsively invited Charlotte to come for a drink and meet her friend Nils Larson – or was the the name Lasson? Lawson? – an old old dear friend. Nils was short, squat-bodied, energetic, with a gnomish head and bright malicious eyes; linked to Ceci, it appeared, in a way that allowed him to be both slavish and condescending. He was a 'theatre person'; his bubbly talk was studded with names of the famous and near-famous. Never once did he mention Paul Riegel's name though certain of his mannerisms – head thrown back in laughter, hands gesticulating as he spoke – reminded Charlotte of certain of Paul's mannerisms. The man was Paul's elder by perhaps a decade.

Charlotte stayed only an hour, then made her excuses and slipped away. She had seen Ceci's friend draw his pudgy forefinger across the nape of Ceci's neck in a gesture that signaled intimacy or the arrogant pretence of intimacy and the sight offended her. But she never told Barry and resolved not to think of it and of whether Nils spent the night at the Riegels' and whether Paul knew anything of him or of the visit. Nor did Ceci ask Charlotte what she had thought of Nils Larson – Lasson? Lawson? – the next time the women spoke.

Barry returned from Virginia with droll tales of family squabbling. His brother and his sister-in-law, their children, the network of aunts, uncles, nieces, nephews, grandparents, ailing elderly relatives whose savings were being eaten up – invariably the expression was 'eaten up' – by hospital and nursing home expenses. Barry's father, severely crippled from a stroke, was himself in a nursing home from which he would never be discharged, and all his conversation turned upon this fact which others systematically denied, including, in the exigency of the moment, Barry. He had not, he said, really recognized his father. It was as if another man – aged, shrunken, querulous, sly – had taken his place.

The elderly Mr Carson had affixed to a wall of his room a small white card on which he'd written some Greek symbols, an inscription he claimed to have treasured all his life. Barry asked what the Greek meant and was told: *When my ship sank, the others sailed on*.

Paul Riegel returned from Berlin exhausted and depressed despite the fact, happy to his wife and friends, that a book of his was on the paperback bestseller list published by the *New York Times*. When Charlotte Carson suggested with uncharacteristic gaiety that they celebrate, Paul looked at her with a mild quizzical smile and asked, 'Why, exactly?'

The men played squash, the women played tennis.

The Carsons had other friends of course. Older and more reliable friends. They did not need the Riegels. Except they were in love with the Riegels.

Did the Riegels love them? Ceci telephoned one evening and Barry happened to answer and they talked together for an hour and afterward, when Charlotte asked Barry what they'd talked about, careful to keep all signs of jealousy and excitement out of her voice, Barry said evasively, '. . . A friend of theirs is dying. Of AIDS. Ceci says he weighs only ninety pounds and has withdrawn from everyone: "slunk off to die like a sick animal". And that Paul doesn't care. Or won't talk about it.' Barry paused, aware that Charlotte was looking at him closely. A light film of perspiration covered his face; his nostrils appeared unusually dark, dilated. 'He's no one we know, honey. The dying man I mean.'

When Paul Riegel emerged from a sustained bout of writing the first people he wanted to see were the Carsons, of course, so the couples went out for Chinese food – 'a banquet, no less!' – at their favorite Chinese restaurant in a shopping mall. The Dragon Inn had no liquor licence so they brought bottles of wine and six-packs of beer. They were the last customers to leave and by the end waiters and kitchen help were standing around or prowling restlessly at the rear of the restuarant. There was a minor disagreement over the check which Paul Riegel insisted had not been added up correctly. He and the manager discussed the problem and since the others were within earshot he couldn't resist clowning for their amusement; slipping into a comical Chinese (unless it was

Japanese?) accent. In the parking lot the couples laughed helplessly gasping for breath and bent double and in the car driving home – Barry drove: they'd taken the Carsons' Honda Accord, and Barry was seemingly the most sober of the four of them – they kept bursting into peals of laughter like naughty children.

They never returned to the Dragon Inn.

The men played squash together but their most rewarding games were doubles in which they played, and routed, another pair of men.

As if grudgingly Paul Riegel would tell Barry Carson he was a 'damned good player'. To Charlotte he would say, 'Your husband is a damned good player but if only he could be a bit more *murderous*!'

Barry Carson's handsome heavy face darkened with pleasure when he heard such praise, exaggerated as it was. Though afterward, regarding himself in a mirror, he felt shame: he was forty-two years old, he had a very good job in a highly competitive field, he had a very good marriage with a woman he both loved and respected, he believed he was leading, on the whole, a very good life, yet none of this meant as much to him as Paul Riegel carelessly complimenting him on his squash game.

How has my life come to this?

Poppy developed cataracts on both eyes. And then tumorous growths in her neck. The Riegels took her to the vet and had her put to sleep and Ceci had what was reported to the Carsons as a breakdown of a kind: wept and wept and wept. Paul too was shaken by the ordeal but managed to joke over the phone about the dog's ashes. When Charlotte told Barry of the dog's death she saw Barry's eyes narrow as he resisted saying Thank God! and said instead, gravely, as if it would

[161]

be a problem of his own, 'Poor Ceci will be inconsolable.'

For weeks it wasn't clear to the Carsons that they would be invited to visit the Riegels on Nantucket then, shortly before the Riegels left, Ceci said, as if casually, 'We did set a date didn't we? For you two to come visit?'

On their way up – it was a seven-hour drive to the ferry at Woods Hole – Charlotte said to Barry, 'Promise you won't drink so much this year.' Offended, Barry said, 'I won't monitor your behavior, honey, if you won't monitor mine.'

From the first, the Nantucket visit went awkwardly. Paul wasn't home and his whereabouts weren't explained though Ceci chattered brightly and effusively, carrying her drink with her as she escorted the Carsons to their room and watched them unpack. Her shoulder-length hair was graying and disheveled; her face was heavily made up, especially about the eyes. Several times she said, 'Paul will be so happy to see you,' as if Paul had not known they were invited; or, knowing, like Ceci herself, had perhaps forgotten. An east wind fanned drizzle and soft gray mist against the windows.

Paul returned looking fit and tanned and startled about the eyes: in his walnut-brown face the whites glared. Toward dusk the sky lightened and the couples sat on the beach with their drinks. Ceci continued to chatter while Paul smiled, vague and distracted, looking out at the surf. The air was chilly and damp but wonderfully fresh. The Carsons drew deep breaths and spoke admiringly of the view. And the house. And the location. They were wondering had the Riegels been quarreling? was something wrong? had they themselves come on the wrong day, or at the wrong time? Paul had been effusive too in his greetings but had not seemed to see them and had scarcely looked at them since.

Before they sat down to dinner the telephone began to ring. Ceci in the kitchen (with Charlotte who was helping her) and Paul in the living room (with Barry: the men were watching a televised tennis tournament) made no move to answer it. The ringing continued for what seemed like a long time then stopped and resumed again while they were having dinner and again neither of the Riegels made a move to answer it. Paul grinned running both hands roughly through the bushy patches of hair at the sides of his head and said, 'When the world beats a path to your doorstep beat it back, friends! *Beat it back for fuck's sake!*'

His extravagant words were meant to be funny of course but would have required another atmosphere altogether to be so. As it was, the Carsons could only stare and smile in embarrassment.

Ceci filled the silence by saying loudly, 'Life's little ironies! You spend a lifetime making yourself famous then you try to back off and dismantle it. But it won't dismantle! It's a mummy and you're inside it!'

'Not *in* a mummy,' Paul said, staring smiling at the lobster on his plate which he'd barely eaten, 'you *are* a mummy.' He had been drinking steadily, Scotch on the rocks, and now wine, since arriving home.

Ceci laughed sharply. '"In," "are," what's the difference?' she said, appealing to the Carsons. She reached out to squeeze Barry's hand, hard. 'In any case you're a goner, right?'

Paul said, 'No . . . *you're* a goner.'

The evening continued in this vein. The Carsons sent despairing glances at each other.

The telephone began to ring and this time Paul rose

[163]

to answer it. He walked stiffly, and took his glass of wine with him. He took the call not in the kitchen but in another room at the rear of the house and he was gone so long that Charlotte felt moved to ask if something was wrong? Ceci Riegel stared at her coldly. The whites of Ceci's eyes too showed above the rims of the iris giving her a fey festive party-look at odds with her carelessly combed hair and a tiredness deep in her face. 'With the meal?' she asked. 'With the house? With us? With *you*? I don't know of anything wrong.'

Charlotte had never been so rebuffed in her adult life. Barry too felt the force of the insult. After a long stunned moment Charlotte murmured an apology, and Barry too murmured something vague, placating, embarrassed.

They sat in suspension, not speaking, scarcely moving, until at last Paul returned. His cheeks were ruddy as if they'd been heartily slapped and his eyes were bright. He carried a bottle of his favorite Napa Valley wine which he'd been saving, he said, just for tonight. 'This is a truly special occasion! We've really missed you guys!'

They were up until two, drinking. Repeatedly Paul used the odd expression 'guys' as if its sound, its grating musicality, had imprinted itself in his brain. 'OK guys how's about another drink?' he would say, rubbing his hands together. 'OK guys how the hell have you been?'

Next morning, a brilliantly sunny morning, no one was up before eleven. Paul appeared in swimming trunks and T-shirt in the kitchen at noon, boisterous, swaggering, unshaven, in much the mood of the night before – remarkable! The Riegels had hired a local handyman to shore up some rotting steps and the handyman was an oldish gray-grizzled black and after the man was paid and departed Paul spoke in an exaggerated comical black accent hugging Ceci and Charlotte around their waists until Charlotte pushed him away stiffly saying, 'I don't think you're being funny, Paul.' There was a moment's startled silence, then she repeated, vehemently, *'I don't think that's funny, Paul.'*

As if on cue Ceci turned on her heel and walked out of the room.

But Paul continued his clowning. He blundered about in the kitchen pleading with 'white missus'; bowing, shuffling, tugging what remained of his fore-lock; kneeling to pluck at Charlotte's denim skirt. His flushed face seemed to have turned to rubber, his lips red, moist, turned obscenely inside out. 'Beg pardon white missus! Oh white missus beg *par*don!'

Charlotte said, 'I think we should leave.'

Barry, who had been staring appalled at his friend, as if he'd never seen him before, said quickly, 'Yes. I think we should leave.'

They went to their room at the rear of the house leaving Paul behind and in a numbed stricken silence packed their things, each of them badly trembling. They anticipated one or both of the Riegels following them but neither did and as Charlotte yanked sheets off the bed, towels off the towel rack in the bathroom, to fold and pile them neatly at the foot of the bed, she could not believe that their friends would allow them to leave without protest.

With a wad of toilet paper she cleaned the bathroom sink as Barry called to her to please hurry. She examined the claw-footed tub – she and Barry had each showered that morning – and saw near the drain

[165]

a tiny curly dark hair, hers or Barry's, indistinguish-
able, and this hair she leaned over to snatch up but
her fingers closed in air and she tried another time still
failing to grasp it then finally she picked it up and
flushed it down the toilet. Her face was burning and
her heart knocking so hard in her chest she could
scarcely breathe.

The Carsons left the Riegels' cottage in Nantucket
shortly after noon of the day following their arrival.

They drove seven hours back to their home with a
single stop, silent much of the time but excited,
nervously elated. When he drove Barry kept glancing
in the rear view mirror. One of his eyelids had
developed a tic.

He said, 'We should have done this long ago.'

'Yes,' Charlotte said, staring ahead at dry sun-lit
rushing pavement. 'Long ago.'

That night in their own bed they made love for the
first time in weeks, or months. 'I love you,' Barry
murmured, as if making a vow, '. . . no one but you.'

Tears started out of the corners of Charlotte's tightly
shut eyes.

Afterward Barry slept heavily, sweating through the
night. From time to time he kicked at the covers, but
he never woke. Beside him Charlotte lay staring into
the dark. What would become of them now? Something tickled her lips, a bit of lint, a hair, and though
she brushed it irritably away the tingling sensation
remained. What would become of them, now?

THE DEATH
OF THE POET

Rasaad Jamie

The body, with the length of copper piping tightly and obscenely lodged in the rectum, is found by my father on his way home from the night shift at the waterworks. It's just getting light. The body dangles like a piece of grey padded cloth over the rusty cement mixer, abandoned years ago by the council, in a ditch at the side of the road. The foot and a half of protruding pipe beckons humiliatingly. A hadji, who'd been to Mecca twice, my father refuses to mention it again after he makes a detailed statement to the white police sergeant in charge of the case. Lotus River is crawling with police. This surprises a lot of people; after all it's only him. Nobody thought that they would care. The area around the cement mixer is completely sealed off. Plainclothes men go from house to house asking questions. After the police doctor glances at the body, two men in grey coats remove the pipe with a pair of giant pliers, wrap the body in a piece of plastic and drag it to one of the vans. The television and newspaper people arrive. They're herded on to the field across the road. The sergeant reads them a short statement. They film and photograph the cement mixer peering at them from the ditch. They get into their cars and drive off.

In the tellings and retellings, my mother's eyes intently fixed on my face, I embellish, shape and transform the morning so that I am looking forward to my next recount with a barely contained excitement. My father, always fearful of depravity, had made her

[169]

stay in the house this morning. She is a big woman. In a generous, cumbersome way, she goes about her duties as a Muslim wife and mother with a surprising efficiency. I take after my father. Small and intense, without the solemnity. But that's only because I am eleven, you see. She suspects that I will grow up into a stern and severe believer in the twin values of his light blue kaftan and clean, richly embroidered prayer mat, and that every evening at six o'clock I will boldly and insistently exhort the tired and reluctant Muslims of Lotus River to prayers from the minaret of the damp, half built mosque in Accacia road.

I don't feel like going to school today. I don't think I shall. She will want me to tell her everything about this morning again. She hasn't sworn me to secrecy or anything. She would never be able to get herself to do that. It would be too crucial an admission; it would upset the delicate balance between connivance and collaboration on which our conspiracy is based. She senses my willingness, the way in which I comprehend and accept her predicament. She's about to tell me about her dream last night, but breaks off in mid sentence as if she has second thoughts. This often happens. I have learnt not to press her. She always tells me in the end. With her it's a need, all due to her superstitious conception of my precocious discretion. She sees me as a knowing monkey, intuitive and without intent. It started with my accidental discovery of her smoking. My father foams at the mouth at the idea of a Muslim woman touching a cigarette and turns to violence at the thought of her putting it to her lips. Sent home from school one Friday morning to collect my incomplete project on South African prime ministers since the Republic, I came upon her anxiously puffing away behind the latrines in the yard. She gaped at me, rigid with fear and disbelief. We have never spoken about it, but I date our conspiracy from that moment when our eyes met for two seconds through the stench of the latrines and the sweet, thick smell of low quality tabacco. Still she views me nervously, as if with the onslaught of adolescence I will yield my powers of discretion for a batch of pimples and a tuft of pubic hair.

I am coming home from Koran classes at the mosque in Accacia Road with Sammy Abrahams. He doesn't go to these classes. He's a Christian who doesn't really care. He has refused to go to Sunday school so often that his mother doesn't even bother to send him any more. He has waited for me outside the mosque all afternoon because he wants to tell me something. He thinks his sister is pregnant. She's only fourteen. He makes me promise not to tell anyone by forcing me to stick the tip of my forefinger into my mouth and then pointing it to the sky so that God is our witness and would strike me dead if I breathe a word. The wind is cold against the tip of my finger as I wave my hand in the air. 'She's fucking the boarder,' he says blatantly, assured of my silence. His hands are deep in his pockets, his head lowered. His attitude becomes very matter of fact. He's enjoying himself. His father was run over by a furniture removal lorry five years ago. They took in the boarder a year ago to make ends meet. It's only Sammy, his mother and his sister. He sees himself as the man of the house, although he's only twelve. He likes to pretend that he's burdened with responsibilities. He's going to report the boarder to the Coloured Welfare Authority. He's thinking of arranging a backstreet abortion for his sister. Under no circumstances will he allow his sister to marry an out-of-work bum like their boarder who owes them four months' rent already. Married to Sammy's sister he would stop paying rent altogether.

Towards afternoon it is warm and sunny. My father and I are drowning a litter of kittens in a huge aluminium bath tub. We fill it to about two inches from the top by running a hose from the tap at the side of the house. An ambulance reverses into the Octobers's yard. We don't immediately stop what we are doing, but it is slower, less deliberate, allowing us to take in everything but, as good Muslims, appear not to take too acute an interest in the affairs of our neighbours. My first thought is, perhaps something has happened to October. Maybe he has stuck his finger too far up his nose right into his brain, causing a haemorrhage. He's always picking his nose, even when he is engaged in a religious argument with my father across the fence. My father puts it down to the inherent depravity of the Christian religion, and is forever reminding me that in Mecca you can have your hand cut off for that kind of thing.

So we expect the ambulance men to take October out of the back, a heavy bandage around the upper part of his face and tubes, attached to bottles of blood, coming out of his head. My father, because of his position at the mosque in Accacia Road, doesn't want to let on that he is interested in such things, and tells me to get on with it. Our cat uncannily produces a litter every two months. My father refuses to let her be spayed. If Allah had meant cats to be spayed he would have done so himself, or made all cats one sex. I enjoy the feeling of drowning them and knowing that I am fulfilling the will of the almighty. I put them into the sack one at a time. The second one licks and nuzzles my finger. Our cat is sitting on the fence washing herself. She has witnessed the sight all too often. We might be digging a hole in the garden as far as she is concerned.

The man coming out of the back of the van is not October. He's small. October is like a bus. My father stops blessing the water in the bath. The stranger is sitting on a stretcher like some ancient king, carried by his underlings. Only he is coughing and that spoils the effect somewhat. Sharp, hollow coughs which ring across the yard. 'He will die soon,' my father says. He knows. He has attended the death bed of every Muslim in Lotus River for the last ten years. He has acquired an ear for such things.

They carry him into the shed at the end of the Octobers's yard. He looks like a child, no bigger than myself. But he coughs and struggles for breath as if he's a thousand years old. We suspect that he's a relative of October's, even an illegitimate son, because October is a Christian who drinks from time to time. The kittens have escaped from the sack on the ground and are making for their mother, who stops washing herself for a moment and looks at them crying at the bottom of the fence. I go over, pick them up and put them in the sack again. My father ties the sack with a piece of wire, praying all the time. From the sack their cries are faint. At a nod from my father, I drop the sack in the bath, pushing it right down to the bottom, so that the water comes up my arms to just under my armpits, wetting the sleeves of my short sleeved shirt. I wonder whether the Octobers are allowed to rent out the shed. Why don't they take him into the house with them? The ambulance men seat him on a chair in the doorway and he is looking across the yard at us. Most probably he thinks that we are washing something. My father prays in a low murmur. I remember the kittens at their birth, like a ball of soft hairy worms.

[173]

We always drown them two weeks after they come into the world. It has something to do with Mohammed's sojourn in the desert. They always squeal and squirm when you put them into the sack. I enjoy the feel of them wriggling under my hands, a quivering soggy mass. I used to cry when my father chose to drown them himself. He hasn't done that for a long time. He prefers to pray now. I even slaughter the chickens while he prays. The ambulance men prepare to leave. They're still looking at us. It must seem strange to them. A little boy up to his arms in a tub of water and a bearded man in a light blue kaftan, staring and humming into a Koran.

It's quite hot and we are sitting on the beach, except Salim. My father is in a bad mood. He hates the sea because he is so small and thin. He refuses to remove his clothes. Most people stare at his kaftan and fez. I get up to play in the sand as far away from him as possible. But people still look at me because of the white skull cap.

Salim is wading out into the water. He is the only one of us who can swim. My father says that he can too, but can't because he is an elder at the mosque in Accacia road. The water is up to Salim's waist now. He looks around to see if anybody's watching. I wave to him. He waves back. He wears one of those bathing caps because my father refuses to let us bare our heads, even when swimming. He looks around at the girl wading a few feet behind him. She's looking the other way. He waits until she turns in his direction, and then pinches his nose as if to seal it, and dives. It works. She waits to see where he will emerge. After a long time he pops up about seven feet to the left of her. She must be smiling at him because he has a big grin on his face. He waves to me. She looks around to

[174]

see who he is waving to. I don't wave to her, even
though I have an urge to do so. He dives again and
again, in different styles, each time a bit more flam-
boyantly. He even throws himself over backwards,
clumsily, but his enthusiasm lends an air of off-handed
calculation, even of expertise, to these somersaults.
The girl is thrilled with his performances. I can almost
hear the ring of her excited cries from where I am on
the beach. Her hands shoot up with a pumping motion
each time he lands with a splash. I imagine these cries
are like music to his ears. All the time he goes out
further. The girl can't be Muslim, at least not a good
one, loyal to the Faith, or else she wouldn't go about
without a scarf and in that skimpy bathing suit.
Suddenly I can't see my brother. I look in the direction
in which the girl is looking. Yes, there he is. Waving
his arms. He is being swept out to sea. I call to my
parents who are arguing. It takes them something like
three minutes to realise what is going on. My mother
starts to scream, goes into a fit and collapses. My
father pays no attention to her, writhing in the sand.
He goes over to one of our bags, takes the Koran with
the red cover from it, sits down, searches for the
appropriate text, finds it and starts reading. About
four feet away from my father, squatting and hunched
over the Koran, my mother is lying sprawled out,
oblivious like a sack. My father is soon a conspicuous
light blue on the white sand because everybody is
crowding near the edge of the sea to watch my brother
bobbing up for the second time. Three men try to
swim towards him but he is too far out. I don't know
where the girl has disappeared to. There is no sign of
her. Someone told me that people who drown go down
and come up again three times and if they are not
rescued before then, that's it. But my brother comes

[175]

up five times before he disappears forever, desperately waving his arms out in the distance. In the evening we are taken home by ambulance. My father blames my mother for dragging us out there when he and the Muslim Faith were against it from the start.

Nobody tells us that he's a poet. Suddenly it's just in the air. Everybody knows. Nobody in Lotus River has heard of him or any other poet for that matter, except maybe Shakespeare, but he's white and dead and famous with the schools and universities behind him. *Him*, most people think he's a bum. Any Coloured who thinks he's a poet must be a good for nothing loafer or a deranged bum. My mother wonders whether he has a wife or ever had a wife. She watches him through the kitchen window. He often sits on the milk crate against the wall of the shed, reading in the sun. The shed is filled with books, Mrs Olivier tells my mother. She's sure they're all dirty and banned. My mother finds the idea of a man being at home all day difficult to cope with. That would never happen with my father. After his heart attack four years ago, when everyone from the doctor to the social worker had urged him to take it easy, he had gone out every morning looking for work until he found the job cleaning machines and shifting barrels at the waterworks. And it's shift work. But look at him, sound and healthy as any man half his age and ten times as religious.

Orville Jacobs tells my father that the man in the shed is actually under house arrest. That will change a few people's opinion of him. He can't go out to work even if he wants to. Orville thinks he does a bit of book-keeping to pay the rent and to get by. Orville thinks that everyone with a bit of schooling simply keeps books while he kills himself digging up and repairing roads for the council. The Octobers are over-charging him for that shed, even though he's October's nephew. My mother wonders what it is about certain Coloureds that as soon as they get a bit of education they no longer want to work as teachers for the Department of Coloured Affairs. They want to run the country, tell the white man what to do. She plans for me to leave school around standard eight, perhaps apprentice me as a carpenter somewhere. The idea is for me to earn a decent wage as a skilled man so that I'll be able to support them in their old age. There is nothing that Allah detests so much as a son who doesn't bring in good money.

People sometimes come to see him. They have to go into the shed one at a time to talk to him. At the same time my mother begins to notice them watching him. Two cars parked prominently and defiantly at each end of the road. Her interest, once aroused, grows keener to the point of obsession. When I come home from school she tells me about his day: who came to see him, for how long, how many times he went to the makeshift toilet which stands faltering in full sight of our kitchen window. I often run into him circling the small field at the end of the road. He gets sick of being cooped up in the shed all the time. In this way he defies his banning order, but nothing ever happens. The one car informs the other by walkie-talkie. He's still on the field. Some kid passing him now. When I get home I tell her I saw him skirting the football pitch.

It disturbs my father that he is taking so long to die. We're all waiting for one or both of his lungs to collapse, for his chest to seize up, and for clots of blood and shreds of lung as big as my fist to bubble at his mouth, for him in a moment of illumination

[177]

afforded only by the proximity of death to call for my father to convert him to Islam before it's too late, and to die with a smile on his face. But he should have done that already, so my father decides that Satan looks after his own, for the word is also getting around that he doesn't believe in God. Crowding the kitchen window, the three of us watch Pastor Roberts, a man who is thoroughly acquainted with the temptations and pitfalls that an education holds out for Coloureds. Himself educated at the University of the Western Cape, he is conversant with all the arguments from communism to black power, from drugs to group sex. He emerges three hours later, shaking his head. My father scratches his beard, screws up his eyes and blames it on the audacity of the Christian religion to elevate Jesus to the level of God. The truth is he's a minor prophet, a lot less significant than Mohammed.

'People know about him. He has written books,' Orville Jacobs says to my mother. His eyes, coated with a transparent slime as thick as jelly, protrude as if they are about to pop out of his head. It's almost impossible to talk to him and look him in the face, so my mother stares out of the kitchen window at the shed. The door is shut. He must be circling the field. 'You might say he's famous,' Orville says without taking his lips off the rim of the cup. My mother will get rid of it, saucer and all, as soon as he leaves. 'He's known overseas. That's why he was banned and put under house arrest in the first place.' Orville almost shouts. 'He was getting too well known,' he says knowingly. He likes to give the impression that he's politically involved, that he knows what's going on. An uncle or a cousin of his was killed during a riot on Robben Island. No one knows for certain whether this relative was a political prisoner who tried to blow up a police station, as Orville claims, or whether he was just out there for the day doing maintenance work for the council and was shot by mistake. All this happened before Orville, his mother and his four sisters came to Lotus River. He is the only friend my father has, Christian or otherwise. Except for one or two points concerning religion, they agree on almost everything. Some weekends he even helps with the building of the mosque. After Orville leaves, my mother tells me she sees *him* scribbling in a notebook. She doesn't know where he hides it. The shed is turned upside down and searched quite regularly. He must have found a good place for it. One where they won't dream of looking, she says, dropping the cup and saucer into the bin.

We are watching the ten or so white men searching in and around the shed. People come running from all over to see. This happens about once a month. Soon the whole of Lotus River will be here. 'Security Police' Orville Jacobs says to my father, who pulls his beard and nods as if he knew all along. We watch them take the furniture and the books outside. They take the two cupboards apart. Three of them get on the roof of the shed, and examine it, inch by inch. He stands to one side, watched over by another white man, alert and severe looking. The one in the green suit slits the mattress along its side, reaches into the opening with his hands as if into a belly, showering the yard with brown hair. My mother wants to know — will they repair it or refund him? My father signals for her to be quiet. They start to take the old fridge, which stood at the side of the shed for the last ten years, apart. One of them approaches the pile of books, picks up one, carefully leafs through it and then tears off the cover to see if there's anything in the spine. 'It's going

[179]

to take him all day,' my mother whispers. Four others take spades and start to dig holes in the Octobers's yard. 'Someone must have tipped them off,' Orville says to my father. 'They seem convinced that there's something to be found.' He stands to one side shivering in his vest. They won't let him put his clothes on. 'That bastard is just waiting for him to make a run for it,' Orville says. I have never seen anyone being shot before, except in the films. I desperately wish he would make a run for it. But he just stands there, one hand in his pocket and the other pulling nervously at the short, oily curls around the bald patch on top of his head. With his short limbs and protruding stomach, he looks dwarfish, ridiculous amidst the efficient bustle of the white men.

This morning we watched him being taken away. 'For questioning,' my mother says. Suddenly, like Orville Jacobs, she too is familiar with such matters. There was hardly any expression on his face as he got into the back of the van, flanked by two men. He was dressed only in a thin white sweater and baggy blue pants. His lips moved as if he is praying or talking to himself. It's my mother's idea that we should have a look inside the shed while the Octobers are away at work. 'He never locks it,' she says. He has a little bird inside the shed. It cries and claws to the side of the cage as we come through the door. My mother tells me to put water in its tiny bowl. I feed it a packet of bird seed that I find on the table. It's small inside the shed. Bed, table, one of those double burner paraffin stoves. A wall of clumsy shelving made out of stacked bricks and long strips of board. He has nailed a tomato box against the wall over the table on which are standing two bottles of ink and a glass jar of assorted pens and pencils. I want one and, as soon as my mother looks out of the door to see if anyone's coming, I snatch at the black fountain pen and knock over the jar, scattering everything in it on the floor. 'What's that!' my mother says alarmed, ready to run. I go down to pick up the scattered pens. I find the black fountain pen and quickly put it in my pocket. There are stones of different shapes and sizes, pieces of bark, bones and a bright red plastic canister. I remember the canister. It used to lie on the rubbish dump across the road. He collects these things while he circles the fields. His books, torn and hopeless, are stacked about on the floor, some in boxes. There is a photograph of a white man with glasses and curly hair on the crate next to his bed. My mother picks it up and looks at it for a long time. The bed is still unmade. My mother moves towards it to make it out of habit, but checks herself. It's really like a hen coop in here, it's so small. I notice a typewriter under the bed. The keys are stiff, clogged with dust and rust. It hasn't been used for years. The bird jumps about in the cage screeching. It seems as if it will never stop. 'God knows how he stands the noise,' my mother says. 'I would have strangled that damn thing long ago.'

He came back this afternoon. He's sitting on a milk crate, his mouth moving. My mother thinks he's praying. I think he's just talking to himself because it's so cold and he's wearing nothing but that thin sweater and that silly pair of pants. It's getting dark. Soon he'll be able to see us watching him because of the light in the kitchen, and we'll only be able to see the glow of his cigarette.

'I come into the kitchen,' she says, about to tell her dream at last, 'it must be about four in the afternoon because I am thinking about lighting the fire and preparing your father's food for the night shift. *He* is

[181]

sitting at the table. I think it's your father, wondering why he's not sleeping or praying in the bedroom. But it's him. "I see you look at me through the window," he says. He looks very tired. I don't know what to say to him. I want him to go because it is about time for your father to wake up and go to work. "I see you watching me through the window," he says again, just sitting there. I grow anxious because I can hear your father praying in the bedroom. He just sits there. I become desperate and take hold of him. He clings to the table. It's all so difficult. I don't want to alert your father. I try to tear his hands away from the table. I hit him over the knuckles with the heavy spoon. I see him open his mouth. I know he is going to scream and arouse your father. I cannot allow that. I quickly drop the spoon and seize him at the throat with both hands. His mouth opens and closes silently. I sigh with relief as I watch him gasp for breath. Suddenly he goes limp and hangs from my hands as if there isn't a bone in his body, just like a sack. As I wonder what to do with the body I hear your father's footsteps coming towards the kitchen.'

She's shaking badly. I see her lighting a cigarette in the kitchen for the first time. I open both windows to indicate something of the nature of my comprehension. I can't console her openly. It won't do. Allowances for such an eventuality are nowhere to be found among the multitude of our mute but lucid understandings.

THE INTERROGATOR'S DIVORCE

Paul Sayer

Where, you might ask, is the state of Judpara?

On the map it skews like a three-fingered hand, not two hundred miles across at its widest point, barely fifteen miles broad at its most vulnerable forequarter. Our climate is mild with short summers and unspectacular winters. We are a long way from the sea. A handsome lake is the nestling jewel in our flatlands but the mountains, such as they are, barely trouble the horizon and are smothered by scrub. But Judpara is a very real place, real indeed, and being just forty years on from the revolution that cast off our tyrannical rulers, it is still in the process of vigorous renewal and reinvention.

Divorce is frowned upon here – the family unit is very much both the foundation and the superstructure of our democracy. Imagine, then, my dilemma this day as I pore over the papers from my estranged wife's legal representatives which inform me that the term of our separation is now over and we may apply for the annulment of our wedding vows. Torn between loyalty to my country and the dissolution of the love affair of my life – and it was that, my dear Yvette, it was that – I realize I have now reached the impasse I have been dreading these seven long years.

I should explain my position for I am not of the common classes of our country. Rather, I am in an honoured and elevated strata, a servant of the people, yes, but also their watchdog, their conscience.

My name is Beaumont and I am an official interrogator whose *rôle* involves the ascription and arrest of

[185]

subversion and civil disobedience. My tasks of late have been many and arduous for there is much new antagonism being shown against our government. Try and understand me when I say that should news of my failed marriage leak out, then I become vulnerable, suspect in the eyes of my superiors – not that there is a single one of them who has not at some time contravened against the socially accepted boundaries of our civilization.

This morning I have arrived for work as usual. I am alone on the ground floor of the small converted warehouse that serves the purposes of my calling. I fumble with the papers in my hand like an adolescent. I pause before the mirror as if to check for signs of my own duplicity and see only my old face, its reptiloid features seeming more pointed than ever. I am unhappy, I say to myself. But not bewildered. The cold air in this place informs me that Ramon, my one assistant and apprentice, a doleful sort, has not yet arrived. He is late and might shamble in at any moment, catching me in this hesitant pose. I cannot risk that. The bare wooden staircase to my office beckons me and I climb up to seek temporary sanctuary there.

Now I can sit back in my comfortable chair and idle a while, reading again the documents that were delivered to my home this morning. I note that we have agreed, my darling Yvette, that I kept you short of money. This, of course, is untrue, but it helps to conceal our simple hatred of each other. And we have made no mention of my whore Charlene. That is good too. With the plain facts before me I feel more reassured. I might get away with this yet. I am not the first, nor shall I be the last. But it will be a difficult, unseemly business, this.

A door in some far part of the building is closed
with a thud. He is here. I slither the papers away into
my desk drawer. He rushes into the office without a
word and I sense the sulkiness in him that I despise.
See how he slumps behind his desk, loose and gangly.
I loathe that posture of his. Where do they find them
these days? How could those popsies in the recruit-
ment centre in Telfa ever have dreamed this boy to be
capable of the serious, vital work of interrogation? Six
months he has been with me, and for what use he's
made of that time I might as well have worked alone.
Even the most rudimentary tasks – those I performed
with zest when I was his age and in his position, such
as cleaning the interview room after an untidy session
with a suspect – he does in a dilatory and self-absorbed
way. He knows when to keep quiet though, I'll give
him that. He is quiet nearly all of the time and it suits
us both, I think.

This morning, my senses heightened a little by my
own predicament, I divine something different about
him, an aggression, a look of resentment which
interests me. He glances up at the notice board and
sees that we only have Bovingdon, the dull pilferer, to
deal with this morning – and he not for another hour.
Ramon's discomfort may be made worse by the
thought of this blank time, this period when I should
be contriving some vigour and haste, some sham
industry to discourage any ideas of idleness. But I do
not have the energy today. 'Tell me, Ramon,' I ask.
'Forgive me for never asking before, but are you
married?'

'No, Mr Beauont. I am not married,' comes the
reply accompanied by a sigh that surprises me.

'Do you want to know why I ask?'

'I think that, in your way, you're about to make

[187]

some reference to my lateness. I slept in. That's all. It happens from time to time.'

See how defensive he is? Like all the young. 'Forget it,' I say. 'I shall make no mention of it in my report. You are a good timekeeper, I have noted it before. But I should like to know more about you. We get so few opportunities to talk informally.'

He leans back on his chair, casting a rueful eye at the radiator which, had he been here first as he should have been, he would have turned up to its highest setting. He stifles a shiver, writhing in his heavy suit. He hates this place, despises me. I, of course, have an eye for such things. 'I like a quiet life, Mr Beaumont,' he offers reluctantly. 'There isn't much to tell you that you wouldn't already know. I am an only child. My parents live in the East Sector of Loser. I have lodgings on this side of town, two streets from the Hall of Commerce. I live alone. I work here. Is that enough?'

I smile and nod in appreciation of this little out-burst. I shall not press him further: conceding him this small victory might pep him up a little, bring him to life. He should be encouraged by all this.

'To work then, Ramon,' I say. 'As you can see, we have a quiet morning and hopefully it will stay that way. Bovingdon will be here at ten-thirty, but I shall spend no more than half an hour with him. I see nothing new emerging from that dreary rodent.'

He scribbles something, perhaps notes about the tedious case we are soon to deal with, though we both know our minds are locked in that early tension between us and we are quite unable, as yet, to address our minds properly to the day's work that lies ahead.

*

Anew, Yvette, I think of the evening of your departure, the benign entertainment to which we treated each other, that little drama when you stood in the hallway of our home with Samuel – him, two years old and already gauche – and I, all pride gone, in my weakness, yes, my frailty, delivered one last, hopeless petition: 'There is still time. Couldn't you come back in a few days and we'll think it through again?'

'There's nothing left to think about. We've been over everything.'

'Are you being fair to the boy?'

'Your sudden interest in his well-being fails to impress me, I'm afraid.'

'But we do love each other, you must admit that.'

'Love? Is that what you call it? I have not heard that word from you before. It must have been a trial for you to wrench it from your throat.'

'But I have *feelings* for you.'

'You have considerations only for the poor light this might show you in with your superiors. I know you too well. Please don't insult me by taking me for one of your terrified "interviewees" as you so quaintly refer to them.'

I nearly wept then, after you had gone. Truly, Yvette, I could have blubbered and blustered, if I'd been the type. But I was more troubled by the hatred you showed me. Was that real? Was there some other reason? Someone else?

The day drags slowly on and before us now we have Bovingdon.

What a bore this man is. If the new subversion that plagues our country was represented by a body this fellow would be no more than a loose hair on its head,

[189]

a spleen cell, a speck of dust in a pore. He was caught house-breaking – he has a long record of futile crime – and should normally have been dealt with by a small court were it not for the fact that the bag of tools he was carrying held some specialist piece, the like of which our intelligence people have noted only once before, in the possession of the Pelargue tunnellers, a dangerous group who attempted to free political prisoners from the Pelargue High Security Settlement.

For the purposes of interrogation, I should explain, the subject is seated in a high-backed chair between the arms of which my fumbling assistant slots a thin tray, quite easy to remove should the one who is being questioned so wish it. This tray simply affords the *principle* of a barrier, though few but the most desperate and foolhardy would ever attempt to lift it. There are no straps or restraints of any kind, please note, for ours is nothing if not a modern and civilized process.

Now here we have this Bovingdon creature sitting with his hands pressing against the tray, unusually scorning the comfort of leaning back. His head is pink and bald, save for long wisps of white hair swept behind his ears. He has an unchanging, vapid expression and his flecked eyes stare straight at my chest. I can smell something on him, his breakfast, perhaps. But what interests me most is this posture of his: head forward and low, in exactly the right place should I want to deliver a blow. Perhaps that is what he wants me to do, thinking that he will have cause to lodge some official complaint later about my physical violation of him, my contravention of his rights. If so, it is obvious that he has no understanding of the law at this high level. Here in this small crucial branch of our country's defence system, few restrictions apply. I step back, arms folded, so that he is forced to look me in the eye. I begin again: 'You had no pass. You are a known criminal and have been in prison many times. Loser is a place you should not have ventured near. Your home is in the Darecq downlands and you know that with your record you cannot travel from there without a pass.'

'They took it from me the last time I was inside, sir. They didn't give me a new one when I was released.'

For the life of me, I cannot help but take on the chiding, paternal voice of a small town magistrate. 'You could have asked. Surely it's not beyond you to remind our busy officials that you must have a security pass?'

'I mentioned it, but they wouldn't give me one. I think they wanted me to stay put in Darecq.'

'And so you should have, Bovingdon.'

'Yes sir.'

This is old territory, covered before in each of our two previous interviews. I turn, as I must, to the question of the implement he was caught with. 'Who makes the tools for the Pelargue tunnellers?'

'I don't know.'

'You have heard of the aborted Pelargue operation?'

'No sir. I have not. I know nothing about it. As I said before . . .'

'Do you realize the consequences of being caught in possession of an item such as this?'

I produce the thing before his eyes, holding it with a tissue. Looking at it again, I'm forced to admit that it seems no different from an ordinary woodworker's clamp, though I am reliably told it is, somehow, a quite sinister piece of machinery.

'I had no idea it was so important. I found it in an alley in the Old Quarter. Lots of things get thrown away in the alleys. If I'd known there was something

[191]

illegal about it I should have handed it straight to the police.'

He is lying, of course. And badly too.

Such a day this is becoming. I am finding it hard to concentrate and I put the tool aside for a moment. Ramon is seated at his desk in the corner, making notes, doodling perhaps. And who could blame him for that? I am bored too.

Now I must confess I am tempted to deliver this Bovingdon a slap, to make him flare a little, though I know in my heart that it will not bring results. I let the moment pass until I can see from behind my fleeting anger. And the plebeian Bovingdon's watery eyes have seen my hesitancy, my frustration. He knows, instinctively, despite his native obtuseness, that he is safe now.

I have had enough. I nod to Ramon who unlocks the big door and beckons the waiting guards inside. 'Take him away,' I say.

Ramon lifts the tray from the chair and at the moment of Bovingdon's abrupt rise to his feet I realize there is something wrong, something substantial that I have not discovered about this ageing recidivist. His eyes flicker away from mine and he looks towards the door. He is still hiding something. I have made too many assumptions about him. There is an intelligence at work here, somewhere, after all.

Often, at this point, I permit the subject to be led from my workroom back to the vehicle that brought him. This period of time, when he believes his ordeal to be over, can sometimes make the interviewee succumb to a rising joy which might well shake him from his stoical resistance to my questioning. If I notice this – and it is a requirement of the seasoned interrogator to be able to spot such slight, vital clues – I will consciously decide on a length of time by which I require the guards to delay his departure. They may choose their own ruse: the feigning of some problem with their vehicle is quite normal. Then, from my upstairs office window I will watch the subject settle into his seat in the van, observing the extent of his relief in the way that he relaxes, his facial expressions, and so on. The most suspect ones are those who make no overt movements at all. Sometimes I might even go so far as to leave the building myself on some make-believe errand, perhaps to lunch, and I might smile at the interviewee as I pass, letting him watch through the thick tinted windows of the van as I disappear down the street. And on my return he might detect the slightest urgency in my step, a whit of perplexity in my countenance as I re-enter the building. Then I will ask for him to be brought back, often going outside myself if I think my sceptical smile might unsettle him further. 'Just a few more points. Mere details,' I would quietly insist. 'If you don't mind.'

This morning the four of them – Bovingdon, Ramon, and the two green-uniformed guards – are waiting for my word. I remain undecided. I am tired, I must admit. Perhaps this once . . .

I shake my head as a sign to Ramon that he may tell the guards to take their charge away. Later I shall file a report stating that Bovingdon spoke the truth to a factor of only thirty per cent. On the strength of this the courts will pass their sentence which, for house-breaking, for being in possession of a suspect implement, for movement without a pass, will be five years, should be ten for the nuisance his petty larceny causes.

I am unhappy. I have not performed well. I return to the upstairs office briefly concerned that Ramon, perhaps with some justification, might suspect me of having become slipshod in my duties.

See, Yvette, how you affect my work? You have much to answer for with your divorce papers, your defiance of me and my position, your utter, utter selfishness.

Twelve-fifteen.

'Go,' I say to Ramon, 'to the Interrogational Records Department in the Sipraloo Chambers and ask for the notes of my interviews with Buzan, Clatters and Qot. I have need of them.'

We both know I only want to be alone. He stands slowly. 'I have a pain,' he says.

'Where? Where is this pain?' I ask, forcing myself to look at his ridiculous expression of discomfort. Wretched youth.

'In my leg. The left one.'

'The exercise might do a leg pain a deal of good,' I venture.

'Yes, Mr Beaumont.'

'Then go. Go.'

'I will.'

He sniffs and departs sheepishly, not bothering with his coat, a martyr to the last.

From my office window I watch him walking down the street, not looking back. He trips over nothing and stumbles to his knees. Then he picks himself up and carries on.

Once again I rifle through this abstracted notice of our latter disaffections. Perhaps I have been rather too generous with you, made things too easy. I seem to be taking the blame for everything. Is there nothing on *your* conscience, my darling viper? Were you really so untainted? You were attractive and I would wager that the years have been kind to your wholesome dark features. I cannot think there has been no one else in *your* life.

Now I am troubled by a few mischievous thoughts. What if I were to object to these proceedings? Even at this late hour I could put a stop to it all, for the law is rigid on its insistence that both parties must be absolutely willing to end the marriage. What if I delayed another three months, another year, long enough for me to have you investigated? I could do that as you must realize, and I am sure such a knowledge has been a source of fear for you . . .

Ah, spite, spite. It will achieve nothing now.

The day does not go well. Now I have been summoned to the Ilakoy airfield to attend an official gathering at the site of some fresh subversive activity.

I wait outside my premises, watching the rainwater dripping from the stark branches of a sturdy old ash in the centre of the empty square. What summer have we had? Every year we ask this, we Judparans, with lamentation in our voices.

What summer? I might hear from an over-relaxed subject come for interrogation . . .

Ramon has not yet returned from his errand. How happy he will be to have the afternoon alone, to set about his favourite business of idling, perhaps ringing his friends on the office telephone. Deceitful boy. And he is intelligent, you know. Such a waste.

The blue staff car arrives and I climb into the rear.

[195]

It is a roomy vehicle, though, and that is something in this age of civil service economies. 'How long to Ilakoy?' I ask the driver.

'Less than an hour, sir,' he says, eyeing me in his mirror, 'Providing the road is clear.'

'And should it not be?'

'Fighting, sir. Over the weekend.'

I have heard nothing of this. 'Away then,' I say. 'Quickly as you like.'

We are soon in the countryside, the piddling mountains behind me and to all sides the flatlands, the green and brown patchwork of fields going to purple in the distant gloom. A little way on I see brief orange reflections among the far low clouds. Leaning forward I watch the skies closely through the rain-mottled window. I count four little sunbursts and what looks like a tree exploding, though I hear nothing.

Why have I not been informed of these 'new' troubles? I feel oddly vulnerable and think that the driver senses something of my plight when I politely enquire as to whether or not he minds if I open a window.

In times gone by, Yvette, I should not have had to suffer your rejection of me: the government has become too liberal with the likes of you, with all of us. Yes, I may be out of tune, shuddering at the new philosophy that allows us our so-called 'freedoms', but I cannot be completely wrong. There is a part of me, quite independent of social and political thinking and influence, that says this openness, this coming and going, this right to 'choose', will be our downfall.

What kind of man will Samuel grow into? I know I had little time for him, but he is often in my thoughts

[196]

now. Sometimes I dream that I am standing naked before the mirror in our bedroom. I am void and still. Sammy comes into the room and asks: 'Are you all right Father?'

I cannot be angry with him for catching me in so indecorous a pose. 'I'm fine, boy. Really.'

'Would you like me to fetch you anything? You don't seem well.'

'Don't worry about me,' I say as I watch my reflection turning into a grotesque apparition before me. 'Run along now.'

'If you say so.'

'I do say so, Samuel. I do.'

The spectre leaps from the mirror and evaporates. The tension that has held me inexplicably is suddenly released and I lie down on the bed. I think I can hear my son beating on the door, miserably wailing, asking to be let in, but then I wake and, of course, there is no one there.

A small transporter aircraft, its silver back broken and its flayed metal innards bared to the elements, is central to the scene of mild chaos I find at the airfield. Officer personnel of the Judparan Air Force yell orders to ratings who run everywhere yet seem to be doing nothing of genuine purpose. This contrived urgency though, combined with the smell of oil and damp, suffices to make the hairs on the back of my neck bristle and ruffle. This proximity to any kind of catastrophe always serves to unsettle me.

There are twenty or so of us – interrogators and apprentices. I know some of the older men and am acknowledged by two of them. I fret over the names of others which are called and which I recognize vaguely from despatches and memoranda. I am given to thinking about the sheltered life I lead in provincial

Loser, paying scant attention to Zibbs, the secretary to the Defence Minister, who is addressing us.

'I am sorry,' he says, 'to bring you here at such short notice. But before the clean-up operation begins, the Minister felt that you should see for yourselves the extent of this new wave of subversion and sabotage. As you will have noticed, the events of last Sunday evening are real enough, though naturally none of this will be reported in the press or on television. Gentlemen, our democracy is being seriously threatened. I am asking you today to take notice of these heinous occurrences and for you all to renew your oaths never to . . . never to . . . rest in . . . er . . .' he shakes bits of limp paper in his hands.

'We should not fail in our duty to our countrymen, to the working classes, in the fight against Imperialism,' offers a bright thing in a very smart black coat.

Zibbs peers down at the glistening young man. 'Precisely, er . . .'

'Adelbert, sir.'

'Well said, Adelbert.'

The older hands among us have already winced at the boy's rhetoric and I, for one, feel positively gloomy as I see him blush and sparkle as he receives the whispered congratulations of his equally youthful colleagues. Naïve as they may be, there is a certain charm in their enthusiasm and I wonder briefly how my own lacklustre charge, Ramon, would have fared in their company.

Zibbs, made eloquent now by a new piece of paper handed to him by his aide, tells us of a military reprisal taking place this very afternoon against a pocket of mercenaries in Uptha, a town dangerously close to my own area. He assures us that these 'foreign' influences will now either be dead or on their way to the Pelargue settlement and that, wonder of wonders, we are to prepare for an even heavier workload in the months ahead.

My bones ache in the cold wind. I stare down at my feet on the muddy grass trying to accommodate the idea of a national crisis in my mind. I am what I am, too old to change my ways, beyond being convinced by this weakly-inspired rallying cry that has come from a philosophy in decline. Thankfully, the meeting is beginning to dissemble with questions from the young men, aimed solely at showing their patriotism, being fired at Zibbs, this rare visitor from central government.

Among the old hands I spot Donner, a former student of mine. Can it be three decades since he left me? We exchange greetings and I notice his grey expression which seems to match my own. This man, one of the best apprentices I ever had, is someone I can trust.

'So where's the real fire?' I ask in our customarily cryptic way of seeking indiscretion, the truth behind official pronouncements.

'The civil unrest?'

'If you like.'

'It's pretty bad. Ours is a small country. We allow our people too much freedom to cross the borders. They find out about life under liberal governments. And there is the resurgence of religious beliefs. Do you know there are people out there ready to die rather than give a simple denunciation of their god? Intelligent, some of them,' he says, rubbing his stubbled chin thoughtfully. 'Maybe we should listen to them. It would cost nothing to review our policy of secularism. But there are many old fools still in power. Time some of them were rooted out.'

This kind of talk dismays me – disillusionment these days, it seems, is not confined to my own personal province. 'Do you air these views openly?' I ask. 'You never know who might be listening.'

'Look at the young men,' he says, wagging a finger in their direction. 'See their superficiality. If the revolution came, who do you think would be the first to swap sides? Already I have my doubts about several of them.' He yawns and rubs his eyes. 'I'm forty-nine and washed up. I cannot learn the new tricks. You should come to Telfa one day. It would open your eyes. I must go. Forgive me if I'm being rude.'

'Shouldn't we keep in touch?' I ask, wanting to hear more from him.

'If you want to,' he says, wearily waving his hand in farewell as he stumbles across the littered airfield to the cars parked by the perimeter gate.

I'm sorry, Yvette, but in my old age, in my wintering body, I feel the past owes me something. Our years together, few that they were, seem precious to me in this hour. I remember your soft skin beneath my thick insensitive fingers, your suppleness and coy laughter. Ridiculous really, the words of a sentimentalist. But do you know, my dear, how lonely old men can be? No, you do not. Neither decay nor the fear of death enter your thoughts. How could you be doing this to me now if they did?

Back at my workplace I slowly climb the stairs.

Ramon is here, back from his 'errand', in the chest-griping heat of the office. Just once I wish he would surprise me by not turning the radiator on at all. I hang up my coat and hat and stride over to the control knob, turning it down three of its ten points. Then in a split second of decision I switch the thing off altogether.

'It's colder than usual today,' he moans.

'Not in here,' I snap. 'When it gets properly cold then we shall use the heater accordingly. Too much warmth will make us soft and prone to chest infections and all manner of minor disabilities the new winter is likely to bring.'

Now he sulks. One day I shall strike him, I'm sure I will. But wait, what is that stupid expression on his face? I sit at my desk and we face each other in silence. At last, hardly able to control my temper I say: 'Oh spit it out. Spit it out. I can tell you have something in your small mind that I should know about.'

He stiffens in the teeth of my aggression – we have never sunk so low before in our relationship. 'You've had a phone call. They want you to ring them back. It seems urgent.'

'I suppose it would be pointless my asking who the caller might have been?'

'I've put the number in your diary.'

I open the book on my desk. The number is not familiar.

'They must have said who they were.'

'No.'

'My dear boy, this could be very important. Do try and remember where you are working. Have you checked the number with the central tracing department in Telfa?'

'I think it may be personal.'

And of course he knows who it was. He will undoubtedly have checked the number if he thought it was confidential. Satisfied with seeing my discomfort he reminds me that it is five'o'clock and asks if he can go. I have no choice but to let him. I shall deal with him some other time. 'Go. Go.'

He is out of the office in seconds. I await the closing of the door downstairs before taking the papers from my desk and ascertaining that the number is indeed, as I suspected, that of the Marriage Registration Bureau in the Loser Offices of Affinity.

So now you have decided to make your move. Clever girl. Have you sensed my frailty from that squalid den I know you occupy in the Eastern Quarter? The clerk on the other end of the line makes maudlin prevarications about the size of his caseload and asks if I object to the divorce proceedings being heard at a late and unusual time. I state clearly that I have no quarrel with the hour and that I am ready to answer all that the magistrate might ask.

Is it my weakness to see you again that makes me decide this? Tonight then, after hundreds of nights spent grieving over your departure, we shall meet again for the occasion of our parting. If I should so wish it, remember. If I should so wish it . . .

The court is as spiritless a place as I could imagine: grimy cream walls, the lights bright against the autumnal gloom outside the curtainless windows. By day it will be used for criminal cases such as Bovingdon's. He may even be here, locked in the bowels of the building, scratching himself, feeling the features of his face in the dark of his cell.

Yvette sits between two clerks, her heart full of cinders.

The magistrate reads my wife's declaration of intent

in acrid tones, weakly imbuing it with the State's disapproval of the failure of a marriage and its conse- quences for our society and our planned economy. He cites my calling as that of civil servant and Yvette offers a look of loathing. I can barely concentrate on his words, feel quite indifferent to them, preferring to watch my wife, to note the greyness in her hair, the slight emaciation and stooped posture that the last seven years have wrought on her. She may have hated my calling, but if nothing else, I did at least keep her properly dressed and nourished.

Fighting against sleep, it seems, the magistrate shuffles papers, rubs his eyes and begins his brief résumé of our marriage. I can hardly make out his words, my head being filled with many memories, thoughts about myself, about a time past that may never have existed, except in my imagination. At last he seeks my response to Yvette's request for the dissolution of our married state.

What shall I do? Keep the longing alive? I have that at least, the desire for you, that shifting rootless wish. I am an old man now and old men need their dreams. The whole court is quiet while I consider the options. Everyone is looking at me except Yvette. I totter on my feet at the end of this long and trying day, this season of disaffection when I know I am wearying of all the lies, the deceit, the circumvention I deal in myself.

'Where is Samuel?'

I hear my own words. I see the faces around me woken from their half-dozing.

'Where is my son?'

What am I doing? Am I going mad?

'Do you have something you wish to say?' asks the

[203]

magistrate, surprised as we all are by my obscure articulations.

I must get a grip on myself. 'I'm sorry,' I say, in a more familiar voice. 'A ghost has been walking over my grave, I fear. I consent to all that my wife requests.'

Taking advantage of my professional status – a State interrogator is subordinate to few in this land – knowing I will not be opposed, I leave the court before the remainder of the proceedings are instigated.

On the steps outside I button my coat against a sharp wind and set off across the square. Somewhere to the north there is gunfire. Perhaps there will be revolution after all. And maybe the sun will fall from the sky. I walk on through the dark empty streets, indifferent to it all, asking only for a little more time – time to reflect on the history that enslaves me, dogs us all, time to contemplate what remains in my heart, my soul, or some other cold cavity.

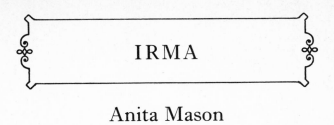

IRMA

Anita Mason

The last tourist of the day was standing just inside the high wrought-iron gates. He was spindly, with a fair skin over-exposed to the sun, and Irma put him down as English. She didn't get many English people. They were careful with their money, but at least none of them had ever put their hands on her breasts. She whistled to attract his attention, and called him over.

She was obliged to do this because if she left her place at the top of the steps Senhor Coelho would rush out from his cupboard and put up the 'Closed' sign. He tried to do this every afternoon at twenty to five, although the building didn't close until five o'clock. He said it was not possible to show someone round the rooms in twenty minutes. Irma knew this was nonsense. It was perfectly possible if you talked quickly and kept up a smart pace.

And in any case, it was necessary.

She ushered her tourist through the panelled hall, past the malevolent stare of Senhor Coelho and into the first of the reception rooms. As they entered it, he drew in his breath. They often did that. She had done it, too, the first time; and then later, when she had a spare few minutes, she had sometimes crept back to look; and in the end they had become just tiles on a wall.

She envied the strangers she brought into this room, who were seeing the tiles for the first time. She would say, in whatever language it was (she could do the talk in four), 'They are very beautiful', and watch the response with some eagerness, as if she could draw their perception into herself.

The tiles had been made in Portugal in the seventeenth century by a Delft tilemaker, a Dutchman, she said. There were friezes in all the ground-floor rooms and passageways. The tourist commented that the subjects were not religious. This was true: one room was decorated with hunting scenes, another with battles, and the third with street scenes of Lisbon. She loved their worldliness, the fact that they had nothing whatever to do with the Third Order of St Francis.

And their boldness. For these were not decorative tiles, they were paintings. They were art. And the blue, so rich and sensuous, yet so pure . . . You never saw a blue like that. And yet when she thought of blue, it was that blue.

These things weren't in the talk Irma had memorised. The talk was full of names, dates and figures; there was a great deal of information in it and she thought it was good value. Sometimes her attention would drift when she was giving it. She would start thinking about Joaquim or dinner, and come back and find herself in the middle of a sentence and wonder how she'd got there.

There was nothing in the talk that explained the tiles. There was nothing in it that explained anything else either.

'They are very beautiful,' she said in English.

He nodded slowly. He was absorbed.

Irma beamed. For a moment she looked at the tiles with him. Then she turned and walked out of the room, her high heels tapping on the stone, because there was no time to waste.

The rooms on the ground floor contained some antique jacaranda wood furniture and a collection of documents relating to the foundation and early history of the Order. Irma pointed out the Charter, the Cardinal's desk, the founder's portrait, some rare porcelain which had belonged to the Founder's nephew's wife, and a case of militaria from the Paraguayan War which was taking shelter from the repairs occasioned by subsidence at the Civic Museum.

They climbed the mahogany staircase, where sombre oils of great men hung on the walls. Irma wondered what time Joaquim would be home from the studio. He was a wood-carver, and his hours of work were erratic.

Below them, Senhor Coelho coughed with a sound like a door grating.

'The Chapter House will close in five minutes,' he said.

'It will not,' retorted Irma.

They went into the treasury, dominated by a wall-length case of braided vestments and silver plate. Irma was wrinkling her nose again, she always did. It was the silver-topped canes in the corner. They were crowned, not by a knob you could straightforwardly grasp with your hand, but by a sort of hook in which you rested your wrist so the hand could dangle elegantly. These canes seemed to Irma to sum up everything about the people who had owned them: what the hand looked like was more important that what it did (indeed, it could probably do nothing anyway), and even in dangling it had to have assistance.

She began to talk about the collection of plate, some of which dated from the seventeenth century. Candlesticks, processional crosses, chalices so thickly set with jewels you could scarcely see the silver, massive crucifixes plated with gold. Irma felt awe towards these objects but did not much like them; they were too

[209]

heavy and ornate to correspond to her idea of beauty. She wondered what St Francis would have thought of them, too. The case in which they were displayed was connected to an alarm in the police station. Irma told her tourist this, but did not tell him the wiring was broken. She had been reminding Senhor Coelho for weeks.

Senhor Coelho's heavy shuffling tread, accompanied by Senhor Coelho's heavy breathing, bore down upon them from the staircase. Irma gathered up her tourist and took him downstairs, where she led him through the courtyard and into the church.

'We have two minutes,' she said. 'You must see the altar. It is covered in eighteen kilos of gold leaf: can you see? Very fine work.'

His eyes travelled over it, the hundreds, thousands of perfectly carved leaves and scrolls and curls and arabesques, all covered in gold beaten so thin you could wrap it round your finger.

'Brazilian gold,' she said. 'Mined by slaves. The money to build the church came from plantation owners. There are two rooms at the back for the slaves to stand.'

She walked out, beckoning him, just as Senhor Coelho came puffing in at the side door, and was able to give him another two minutes on the façade: highly ornate carved sandstone, the only example in the country of Spanish Baroque.

On the stroke of five she stopped talking, threw back her head and ran her hands through her hair. It sprang under her fingers. She smoothed down her dress, and put a cigarette between her lips.

'What do I owe you?' asked the tourist, and reached for his wallet.

'People usually give me between one thousand and two thousand cruzados,' said Irma.

They were supposed to put it that way, Irma could never understand why. It gave the mean ones an opportunity to be mean, and confused the others.

He gave her fifteen hundred, as she had known he would. It was fair. She tucked the notes into the top of her bra, and asked him if he needed to change money.

'Not at the moment,' he said.

In case he did later, she gave him her card with the address of Paco's shop and said she would be there most evenings until eight. She said he must on no account try to change money with the touts at the top of the cliff railway who offered more than the official black market rate because they weren't genuine traders but thieves. A few days ago an American had been robbed of everything, even his fountain pen, she said.

He thanked her and said goodbye. She said, 'Enjoy your visit,' and went and had an ice cream in the café overlooking the harbour. It was expensive there, but she was a friend of Marta, the waitress, and paid a price which had been agreed between them and took into account the complexities of a fifteen-year relationship.

Having finished the ice cream and exchanged news with Marta, Irma smoked a cigarette and looked down on the tumble of roofs where the old quarter descended precipitately to the waterfront. From where she sat, she could just see the steep curve of the street in which Joaquim had his studio.

Joaquim had achieved some fame with his carvings. Eight years ago his work had been included in an

[211]

exhibition of Afro-Brazilian art which had toured nationally. Irma kept the press clippings in a folder in the glass-fronted bookcase at home. The reviewers had called his work 'powerful' and 'African in its ageless inspiration'.

Joaquim's studio was the subject of a long-standing disagreement between himself and Irma. She was sure its location was the principal reason why so little of his work was bought by visitors. They simply didn't go to the place. You couldn't blame them; certainly the area was picturesque and had once been the artists' quarter, but it was now the thieves' quarter, and even if the guidebook was silent on its villainous reputation, hotel-keepers and taxi drivers weren't.

Moreover, the building of which the studio occupied the first floor had gone beyond the stage of being picturesque. It was rotting. The roof undulated, the ground-floor windows were broken, the balcony sagged and threatened passers-by, and the staircase – should you venture so far – was without a stair rail and shrouded in gloom.

The landlord said there was nothing he could do. Joaquim said it was not worth making a fuss about. Irma said the state of the building was hardly such as to attract people inside. Joaquim said that anyone who really wanted to visit the studio would not be deterred by the approach to it. He did admit that the lack of a signboard outside was a disadvantage. There had been one, he had painted it himself, but someone had stolen it.

Find a studio nearer the centre of town, Irma urged. She knew of several places that would be suitable. What was the use of the guidebook praising his work – the animal carvings, the Candomblé cult figures, the Negro heads – if he hid himself away where no one would see it? It wasn't the money. She knew he must do the work for its own sake; but she wanted it to be *seen*. She didn't even see it herself: he never brought it home.

He looked shocked. He had a spiritual affinity with his studio, he said. He couldn't just transplant himself.

At ten to six Irma left the café and went to work in Paco's postcard and souvenir shop. Paco was her brother-in-law. He was small and thin, with a straggling moustache and a worried air. He was always on the verge of a transaction which would establish the fortunes of the shop; for a remarkable variety of reasons, none of these transactions ever proved the success it should have done.

The previous day he had gone in his car to collect a load of cut-price crucifixes which he assured Irma would sell out within days, but the vendor had not kept the appointment. The space in the window cleared for the crucifixes had been filled with stripy yellow cats instead. As Paco said, the advantage of a souvenir shop was that you could sell anything. The Friday before, it had been watches: not the kind you could buy for a thousand cruzados in the street, which lasted two months and then you threw them away, but quality watches, rejected by the manufacturer because of some small flaw, and available for a fraction of the normal price. Paco had rejected them too, when the glass fell out of every one he picked up. He had not been so quick with the musical cigarette boxes that could only play three notes, and they were on special offer beside the till. Paco had tried to stop them playing anything at all, reasoning that a silent cigarette box was preferable to one which started to play a tune and stopped after three notes, but he was not good with a screwdriver and all he had managed to do was drive it into his thumb.

Irma was fond of her brother-in-law and knew him to be a good man, but she could not understand why he had chosen to run a business when everything about it seemed to cause him anxiety.

She would have loved a business to run. She would have made lots of money and given work to lots of people, and she would have hundreds of satisfied customers. She sat on a stool behind the counter and ran her eye over the shelves, waiting for Paco to go out.

She had suggested to Joaquim that he let Paco have some of his carvings to sell. Joaquim had been indignant. He declined to sell his work through shops at all, saying they took too large a percentage of the price and if people wanted to buy his carvings they could come to the studio; but least of all would he put work in his brother's shop. He was an artist, he said; what Paco sold was rubbish.

He did not say this to Paco, with the result that Paco, to whom the idea had also occurred, never understood why Joaquim would not give him his carvings to sell and from time to time asked for some, and Joaquim always said he had none to spare. Or rather, Irma said it, since it was through Irma that this conversation was carried on.

Paco was arranging dolls on a shelf by the door. The last doll kept falling off. Paco kept picking it up and putting it back. When it fell off for the fourth time he picked it up and put it on the counter.

'I'm going out for an hour,' he told Irma. 'I'll be bringing back some ashtrays.'

'More ashtrays?'

'These are something special, Irma. Wait till you see them. They're onyx. Each one has a silhouette of the church of Carmel in silver – well, it looks like silver – mounted on the side.'

'That sounds nice,' said Irma, thinking that when you wanted an ashtray surely all you wanted was somewhere to put your ash.

'No one else has them,' exulted Paco. 'They'll be unique to this shop.'

He left. His car bumped off the pavement, drawing the inevitable hoot from the car it forced to swerve. Irma served a customer with two postcards and a keyring with a plastic Christ which had swivelling eyes. Outside, dusk fell and the sounds of evening began.

At seven o'clock an American couple came in wanting to change a large sum of money. Irma shut the shop for five minutes and took them into the back room where the safe was. After they had gone, she did some arithmetic on a scrap of paper. She had enough to pay the rent for the flat, and she would have the rent for Joaquim's studio by the time it was due.

She had been supporting them both for so long she hardly gave it a second thought. She knew he couldn't do it. Money was simply beyond him. He made no effort to sell his work. She accepted it. He was her husband, and he was an artist, and it was a privilege to share your life with an artist. And she understood money: oh yes, she understood it well.

She thought about it only when she had to pay the rent for the studio. And then exasperation at the landlord who exploited him and at the inexplicable inertia that kept him from exploiting his talent would

[215]

seize her; and she would resolve, as she did now, to speak to him about it again.

The English tourist was waiting at the gates of St Francis when Irma arrived the following morning. It was a minute to ten. Through the bars of the gate, she could see the bald head of Senhor Coelho, pointedly motionless at a window.

'I have to catch a plane this afternoon,' the tourist said, 'but I wanted to have another look at the tiles before I go. There wasn't much time yesterday, was there?'

In the six years that Irma had been a guide at the Chapter House, no one had ever come back to look again at the tiles.

She pressed the bell, and leant on it until she saw Senhor Coelho come out, keys gripped in his fist, and begin his slow progress down the steps.

Inside, she and the tourist looked at the tiles.

The blue was not one blue, but many. It was like music: the different instruments, the same tune. They became in the end the same blue.

The blue of the figures and the white of the ground, they were the same thing, too. She saw how they answered each other. How, if one was there, the other must be.

And the glaze that had a milkiness to it.

'They are very beautiful,' she said.

'Yes,' he said. 'They are very beautiful.'

She accompanied him to the top of the steps and wished him a good journey. She said he must come back to Brazil, and back to St Francis, and come and have dinner at her house.

'I'll try,' he said, laughing, but visibly pleased. 'It's

a long way.' He was here to visit his brother, working on a contract in Rio.

He reached for his wallet. 'No,' said Irma. 'You are welcome. Thank you.'

Paco had cleared most of the contents of the window on to the floor around his feet and, thus impeded, was struggling to get at the stripy cats, which were right at the front.

Irma hitched up her skirt and climbed into the window. She threw the stripy cats at him. He caught them and put them on the counter.

'Duster,' Irma said.

He threw her a duster. She ran it over the window space and the pane, making a mental note that this area should be dusted more frequently. She climbed out of the window holding the laden duster.

'What's this in aid of?' she enquired.

'New stock.' She noticed for the first time Paco's suppressed excitement. 'I'm going to arrange the window round it.' He picked up a box from the floor. 'You'll never guess what I've got in here.'

'Ashtrays?' said Irma.

'Ashtrays!' said Paco with contempt.

He unfolded the cardboard flaps and brought out a small object. He placed it with a flourish on the counter next to the stripy cats. It was a wood carving of a monkey.

Irma stared at it.

'It's Joaquim's!' she said with delight.

'He was here this afternoon. He's given me about twenty pieces to sell.'

A smile started deep inside Irma.

[217]

'Why didn't he say anything to me? I was talking to him about selling his work last night.'

'You know Joaquim,' said Paco. 'He has to do things his own way.'

That was true.

Irma sat on the stool and for a few moments gave herself up to the pleasure of watching Paco take out the carvings one by one and set them on the crowded counter.

Monkeys, oxen, deer, storks, alligators.

They would sell easily. The American couple last night would have bought one. She picked up a deer: something about it surprised her, but before she could examine it a customer came in.

Paco said, 'I'm going out for an hour. Can I leave you to do the window? You're better at displays than I am.'

'Yes,' she said. 'You go.'

Alone in the shop, she did not immediately start on it, although there were things all over the floor and things all over the counter. She sat and looked at Joaquim's carvings. It was a long time since she had seen any of them. He did not like her to go to the studio.

As she looked at these carvings now, it seemed to her that they were not particularly good. The deer, for instance: there was a roughness about it that had always been characteristic of his work, but she saw for the first time that it was not a necessary, an expressive roughness. It had nothing to do with the deer. It was simply the only way he could carve. She picked up the monkey. Its arms were wrong.

She sat there a little longer, unwilling to move. It grew dark.

Irma stood up, smoothed down her skirt and began

[218]

to put the clutter of things on the floor into the box. That done, she arranged a display of the wood carvings in the centre of the window and grouped other articles around them. She wrote out a notice with Joaquim's name on it and placed it with the carvings. She swept the floor and found a home for the stripy cats.

She changed money for some tourists who came in, jammed a coathanger over the end of the shelf to stop the doll falling off, and began to make a pyramid of Paco's ashtrays.

THE CONVERSION

Haydn Middleton

I didn't know that the old woman next door was moving out until I saw her son and grandson filling up a skip with her leftover rubbish. That was early this February. 'When did she leave?' I asked the son over the fence.

'Last week,' he said. 'We've had a granny flat built on for her.'

I nodded at the middling-sized detached house. 'So who are the new people?'

'Youngsters like yourselves,' he said. 'Late twenties I'd say.'

It was two weeks before I caught sight of any of the new occupants. I was emptying the swingbin one Friday night at the back of the house when I looked up and saw someone smallish and long-haired high up a ladder, pulling at a section of the guttering.

'Hello,' I called over. 'Are you the new people?' The long-hair nodded; it was too dark to see his features properly. 'Have you moved in now?'

'No, no,' he told me. 'There's plenty of work to be done inside.'

'The old lady before you hardly ever seemed to be there,' I said. 'She used to spend a lot of time at her son's place.'

'Is that right?' He turned a little towards me on his ladder.

'Look,' I said 'you must come round for a drink. This Sunday?'

He just kind of tilted his head, didn't say anything.

[223]

'Around midday then?' I said, and left it at that.

Between Saturday morning and Sunday lunchtime, I kept a sort of watch on the back garden. Once or twice I saw my new neighbour again, carrying pipes or stacking rotten pieces of fencing, presumably for a bonfire. He reminded me of a pop star, but I couldn't quite place which one; perhaps it was just the blonde shoulder-length hair and biggish jaw. He was a pretty boy all right though, as Mary my wife soon pointed out, a bit boldly for her. There was also occasionally a second man helping him out, but no sign of a wife.

At ten past noon on Sunday the doorbell rang. The two men were on the doorstep. Mary, David, my eight year old and Stephen, who is five, were waiting in the lounge. I brought in the visitors and quickly made the introductions.

'I'm pleased to meet you all,' said the pop star, warming his back at the fire. 'I'm Norton. And this is one of the others: Gabriel.' At that Mary smiled, and I just nodded. Stephen, raring to go, stepped up with a bowl of peanuts and offered them to the men. Both took a handful.

'*One* of the others?' I repeated, smiling. 'So how many of you are there?'

Gabriel, a tall dark-skinned guy in a denim shirt and jeans, shrugged. 'It's difficult to say,' he answered, 'at this stage.'

'Why don't you get some drinks, darling?' Mary suggested when I looked a bit nonplussed by that.

'Yes of course. What will it be: beer, spirits?'

'Oh, mineral water will be fine for me,' said Norton.

'Me too,' said Gabriel.

I'd bought no mineral water at the supermarket on the previous morning. 'I have tonic,' I said. 'Will that do?' Both nodded. I went into the kitchen to pour

[224]

vodka for myself and Mary, and tonics for the guests. When I cut off some slices of lemon I noticed that my hands had started to shake.

'I'm just a housewife,' Mary was saying, quite full of herself, as I re-entered the room. 'But my husband is a salesman. He's away on business a lot. So it'll be reassuring from now on to know that there isn't just that little old lady in next door.'

'What work do you two do, then?' I asked as I passed them their drinks.

'We're both between jobs,' Norton said.

'Well, that's what we say,' Gabriel smiled. 'In fact, neither of us intends to work again if we can help it.'

'I see.' David came up with crisps. 'So what *did* you do?'

'This and that.'

'Nothing we're especially proud of.'

I grinned at Mary, who smiled back. 'Come on,' I said. 'Out with it.'

'No, really,' Norton replied. 'It's not worth discussing.' And that was that. For an hour we chatted on about local parks, pubs, schools – anything, everything – and neither of them gave away a thing. 'So what do you think they are,' I said to Mary as soon as they'd gone. 'Ex-cons?'

She shrugged, apparently uninterested. Right from the start her attitude to them had been out of character. Mary had always been by nature a difficult, suspicious, actually rather unsociable woman.

'And what are they going to do in there?' I said 'Set up a commune?'

Mary grinned, then she came over and took my arm, all moony. 'Don't worry,' she whispered. 'Don't start worrying now. I liked them. They were just so

[225]

. . . I don't know . . . so *calm*. They made me feel calm too.'

That brought me up short. You see, I knew what she meant: they *were* very calm, almost still, and I could see how that could rub off; but there was me with my hands shaking and my heart pumping fit to burst. Anyway, I was away for the next three weeks, selling around the far end of the country. Whenever I rang home I would ask what progress was being made in next door. 'They're doing some knocking through by the sound of it,' Mary told me during our last conversation.

'Is the noise too much for you?' I asked, stiffening straight away.

'No, no,' she said. 'I rather like the sound of activity after so long.'

'How many of them are there now?' I said.

'Usually just the two. You know – Norton and Gabriel. There were some others last night, though. Girls as well. They had a big bonfire.'

'Did the smoke come over?'

Mary laughed. 'No, dear. You mustn't fret so much. It was all very festive. I went out and chatted with them for a while. And then much later . . .' She paused, and chose not to go on. 'Oh, look,' she laughed again, really coyly now. 'I'll tell you when you get back.'

'Tell me now,' I said. 'What is it? I want to know.'

'Nothing. Nothing at all.' But her voice sounded dreamy, and when I got back, three nights later, I asked her, even before taking off my car coat, to finish what she'd started to say on the phone.

She blushed, her eyes glued to mine. 'It was when I was going to bed,' she said, 'when I was pulling the curtains. I looked down, and there, in the glow of the

[226]

dying bonfire, was Gabriel – making love to one of the girls.'

'In the garden, you mean?' I couldn't believe this. 'Out in the open?'

Mary looked hurt. 'It wasn't like that at all.' She looked away; I couldn't remember the last time she had talked about sex off her own bat. 'It was really quite beautiful – just the two of them – loving each other . . .'

'You're telling me,' I said, incredulous, 'that you stood there and watched it?'

'Well no, not really. But they noticed me, you see, and waved. So I waved back. It seemed stupid to pretend that it wasn't happening.' She turned away toward the kitchen window. 'I've never seen anything quite like it . . .'

I laughed but not in amusement. In fact I suppose I was already afraid. Perhaps I'd been afraid right from the off, from when my hands and my heart had started to go. Still, the next weekend I buttonholed Norton up his ladder again. He was taking off roof tiles, his hair tied back in a ponytail. 'How's it going?' I shouted over.

He smiled at me. 'Oh . . . slowly!'

'You're making some structural alterations inside, are you?'

He nodded, made no apology about the noise, and went back to the tiles.

'Well, give me a shout,' I said in the end, 'if you ever need a hand.'

He smiled again but said nothing. I was palpitating all over.

'What did you talk to them about,' I asked Mary that evening, 'when they were having their bonfire? Did you find out anything?'

[227]

Mary shrugged. 'I can't really remember what we said. Nothing very serious. Just chitchat, you know. They gave me a mug of mulled wine over the fence.' She paused, giving me a long look. 'David was around there a couple of days ago, though . . .'

'*Our* David!'

'He was out in the garden and Gabriel invited him in, apparently, to look at what they were doing inside.' She looked at me again, not exactly defiantly but quite coolly for her. 'Well, David said that they hadn't just taken out a couple of the walls, but some of the ceilings too.'

I blenched. Since the internal work had begun next door, all the curtains had been closed so I'd never been able to look inside. 'I don't want David in there again on his own,' I said, suddenly feeling completely helpless and strangely jealous of my son, 'not while there are walls and ceilings coming down . . .'

A fortnight later my next long-distance business trip came up. I was away from home for three nights. In bed, on the night I got back, Mary turned to me. 'Norton asked us into next door last night,' she said. 'There was another houseful, a kind of party. A working party, really – because everyone was getting on with the conversion.' In the dark, her eyes were bright, burning. 'And you'll never guess what, dear – they're building a swimming pool in there, an indoor one, and . . .'

I interrupted her. 'This is going beyond me now,' I said. 'A swimming pool? You can't *do* that. You can't just turn a house into a swimming pool.'

'Well, they are. They seem to know exactly what they want and how they intend to go about it. They're doing all the work themselves.'

[228]

I said nothing. Now I really was worried. Swimming pools have always worried me. I can't swim, you see, even though I made sure that David and even little Stephen learned. And the wonder in Mary's voice had gutted me; that and the damned calmness. On the next Saturday, I decided, I would go round and check all this out for myself.

It was raining when I threaded my way between the half-dozen cars outside my neighbours' home. The curtains were still closed, although I could see the glow of lights beyond. Two huge skylight windows had been fitted into the roof. As I waited for the bell to be answered, it felt odd somehow to think that Mary and the children had already been inside. Odd and kind of heart-wrenching; but I thought that that would pass as soon as I got in there myself: one way or another, it was important for me to do what they had done. A tall red-haired girl of twenty-three or twenty-four drew back the door. It was eleven-thirty in the morning but she appeared to have just woken up. She was dressed in panties and a white tee-shirt that barely covered her midriff.

I smiled. I hadn't been expecting a girl. I don't quite know what I *had* been expecting. Behind her I could see nothing but rubble and dust; there were no sounds at all. 'Is Norton there?' I asked, stepping forward. 'I'm from next door.'

'Norton's away,' the girl replied. 'Can I help?'

Before I could speak, a muscular guy edged into the doorway, naked but for a handtowel tied at his waist. He eased the girl aside, then raised a palm to greet me. 'Hi,' he said. 'I'm Paulus. What can we do for you?'

My hair was getting soaked in the rain. I longed to be asked in but Paulus was blocking the doorway.

[229]

Mary and the children had been asked in, I kept on thinking. I ran a hand across my brow; I knew it was all going to come out. 'Look,' I laughed, 'look, Paulus, can you just tell me what's going on in this house? I mean, from what I hear you're gutting the place . . .'

Paulus raised his palm again, grand as you like. He smiled. 'Nothing we do here will have any effect on your own property. You have my word on that.'

His promise hung in the sodden air between us. I could only grin back. 'But a *swimming pool*,' I went on. 'I mean, are you intending to live here or just use it as a kind of leisure centre? I'm interested, that's all. I want to know what I'm living next door to.'

'We'll be here,' Paulus replied, nodding, his expression grimmer now. 'You can regard us as your neighbours.'

'But what's "us" anyway? How many of you are in there, for God's sake?'

Paulus turned his head aside. It took me a moment to realize that he was making a headcount. 'As of now,' he said, meeting my eyes again. 'Fourteen. That could change though – up or down.'

'Fourteen,' I said. 'Fourteen!' And then, I'm afraid, I just lost my rag entirely. 'You know that you're a smug, patronizing son of a bitch, don't you?' I said to him. 'You know that, don't you?'

Paulus didn't flinch. He actually seemed to be considering a reply. But I wheeled away before he could speak, hyped up to breaking point.

There was then a kind of ceasefire for a week. I saw nothing of any of the neighbours in all that time, although I was sure that they were inside because the cars were still there. Expensive cars, too, some of them . . . I might as well admit here that in the previous month or so I'd been having a thin time of it on the road. My sales area had never been particularly fertile, but in that month my total commission fell to an all-time low. I was trying hard enough. But I suppose this neighbour business was playing on my mind, hampering my performance. Anyway, I knew I was going to have to account for myself to the marketing manager at the upcoming sales conference, and that just put me even more on edge.

After the week was up, I went off for my longest spell away from home. Twenty-four days. I didn't want to go. I suppose I sensed that something was going to happen while I was away.

I didn't ring Mary as often as usual; whenever I did, she sounded only vaguely interested in what I was doing, and non-committal about what she was doing herself. I guessed that she was spending more time in next door and didn't want to tell me. I agonized constantly about David or Stephen being trapped under falling doors or walls. My dreams were all about water, about the children drowning and me just watching, unable to save them.

When I got back home on the Friday evening, I couldn't see the house next door behind a row of construction trucks and lorries. Norton was standing at the fence between our two drives, though. He was standing hunched with his hands in the pockets of a kind of kagoul, but when he saw me he straightened up at once and smiled.

'I'm sorry you had some cross words with Paulus,' he said.

'Oh,' I said waving it off, not wanting to talk. 'That doesn't matter now.'

'Not to you, perhaps,' he went on. 'But it upset Mary quite a bit.'

[231]

'*Mary?*' I said, furious. 'Are you talking about my wife, buster?'

Norton smiled at me as if I was about four years old. 'You've made it very difficult for her, you know.'

I'd had enough of this. I turned away. But when I looked up at our house I saw that none of the lights were on. I turned back. 'Look,' I said. 'If you've got something to tell me you'd better just say it. Now.'

He raised both his palms. 'All right.' He took a breath, then he said it: 'Mary felt that you were creating a two-camps situation – you know, there was your camp and there was ours. Well anyway, Mary's chosen, for the time being, to come into our camp. And she's brought the boys.'

I gaped at him. Crazily, I was still trying to place which pop star he looked like. I realized that he had been waiting there for me, sent out by Mary. It felt like hours before I could pull myself together sufficiently to say a word. 'Tell, Mary,' I murmured, 'to come out here this minute.'

'Well, you see, she won't,' Norton came back. 'Not this minute. She's still quite upset. She says she needs some time and space to sort herself out.' And with that he turned away, and disappeared behind one of the lorries – and I just watched him go.

Well, what happened next was that I slept on it – very badly indeed – and first thing the next morning, before I left for the sales conference, I called in the police. The two uniformed men spent five minutes in the house with me first. I gave it to them straight: that although my wife and children mightn't actually have been abducted by the fourteen, they had somehow been hoodwinked into moving in with them – and I wanted them all back damn quick. I felt I was on safe ground. I did, really, though even then I felt that I was in some way *betraying* someone or something.

The officers said very little until we knocked on the neighbours' front door. The construction trucks were still outside. 'Looks like they're giving the place a pretty thorough overhaul,' said the taller policeman as we waited for someone to come to the door. I was about to tell him about the swimming pool when the door opened and it was Mary.

'Hello,' she said, smiling at the policemen but ignoring me. I felt like lunging forward and gripping her by the throat. 'What's the problem?'

The shorter officer guessed right away who Mary was, probably from the murderous way I was looking at her. 'You're this gentleman's wife, are you?' he asked. 'Only he believes that you've been brought into this house against your will. Would that be correct?'

Mary looked from him to me and then back to him. I was staring at a person I hardly recognized. I'd never seen such contempt. She was wearing unfamiliar clothes, too: pale jeans and a sweatshirt, with her hair pulled back under a red headscarf. 'No,' she said with this total, eerie control. 'I'm here because I want to be here. There's no question about that.'

The policeman turned and faced me. 'Well, there's not an awful lot more we can do about this, sir . . .' he began, in that ever-so-slightly sarcastic tone that he'd been using on me from the start.

'But my kids,' I said, losing it (and wanting really to say to them: Get me inside, just get me *in*, where it's calm). 'She's got my boys in there. She took them, when I wasn't around. No explanation, no nothing!'

'Again, sir,' they were both stepping away now,

[233]

dissociating themselves entirely, 'this is something you'll have to sort out between yourselves.'

And then I was left facing her, this changed woman in her borrowed clothes and her face full of contempt. 'I'll get a court order,' I threatened her, without really understanding what I was saying.

'Give it some time,' she said back, almost smiling at me. 'Just give me some time. I'm not ready to talk. Norton told you that.'

'Fuck Norton,' I said. 'And fuck all the rest of them, too. You can't do this to me,' I told her. 'I won't take it. You'll regret all this, I can tell you now . . .' I must have ranted on in that vein for quite a while longer. I recall becoming more and more enraged by that glassy, uninvolved look of hers. But what I was also feeling – perhaps, eventually, more strongly than anything else – was *resentment*, at not being allowed into the house. That sounds odd, I know. But I had this notion that if only I could be inside there, with them all, then everything would surely come right. I couldn't see in, because Mary had been careful to pull the door up behind her, but I knew it wouldn't just be rubble and dust by now. And suddenly I knew I had to see inside. I had to have a look.

So I thrust Mary aside and pushed back the door. Straight away Norton and one other man, a black, were blocking my entry. 'Get out of my way!' I grunted at them, pressing forward, and I was about to shout out my boys' names when the two men punched me simultaneously in the stomach.

I doubled up on the front step, clawing at their legs. I'd never fought so hard for breath in my whole life. But I was aware of Mary stepping over me and back into the house, then the door shutting quietly behind her.

[234]

If it had been a normal working day I probably wouldn't have left home after that, but since on that day and on the following two I was due to attend the sales conference in London, there was simply no other way.

Now I knew I was going to get my knuckles rapped for my recent figures. But I hadn't bargained for a total redrawing of the sales map, leaving me with virtually no job at all as far as commission went. The marketing manager let me have it on the first day of the conference, but for some reason I stayed on for the other two days as well, knowing that to all intents and purposes I had been eased out. I suppose I just preferred the safety of the hotel room to going home.

When I did get back, late on that Friday evening, the lorries had gone from outside next door and so had several of the cars. There was smoke rising from the back garden, though, and later on, when I looked out through the boys' bedroom window, I could see that another bonfire party was going on.

I must have stood there watching in the darkness for hours. I counted a dozen or more different figures, laughing, drinking, toasting sausages in the flames. Stephen was there, and David – way, way past their bedtime. They looked happy, carefree, racing up and down on the lawn, flinging their arms from time to time around the adults.

Mary spent a long while hunched against the chest of one of the men I hadn't seen before. But when he went inside, Paulus came up to her and embraced her too. I had no idea what was going on. I remembered Mary telling me how from this very window she had watched Gabriel making love to some girl. I felt stunned, stupefied. She seemed to be so completely one of them. Nothing to do with me any more. A different species, almost. At that moment I honestly think that if one of them had started making love to Mary, I too would have stayed there and watched, just like she had.

Around midnight, when the party appeared to show no sign of ending, I capitulated and went out into the garden, pretending that I was emptying the swingbin. As soon as I glanced over the fence it seemed that every one of them – my boys included – was looking back at me.

'Hello, David,' I called out. 'Hello, Stephen.'

Neither of them spoke back. It's possible that they didn't hear me. I was thinking that Norton and company had given Mary mulled wine over the fence, mulled wine and easy, calming conversation. Mary didn't move from Paulus's side. Then Norton came towards me. Right then I wanted more than anything in the world to be invited to join their party. I could be like them too, the bastards, with their mineral water and their denim and their mulled wine. There didn't have to be two camps. I knew that it could still be all right. I knew that basically it still wasn't too late.

'Tomorrow,' Norton said to me. 'We'll be ready for you tomorrow.'

I looked at him, blank, not needing to spell out my confusion.

'Don't worry,' was all he said, nodding. 'Just wait until tomorrow.'

I went back inside quickly. And as I went, I realized at last that the pop star he looked like was Brian Jones. You know, Brian Jones, the Rolling Stone. For what it was worth, Norton was the spitting image of him, the one who had been found drowned dead in his own swimming pool back there at the fag-end of the sixties.

And that bothered me. I vaguely remembered something about one of the other Stones taking his woman
off him just before it happened. To tell the truth, it
bothered me quite a lot.

Again, I barely slept that night.

I hadn't the faintest idea what Norton had meant by
'ready for' me. But the craziest thing was that when I
woke up for the last time I was thinking: it's all been
a game: I'll go in there this morning and it'll all have
been a game. And that's what I wanted, damn it. I
wanted to laugh – at myself as much as at anyone or
at anything else. To that extent, they'd converted me
already. And I loathed them for it, but I definitely,
absolutely unarguably, wanted to be *with* them.
Loathing them but with them.

It was a fine sort of morning after all the rain we'd
been having. At least there was a bit of blue in the
sky. I took a long time getting up, showering, shaving,
carefully not looking out into the next-door garden.
While I was eating my breakfast I kept on thinking:
this is the end of this particular phase, soon all this
will be over, and I won't be on my own any more; all
this will just be like a dream. That's what I thought.

I went out of the house with my eyes closed. I could
smell a bonfire somewhere. There's always someone
with a bonfire going. My mouth was set ready to
laugh, I know that. I was willing myself to smile. I
was going to be back with David and Stephen apart
from anything else: that was worth a grin. But that
stupid Brian Jones thing was still on my mind, sort of
making me sweat a bit, and then there was the thought
that I'd never even begun to connect with Norton or
Gabriel or Paulus or any of the others . . .

There were no cars or lorries outside the house. For
some reason that made me feel better. I thought there

[237]

would only be the hard core there, the ones who mattered. I didn't especially want anyone peripheral looking in on whatever was going to happen. And all right, I admit it, I felt privileged too – that I was going to be *in there* with the hard core, a kind of summit meeting that had been waiting to happen from the very beginning. This was going to work. This was going to be the start of some new kind of order.

I didn't ring the bell this time but banged on the knocker. I don't know why – I suppose it seemed more assertive or something. No one answered. I banged again, harder. The door swung back a little way, because it had been left on the latch. Puzzled, I waited to see if anyone was going to come or not. No one did. So I pushed the door right back and looked inside . . .

Christ, I always knew that this was going to be the hardest bit. Hardest to explain, I mean, and to describe. As a matter of fact the description part isn't too hard really. I mean, I can say straightforwardly enough what I saw. It's the explanation that's still out of my reach, the explanation of why it affected me in the way that it did.

For a long while I just stood there, looking through narrowed eyes, still on the doorstep. The first thing that had struck me was the brightness. A really beautiful brightness – and I know that sounds fey but that's how it was. It was dazzling in there, not surprisingly, since the roof and an entire side wall now seemed to consist of little except glass. The sunlight on that Saturday morning simply streamed in, picking out the brilliant flecks in the calm deep-blue water and the paler blue ceramic tiling that surrounded it on the floor and walls.

All the inside walls had gone. It beat me how the

place was still standing. And I couldn't see for the life of me where all those people – including my own family – had been eating and sleeping. The house had become no more than a shell, a dome, a thin protective membrane over that most gorgeous L-shaped expanse of water.

The water, that lush water! No, I can't talk about the water yet. Not yet.

There were several huge fern-type plants, one of them suspended from the roof in a sort of wicker basket. The plant in the furthest corner had blue flowers on it, which matched the colour of the tiling. There was no other decoration, although there were a lot of fluorescent-light strips for which I couldn't see any switches.

The pool itself had a single set of banistered steps leading down into it, directly ahead of where I was standing in the doorway. I suppose it must have been only five or six strides away, but it seemed at the start like the gateway to a wholly different world. While I was staring at the water, almost unconsciously I stepped inside the doorway and eased the door to behind me.

It was so peaceful in there! So much more peaceful than I could ever have anticipated. All the outside razzamattazz just seemed to fall away: traffic noise, bonfire smells, worries about jobs and children and wives – all of it. For a few moments I felt like the still, neutral centre right at the eye of the storm. Then the water started to actually make me feel *good*.

I can't explain why. It's quite beyond me. Water has never had anything like that kind of effect on me before. Usually I'm a bit apprehensive of it, what with me never having learned to swim and everything. Yet this water somehow seemed to be speaking to me, soothing me, *inviting* me in a way that had nothing to do with fear. 'We'll be ready for you tomorrow,' Norton had said. And where were they all: the fourteen? my wife and kids? But none of that seemed so urgent any more. Because now I, too, had the calmness that Mary had spoken about. I had it. I'd stilled myself, or the water had. The sheer serenity of the place had got through to me.

I was aware, however, that I was trespassing. And I remembered only too well those punches to the gut that I'd got on trying to make an entry before. And so, reluctantly, thinking that I'd come back when Norton and his crowd eventually showed up, I slid out of there, pulled the door up, and came back here to my own place.

I waited in vain for the rest of that day: no one at all came to the 'house' next door. And it was a bad, long day. Because almost as soon as I took my eyes off the pool, all my old anxieties came swarming back. They wouldn't give me any rest. Eight times, nine times, ten times, I got as far as my own front door intending to go back in there, but each time I lost my nerve. I just couldn't face the thought of them coming back and surprising me in there. I didn't want to be hit again. I couldn't afford to be hit again.

Around ten thirty I took a shower. While I was drying myself, I noticed through the rippled glass of the window that there was a glow of some sort coming from next door, possibly from the glassed-over bits of the roof.

I got dressed again with no feeling in my stomach. This, then, was going to be it. And I felt ready. I was ready for *them* whether or not they were ready for me. All I could think was: I'm going to be back in there, I'm going to feel it all again, that good feeling from the water, the peace.

[240]

I don't remember passing between the two houses. My mind was in a complete whirr. I didn't even properly register that there weren't any cars outside; my eyes were fixed on the house, on the blaze of brightness at the two visible skylights. I smashed on the knocker so hard that the door, ajar again, seemed to shake. No one answered. I knocked a second time, a third time, a fourth.

In the end I thought I realized what was going on here: they were wanting me just to walk in: Norton, Mary, the boys, all of them, probably all waiting there in the pool, treading water or whatever it is you do. So I closed my eyes, screwed myself up, and pushed back the door.

The place was empty. I stepped in, closer to the pool, half-expecting them to all burst up through the surface. Nothing happened. I was the only one in there. Again I looked around for light switches but couldn't see any. I wondered whether they'd been switched on by remote control somehow. It was such a crushing disappointment, I can't begin to describe.

But even while I was racking my brains over what it all meant, I was looking down at the water under that avalanche of light, and incredibly enough all the anxiety was draining out of me again. It just went, like that. Right away – into the water as it were. I could feel myself rising above every piece of crap that had happened to me since I'd first spotted Norton up his ladder.

Like a miracle, it was. It took me so much unawares that I slumped down and sat on the tiled floor, cross-legged, just the way I imagined Paulus or Gabriel or any of those others might have sat.

That water looked so good. So perfectly unmoving, it looked heavy, luxurious, not in any way anything to

[241]

be afraid of. It no longer mattered to me that my wife
had disappeared and taken my family. There wasn't
anything to be fraught about, anything at all. I wanted
to laugh out loud, wanted to thank Norton and his
troupe for opening this up to me, this deep inner
satisfaction that I hadn't even guessed at before.

I sat there for at least an hour, rocking gently,
knowing that in the end I would have to go but
longing not to, longing not to. Oh I'd never known a
spiritual weightlessness like it: 'beatitude' was what I
think they used to call it at my Sunday School. It took
my breath away, filled me up with . . . well, with
nothing. Nothingness. It was quite, quite beautiful.
Quite beautiful.

Before I left that evening, I slipped off my shoe and
sock, and gingerly dipped my toes into the water by
the flight of steps. It was bath-warm, as hot as it could
be without actually giving off steam. The water felt as
heavy, as syrupy, as it looked. And I knew then that
I'd go into it at some point, feel it all around me,
caressing me, coaxing away the last traces of worry.

I left the front door as I'd found it, headed back
home and started to drink. I had to keep myself
stimulated somehow: the comedown from that high
by the poolside would have been just too hard to bear.

Well, that set the pattern: a blurred, blurry pattern.
On Sunday I spent two more sessions in the house
next door, drunk both times as I entered but not
feeling it as soon as I saw the water. The same
happened on Monday and then again on Tuesday. On
Wednesday I paid three visits. I was meant to be out
on the road, of course, selling, but I saw little point in
playing that game any more. The job had ceased to
exist in all but words. I was well off out of it.

Under the vodka I lost track of time. All I knew

was that outside it was light for some while and then it would pass over into darkness – and then, like clockwork, the lights would go on in the house next door. Sometimes I slept for long periods during the daylight hours. But whether asleep or awake, as long as I was away from that water I was completely bunged up with torment and savaged pride and unanswerable questions and all the rest of it. More than I could live with. There was nowhere to turn, nowhere except the water, *my* water. What would I have done without it? And even that wondeful soothing calmness was getting through to me less directly now. I was having to fight a bit for my abandonment, having to get closer and closer and closer to the surface . . .

Anyway, to get to the crux of it, by Thursday morning – this morning, that is – I'd quit the drinking and I went through into next door quite clear-headed, but ground down with all the misery. I knew what I wanted to do. At least, I thought I did.

As soon as I got in the door, I took off my bathrobe, I'd stopped bothering to dress on the previous week-end; there was no point in it, just for that little journey. I'd put on a pair of trunks – ones that Mary had bought me years earlier 'to sunbathe in', although I'd never worn them before.

I went up to the steps, turned around, and holding on hard I lowered one foot and then the other on to the first step below the waterline. At just that moment the front door opened.

It was Norton. He was wearing his kagoul thing, hands in the pockets. He looked as if he was on his way somewhere, not stopping. He didn't come in, but stayed on the doorstep, eyeing me, then my heaped-up bathrobe, then me again.

I looked back. It was all I could do. I couldn't

move, couldn't speak. I was in his house. He had me. I wanted to weep there and then. I wished I had been facing the other way so that I could have been looking at the water, the water . . .

'You can't swim, can you?' he asked me, and it sounded so casual.

I shook my head, as far as I was able. He looked at me with a kind of grin. Brian Jones. The absolute spit. How could I ever not have seen it?

'Are you sure,' he said, 'that you know what you're doing?'

What could I say? I felt like a heel. Why couldn't I have been facing the other way? How could I say: *Yes, I know that I want to drown?* I hadn't even admitted it to myself until that point. Not properly.

I looked behind him, out on to the drive and the road beyond. There was no sign of anyone else. Just a car.

'Mary,' I said to him, and my voice was from another dimension, 'she's not coming back, is she?'

And then it was his turn to shake his head. Brian Jones's turn. He did it slowly, not sympathetically but he wasn't crowing about it, either.

My feet were still in the water. I'd started to cry. Then I knelt at the poolside, lifting up my feet out of the water. My head was down. I was looking at my bathrobe, that was all, and at his shoes beyond that.

'I'll go,' I said when I was able to speak. The moment had gone. I'd missed it. Missed the moment to do what I'd thought I wanted to do. I couldn't see my water. I couldn't turn around. Not then.

'This was all for me,' I said, 'wasn't it. This whole thing. It was all done just for me? To bring me over?'

He didn't answer. Instead he just stepped back, turned, and walked away.

[244]

I heard his car revving as I got to my feet and went for my bathrobe. I knew he wouldn't show for a second time. And besides, I had to come back here, to give this account, for what it's worth, on David's cassette recorder. I don't quite know why I had to do it, actually. For Mary to hear sometime perhaps, to show her that I understand, that I came over in the end and saw it all, felt it all, in the same way as her. Or perhaps it was just for me. Some kind of a justification for what I have to do.

It's dark outside again now. The lights will have come on in next door. It'll be better under the lights. It's always better, stronger, under the lights – the peace of it. I'll open the door and look at the water.

I won't stop looking at the water.

I won't, not until it's all around me. That'll be best. Then I'll know the most perfect peace of all.

I loved you, Mary.

I thank you . . .

THE TELEPHONE CALL

Carlo Gébler

The Harrods cosmetics hall was hushed and scented when Mark called in to buy his wife a red lipstick. Samantha, called Sam, always wore pink which he detested. He chose the same pillar box shade as the salesgirl wore.

'I don't hold out much hope she'll wear it,' he said.

'She might,' said the salesgirl. The name on the shining nametag on her breast was Agatha.

They fell into conversation. Mark invited her to lunch. Agatha accepted, as long as it was only for an hour.

He took her to the Brasserie on Brompton road. When they sat down he saw she wore no blouse under her uniform. Between the lapels there was a lovely triangle of bumpy, freckled skin. He wanted to put his cheek there and feel it.

After weeks of wooing he got his way. One Friday afternoon Sam decided suddenly to go to her mother's. She took the children with her.

At closing time he went to Harrods and told Agatha he had a surprise for her.

He brought her home. She thought it strange to be in the place where signs of his wife were everywhere but said nothing.

He gave her a guide – 'Hotels of England' – and told her to choose somewhere for the weekend. Next thing her uniform was off. In bed he said her skin was like a shark's. As soon as they finished Agatha asked to use

[249]

the telephone. She lived with her mother and didn't want her worrying where she was.

'I'm going away for the weekend. I can't talk exactly,' she said on the phone.

Mother took the hint. 'How nice for you.'

In the end Mark and Agatha didn't go away at all but stayed where they were in the house near Regent's Park, in the bed which he made up in the guest room. They only got up to eat.

When they talked he told about his miserable marriage. Fifteen years of hostility, he said, and yet he had always lacked the courage to break free.

Agatha had been married once herself, she told him. It had all happened when she had been very young – a short marriage which ended unhappily. She had a child. The boy lived with her in-laws in Scotland.

She omitted to tell him how she had suspected her husband of an infidelity. In fact it was only a friendship. In the end her jealousy drove him to what she most feared. It taught her a bitter lesson. Leave well alone and matters sort themselves out; bring them into the light and they only worsen.

She was thirty now and tired of being alone. Who knew where this might lead? Even when she saw him change the bed linen on Sunday morning and thought, He could have waited, she said nothing. He has to, she reproved herself, it smells of us.

In the afternoon they went for a walk in Regent's Park. After thirty-six hours of nakedness she found it strange to be in clothes. She had washed her underwear and it was damp around her middle.

They went into a playground near the mosque. Arab matrons in yashmaks sat on the benches watching brown-skinned children in the pale winter sunshine.

He held her hand. She saw the time on his wrist-watch. He would be bringing her home soon. She imagined sitting in his car outside the flat in Strea-tham. She imagined him saying, 'When will I see you again?' in an insincere way.

In the event, when he got her home, he asked if he could come in. Her mother gave them tea in the front room. It was rarely used and smelt of apples. Her mother had the good sense not to ask how the weekend had gone.

After a year of furtive meetings, he told Agatha he was going to leave his wife and that she had given him the strength to do so. She was thrilled but held her breath.

He left Sam, as he said he would, and rented a flat in a mansion block at the bottom of Ladbroke Grove. There were scenes and outrages. His children were distraught. His wife issued dire threats and once made a feeble attempt to take her life with twenty disprins.

Agatha saw him rarely. He had said that would be wisest during this period of transition and she saw the sense of that.

When they did meet, he talked and fulminated while she listened and nodded sagely. She never said anything unpleasant about Sam.

After six months of vile solicitor's letters and increasing unpleasantness from his wife, Mark's patience broke and he said, 'Oh, to hell with it.' Agatha moved in with him, bringing two suitcases and a doll with a porcelain face.

She met the children, James and Amanda. When they talked about their mother she showed no emotion. 'You coped with that marvellously,' he observed, after they had dropped the children home. It wasn't until they were in bed together that she expressed through her passion everything she had been waiting all day to say.

She was again the perfect partner when she met Mark's friends; when she met his family; even when Sam came on the two of them by chance in a restaurant.

As the outraged and clearly drunk wife weaved towards them, she steeled herself. As Sam screeched into her face Agatha remained perfectly poised in her chair.

When the wine hit her face all she thought was that it was warmer than she had expected. She felt it run down her bare neck and on to her breasts under her blouse. She saw a restaurant of people looking on with that painful English mixture of disgust, fascination and disdain.

She picked up the white starched table napkin and began to wipe herself. She heard weeping. She looked and saw it was Sam. The screaming harridan was now wet eyed and puffy cheeked.

Two waiters began to lead Sam away. Sam was humiliated. She stumbled at the door and was gone.

Agatha dabbed at her neck. Everyone was eating again. Conversation had restarted. She had outfaced her enemy with her silence and she had won.

'You were brilliant,' said Mark. She squeezed his hand in reply. In bed later she asked him to make love to her twice.

Having thrown the wine Sam lost something. Either it had made her decide to throw in the towel, or it had drawn out her anger. Agatha couldn't gauge which, but whatever the cause the change was like a turn on a pinhead. Sam agreed to a divorce. Sam agreed the house could be sold and the money divided. Mark and Agatha began to look for a place to buy.

One Saturday they drove to Tufnell Park. It was a grey, muggy, June morning. Rain seemed about to fall but it never came. On the radio there was a programme on separation. They heard a Radio Four voice saying, 'Divorce invariably involves a drop in living standards,' and Agatha retuned the dial to Capital Gold.

The flat was a conversion in a Victorian house. It overlooked a railway line.

'Divorce always means a drop in living standards,' whispered Mark as they stood in the tiny kitchen. 'Where am I going to put the kids when they come for the weekend?'

She put her arm through his and the next moment a train whistled past. They stood listening as it rattled away down the line.

The train clinched it and they decided to buy. Once it was theirs, Agatha took charge of the decoration. She painted the kitchen marigold yellow; the hallways Russian blue; the bedrooms were apple green; and the tiny front room with the marble fireplace was white.

They planned to marry when the divorce came. Agatha found a new job in an art gallery. The children came every other weekend. They often talked about their mother but, when they did, Agatha only smiled and said the nicest things.

'You handle them so skilfully,' he would often praise her on Sunday evenings. Her only reply would be to squeeze her arms around his back until he called out, 'Steady on.'

Then Mark's work took him to the north for a week.

At one o'clock in the middle of the second night he was away, the telephone rang.

'Who's that?' asked Agatha sleepily.

'I'm Val.' Her voice was a husky parody of a seductress.

'Who?'

'Tell him, I loved lunch and am available anytime.'

The dialling tone sounded. Agatha was awake now. She rattled the bar pointlessly, like a character in a film. Who the hell was Val?

'But I don't know any Vals,' said Mark, when he was back. 'Let's hope she rings tonight.'

She did. Agatha answered and motioned Mark to pick up the receiver in the hall.

'Hi. Val speaking. Where's Mark?'

'I'm so pleased you called,' said Agatha, 'Please keep talking. The police are recording everything you say.'

Val slammed the phone down and then rang back immediately.

'You're a big fat hooker,' she shouted and hung up.

Mark and Agatha held each other and laughed until their sides ached and tears ran down their cheeks. Agatha felt reassured.

In the following weeks and months Val's calls continued.

When Agatha answered, she left messages of thanks for meals, gifts – usually lingerie – and outings. When Mark answered Val alternated between sadness and sauciness. 'Can you talk, darling? No, I don't suppose you can. It was wonderful, wasn't it, the other night.'

They christened Val 'telephone sex'. Mark regaled their friends with stories about her calls. He did a very good parody which started, 'Do you want me on the kingsize tonight or in the back of the Cortina?' Agatha always laughed along without much enthusiasm.

Mark was almost certain who it was – a friend of Sam's – naturally Val wasn't her name – whose husband had left her for another, younger woman. She was acting alone, he believed. Agatha disagreed. Surely the woman had the wife's blessing. She kept

[254]

this thought to herself. Only a few months to their marriage and then she could rest certain she had beaten her old inner adversary.

It was November, the month Mark and Agatha had met.

The telephone rang.

'This is Val.'

'Yes,' said Agatha, 'I can hear. He's not in.'

This was what she always said.

'I want you to give him a message.'

Instead of her usual tone of phoney sexuality, Val was curt and business like.

'Cosmetics, Harrods, one o'clock. Fingers crossed it's as good as the last meeting.'

The line went dead and Agatha felt a tug at the back of her solar plexus.

'Was that telephone sex?' asked Mark, strolling into the kitchen.

'No, wrong number.'

In bed that night when Mark reached over, she said she didn't want to. Later, while he slept, she stared at the ceiling and the band of light cast across it by the street lamp outside.

The tug was now a stab in her middle. It was jealousy.

In the morning she told herself she wouldn't but she couldn't stop herself coming out with it.

'You've seen your wife, haven't you, and you haven't told me.'

She saw his face redden slightly and his Adam's apple bobbing as he looked up from his Sunday newspaper.

After a pause he finally said, 'Yes, but her solicitor was present. We're tying up loose ends and trying to be civilised about it.'

[255]

There followed a long account of an innocent meeting in a pub one lunchtime.

'You're seeing her next week, aren't you.'

'No.'

'Don't lie to me. You're meeting in Harrods, in the bloody cosmetics hall, where you bloody met me. Val rang to tell me.'

He blinked. Agatha knew she was right.

'We're buying the children's Christmas presents,' he said. 'It was the first place that came into my head as somewhere to meet.'

Agatha threw plates. She threw a chair. She emptied her make-up bag and stamped on it, scattering powder, smashing phials of perfume, flattening the lipstick and squeezing the red out.

He had never seen her like this before. 'You've always been so reasonable about Sam,' he pleaded. He was disturbed.

'I hate you,' she shouted, hurling her shoes after him as he retreated down the stairs.

The front door slammed and there was silence.

Tears rolled down Agatha's cheeks. This was a moment very like another, years before, when her marriage had started to fall apart.

She sat in the kitchen and stared at the red lipstick on the cork tiled floor. It looked as if it had seeped from the flattened cartridge. Why did this happen at the very moment when she'd almost won through?

As darkness fell Agatha remained seated, not even bothering to get up and turn on the light.

A LOST
OPPORTUNITY

Francis King

Reynolds yawned and yawned again in anticipation. You must get it into your heads that conversation is like a game of tennis. It's not enough to get your racket to the ball, you must, I repeat must, somehow hit it back across the net. He yawned again. He had given this advice to these Japanese and to so many Japanese before them, but it was seldom that the ball did anything but fall inert to the ground after it and the racket of one of them had met.

The director of the Institute called it a conversation class. But how could one teach conversation in a foreign language to people who could not conduct it in their own? He got up and fidgeted with the chairs, the three sitting-room ones supplemented with others from the dining-room, the kitchen, his bedroom and even the bathroom. Why not follow the example of his French colleague and let them squat on the floor? After all, as the Frenchman had said with one of those contemptuous shrugs of his, the students were more used to the floor than to chairs.

At exactly four o'clock there was a ring at the bell. At exactly four-fifteen Reynolds's maid, hunchbacked, her greying hair coiled into a loose bun at the nape of a neck which had the appearance of crumpled-up brown paper, would come in with the tray clicking with glasses of coca-cola. 'You spoil them,' the French-man said. But to provide a few bottles of coca-cola, so much sweeter in Japan than in the West, was a cheap way of spoiling.

With one or two exceptions, the students would all arrive together, the early arrivals waiting for the latecomers outside the gate. One of the exceptions was always Miss Nishikawa, who invariably rang the bell either five minutes before or five minutes after everyone else, as though deliberately to assert her difference from them.

When Reynolds opened the front-door, the students, as always, giggled, looking anywhere but at him. Was there something irresistibly comic about his appearance or behaviour? There was more giggling on this occasion when, instead of his usual 'Hi! Come in!', he gave a mock Japanese bow and cried out '*Dozo!*', with a wide sweep of one arm to invite them to enter. Heads lowered, they then scuttled in, the men in most cases preceding the woman. Once they were all herded together in the tiny hall, they stooped to remove their shoes, neatly placed them on the racks by the door, and then thrust their feet into the slippers provided.

Conversation is like a game of tennis. To ensure that in this weekly game of tennis the ball at least got off the ground, Reynolds had got into the habit of giving his students a topic in advance. Cheating, his French colleague said – the point about conversation was that it must be impromptu. But if each impromptu was at best merely a few breathless words and at worst a sigh, a giggle and a silence, then cheating was surely justified.

'What was it that we were going to talk about this afternoon?' Reynolds seldom remembered the topic set the week before. He did not remember now.

An elderly woman, wife of a famous physicist, who was both one of the most intelligent and one of the

[260]

shyest people in the class, held out her notebook towards him.

'No, no, tell me! I don't want to read it.'

But this was something that she was clearly not prepared to do. The notebook still extended, so that he could see the miniscule writing covering the two open pages, she gazed imploringly first at the tousled boy on her left and then at the young housewife on her right.

It was the young housewife who eventually said, on an upward note of vague interrogation: 'A Lost Opportunity.'

'Yes, that's it. Right.' Now why on earth should he have chosen that, of all subjects? Perhaps one of the class had suggested it, although it was difficult ever to get them to suggest anything at all.

It was at that moment that Miss Nishikawa entered, having presumably been let in by the maid, who edged in behind her with the tray of coca-colas.

Reynolds was glad to see 'Miss N', as he referred to her when talking about her to his French and other colleagues. Of all his students, she was the one about whom he talked most often, so vividly idiosyncratic was she in comparison with her fellows. She often missed classes and, when she did so, the hour seemed to stretch far longer than when she was present.

'Good afternoon, sir,' she greeted him. A woman of about thirty, still unmarried, she all too obviously dressed, as few Japanese women dressed, to excite attention. Her unusually short tartan skirt – when Reynolds had once remarked jokingly that he had never before realised that she belonged to the Stuart clan, she had screwed up her face in offended bewilderment – revealed sturdy bow-legs, encased in pale-green tights. Her shiny black hair, parted in the

[261]

middle, was gathered by ribbons, of the same pale-green shade, on either side of her jolly face.

'Good afternoon, Miss Nishikawa.'

'The late worm gets the bird,' she remarked as she motioned to one of the two youths on the sofa to shift over for her. Was she attempting to be witty? Or had she merely got the proverb mixed up? As always with Miss Nishikawa, Reynolds could not be sure; and not being sure, he felt vaguely uncomfortable.

Reynolds waited until everyone had a glass of coca-cola. Then he repeated: 'A Lost Opportunity. Now what have you all got to say about that?' (Bloody little, he decided privately, if one was to go by previous experience.)

There was a lengthy silence, during which all of them, sipping at their glasses, seemed determined to avoid his gaze.

'Well?' Silence again. 'Mrs Muto.'

The young housewife looked down at the exercise book open in her lap. Then she looked up and put a forefinger, Japanese-fashion, to her nose. 'I?'

'Yes – you.'

She began to read in a voice so faint and an accent so appalling that it was difficult to understand anything at all. Her lost opportunity seemed to have been the opportunity to visit a cousin of hers, married to a diplomat, in Kampala.

'Kampala? Many people might think that you were lucky to miss that opportunity.'

'Please?'

Reynolds shrugged, deciding to let it go.

The next student on whom he called, the tousled youth, had learned his speech off by heart. He screwed up his eyes under a tangle of hair as he began to recite. His lost opportunity had been the opportunity to learn

Esperanto from a female Australian missionary neighbour.

Reynolds's attention wandered; and as it did so, he suddenly became aware that Miss Nishikawa, plump legs crossed at the ankles and no less plump hands folded in her lap, was staring at him. Why did she so often stare at him? He had once put the question to his French colleague, who had answered 'Women usually stare at men for only one reason.'

Reynolds was not physically attracted by Miss Nishikawa, but he liked her. Secretary to the dean of the law department at the university, she struck him as unique in Japan in dominating her boss, instead of being dominated by him. How had she achieved this? Could it be that the small, frail professor was in love with her? Or had she discovered some secret which she now used for blackmail?

Other women in Japan dominated their bosses, Reynolds's French colleague had once argued. Every office and every university department had its *éminence d'ivoire*. But not openly, not openly, Reynolds had protested. It was the blatancy of her domination that set Miss Nishikawa apart from all those female moles, invisibly burrowing their way to unacknowledged power.

As the youth went on reciting, his face screwed up as though in an agony of regurgitating what his memory had digested, Reynolds remembered his conversation with Miss Nishikawa at a concert on the previous Saturday. She had arrived, as the musicians were already filing on to the stage, at the row in which, fortuitously, he had also had his seat.

'Reynolds-san!'

He had risen to let her pass, as had the elderly couple between him and the empty seat which was presumably hers. Heedless of the elderly couple, she faced him, her back to the seat in front of his and their knees touching, with a smile of delight irradiating at her face. 'I am happy to see you, so happy. I did not know that you like classical music. I thought you like jazz.'

'I like jazz, I like classical music. It's possible to like both, you know.'

She appeared to be dubious about that, as he once again felt her knees against his.

'I think these people are waiting for you to pass,' he said.

'We will talk in the interval. You will buy me a coca-cola – like we drink in your home.'

It was extraordinary that a Japanese woman should be so forward. No wonder that the other members of the conversation class seemed either to distrust or actively to dislike her.

In the interval he bought her the coca-cola.

'Do you think that the soprano is glamorous? Reynolds-san – be frank!'

'I hadn't really considered the matter.' Nor had he.

She laughed. 'I think that you are lying! Every young man must consider such a thing.'

'Not at all. What matters is whether she can sing well or not. Unfortunately, she can't.'

'But she is a very sexy lady. Reynolds-san, do you agree – she is a very sexy lady?'

He shrugged, smiling down into his half-drunk glass of coca-cola.

'Yes, yes! You are smiling! You agree, you agree!'

'Not at all!' But in fact she was right. He had found consolation for the inadequacy of the American soprano's voice in her sturdiness, her air of physical well-being and the beauty of the blond hair worn loose almost to her waist.

'Reynolds-san, now I will ask you a question I have wanted to ask you for a long time.'

'Yes?' Oh, lord, what was it going to be? That roguish smile, her head tilted to one side and the tip of her tongue peeping out of one corner of her small mouth, signalled an embarrassment.

'In England do you have a girl-friend?'

'Of course! Many, many girl-friends!' He laughed. But there was no mirth in his laughter. His one girl-friend had only the previous week married the managing director, several years her senior, of the publishing house in which she had been working.

She looked at him, head still tilted to one side, with a disbelieving, misty pity in her eyes. Then she nodded. 'And in Japan, Reynolds-san? Do you also have many girl-friends in Japan?'

'Of course! Many, many!' But again he was lying.

After that it was a relief when the gong boomed out to announce that the interval was over.

. . . At last the tousled young man had finished. As though after some tremendous physical effort, he lay back in the sofa, arms trailing on either side of him, face pale and glistening with sweat, and mouth agape in what appeared to be an effort to gulp more air.

'Thank you, Mr – er – Morimoto. I mean, Mr – er – Morikawa.' Reynolds always had difficulty in remembering the names of his male students, never those of his female ones. 'Very interesting. Has anyone any comment on that?'

No one had.

'This is a *conversation* class, you know. As I constantly tell you. We don't want isolated statements. Things must be linked. So . . .' He felt a sudden,

[265]

ineluctable weariness, such as all too often overcame him in the course of his teaching. But he pushed it aside, as though it were some cumbrous, leaden object in his path. 'Has anyone here ever studied Esperanto?'

No one responded.

'Has anyone ever thought of studying Esperanto?'

After a long silence, an elderly man, employed in the Post Office, reluctantly put up a hand.

'Yes?'

The man said nothing but kept his hand raised.

'Why did you think of studying Esperanto?'

'No, no, I am sorry, Reynolds-san. I wish only to go to toilet.'

It was with relief that eventually Reynolds turned to Miss Nishikawa. 'Well, Miss Nishikawa, we've not yet heard what you have to say on this subject of a Lost Opportunity.'

'I think that I have something interesting to say.' The other members of the class fidgeted, glanced at each other and then stared down at the carpet. Clearly they disapproved of the immodesty of the claim.

'Good. Then say it.'

Miss Nishikawa neither recited nor read. Hands clasped in her lap, she leaned forward to Reynolds as though, the others absent, she were speaking to him alone. 'A funny story, a sad story,' she said.

Again the other Japanese showed their disapproval and unease by fidgeting and glancing at each other. Plainly each was wondering what was about to emerge from this woman so unlike any other Japanese woman known to them.

Miss Nishikawa gave Reynolds a slow, happy smile. Her eyes held his. Then she launched into her narrative.

Travelling, the previous summer, from Kobe to

[266]

Kyoto, she had found herself sitting opposite a man –
'not young but glamorous, very glamorous, with little,
little moustache and romance-grey hair, cut long,
long.' They had got into conversation, they had at
once liked each other – 'like music, perfect music, me
high notes, he low notes, perfect!' The man was
married, he had three children. Each year he came to
Kyoto from his home on the island of Shikoku, in
order to attend a meeting of the sub-managers of the
company for which he worked. At Kyoto she and he
had left the train together. The man had one hour to
spare before the meeting. 'We went – ' Miss Nishikawa
gave a loud, clear laugh, not raising a cupped hand to
her mouth, as most other Japanese women would have
done. 'I will not tell you where we went! But we have
a good time, happy time.' What did she mean? Had
they merely been for a walk in one of the parks or sat
in a café or saké-bar? Or had they taken a room in one
of the innumerable *maisons de passe*, their tariffs
displayed on their entrances, in which the area around
the station abounded? Reynolds sensed that all the
other Japanese were wondering the same thing. He
also sensed their growing embarrassment, and then
their growing annoyance with Miss Nishikawa for
causing that embarrassment.

'We are together only one hour. Then he must go to
his meeting. But he tells me that each year, on the
first Tuesday of June, his company has such meeting.'
She drew a deep sigh. 'Then we make a promise to
each other, a very romantic promise. Next year, on
the first Tuesday of June, we will meet again. Same
time, same place. Maybe same happiness? Who can
say?' She looked around at the others, but none of
them looked back. Then she looked at Reynolds. Her
eyes were sparkling with what he could only assume

was mischief. 'Well, what do you think I did when that day comes? I go back or not go back?'

No one answered the question.

'Reynolds-san – I go back or not back?'

'From what I know of you, Miss Nishikawa, I think you went back.'

Everyone nodded approval of his answer.

'Wrong, wrong, wrong!' she cried out. 'I do not go back. A Lost Opportunity? Maybe. Reynolds-san must tell me.'

'How can I say?' He turned to the class. 'What do all of you think?'

But what they thought, they were none of them prepared to disclose.

Reynolds concluded the class ten minutes before the hour was over. All at once he found that, with so little cooperation, he could no longer ask another question or make another comment. Even Miss Nishikawa had fallen silent after her account, her eyes uncharacteristically dreamy in a face that was no less uncharacteristically still.

While the others exchanged their slippers for their shoes, Reynolds noticed, with foreboding, that Miss Nishikawa was hanging back in one corner of the hall, her hands clasped before her and her head bowed.

When all of them were ready, they surged together to the door, calling out in ragged unison 'Goodbye, Reynolds-san! Thank you! See you again!' When they had passed beyond the gate, he heard one of them – the tousled boy, he thought – laughing loudly. Then the rest of them began to laugh. Were they laughing at him? Or at Miss Nishikawa? Or at something wholly different?

He turned. 'Well, Miss Nishikawa . . .'

'Did you like my story?'

'Yes, I thought it an interesting story. Revealing. Odd. But whether it was precisely the sort of story to tell on this occasion . . .' How priggish that sounded! He felt a not unwonted disgust with himself.

She smiled from the dark corner in which she was still standing. 'But I do not tell the story right,' she said. 'Not quite right.'

God! Was she now going to tell him explicitly about the sex-hotel to which she and her pick-up had adjourned?

'Not quite right?'

'I lie. I lie about the date. I say first Tuesday of June. Really it is first Tuesday of April.'

'Oh.' The lie hardly seemed to be of importance.

She looked into his face. Then she burst into laughter. 'Reynolds-san – what is today?'

'April the second.' Still he did not get it.

'What day?'

'Tuesday, isn't it?'

She nodded. 'Yes, Tuesday. The first Tuesday of April. You understand?'

He began to understand. 'Then you mean . . .?'

'This afternoon is the afternoon of my rendezvous. Yes.' She nodded vigorously. 'Yes. I do not go. I do not go. Do you know why I do not go, Reynolds-san?'

'Perhaps in retrospect he seemed less attractive than you'd thought him?'

She shook her head. 'No. No. I do not go because I wish to be with someone else . . . I wish to be with you.'

'With *me*?'

Again she nodded vigorously, her small eyes glittering out of a face that now seemed extraordinarily white in the gloom of the corner. 'With you.'

'But you can always come to my classes.'

[269]

'I wished to see you. This afternoon. Now. That was more important than anything else.'

The telephone had begun to ring. Thank God, thank God! 'Excuse me,' he said. 'I must answer that. Your shoes are over there.' He pointed at the rack. Of course she would know where she herself had placed her shoes. The invitation to go was all too obvious.

When he returned from the telephone, she had got into her shoes.

Embarrassed, hardly looking at her, he opened the door.

She edged towards it, her umbrella dangling from a wrist. All at once she looked despondent, weary, afflicted. He had never before seen her look like that.

'Then I go,' she said. 'That was my Lost Opportunity. Now you know. Reynolds-san. See you again!'

'See you again!' Since he had taken up residence in Japan, he had become accustomed to echoing the idiotic phrase.

She descended sideways from step to step, like an old woman afraid of falling, while he looked down at her. Without once turning, she made for the gate.

Slowly he closed the front door. Then he raced up the stairs to his bedroom, the window of which overlooked the bus-stop at which he knew that she usually waited for the bus which would take her to the suburb in which she lived. He stood behind the net-curtain and gazed down at the empty street.

When she appeared, she had raised the edge of the tartan skirt and was tugging at a thread – presumably loose – in its hem. She no longer looked weary, despondent, afflicted. She now looked as she always looked. Had that been a true story? Or had she made it up? He would never know.

Her hair shone in the late spring sunlight. In that

sunlight the skin of her arm also shone, as she raised
it to pick a blossom, small, crumpled and white, from
the hedge of the next-door house. She raised the
blossom to her nose and sniffed at it. Suddenly she
was laughing. As with the others earlier, he wondered
if she was laughing at him.

Still standing at the window and still looking down
at her – now she was motionless, gazing up the road
for the bus – he thought, with a sudden hurt and
anger, of the girl who had married the publisher so
many years her senior.

The bus had arrived. Miss Nishikawa was skipping
– yes, there was no other word for it – aboard.

[271]

MARIA KRIZOVE

Simon Mason

I

Thirty-six years old. Short and paunchy with a pouchy face screwed-up against the nervous drift of cigarette smoke. Footballer's haircut, long and straggly at the back, sparse on top. Black in colour, oily to the touch. Dressed as always in designer tracksuit and sneakers. Lounging at the foot of the shag-piled stairs, picking at a thin growth of beard, waiting for her to come out of the loo. Me.

Yes, here I am. I'm rehearsing my lines. Think of it, me, such an old hand now, a film-maker, an *award-winner*, an intellectual, still putting myself to the trouble. But it's the simple thrill, lust, that keeps me at practice. Work hard, play hard, that's me.

Overhead the flushed toilet makes a genteel swallow (I had it silenced when I took this place), and the door upstairs opens, and she begins to descend the thick shag waterfall of the stairs. What a walk she has. Her stockinged legs like two feline creatures rubbing their backs against each other. When she's halfway down I lift myself off the bannister like a suddenly animated rag-doll, and make a bow, quite ridiculous but pleasantly confusing, and I give her the usual guff.

'Christ,' I say, coarse and fawning, 'Look at you. It's like Hollywood. We're talking perfect entrance. Now where did you learn an entrance like that?'

The question sends one hand fluttering up to her mouth. Usually a good sign.

'Don't deny it,' I guff on (pointing my fag at her), 'but you've done quite a bit of acting in your time, haven't you? I can tell. Look,' (employing my emphatic fag again) 'this new film of mine I was telling you about (wasn't I?). I've been four months trying to find a lead – got absolutely nothing, no one. Started to think she didn't exist. But she does, she certainly does.' (use here of the open palm tilted towards her) 'You. You're perfect.'

You'd think this was a scene from one of my films, wouldn't you, but no, it's a scene from my life. Two days ago it happened. That's what I used to be like, two days ago – all mouth and tracksuit. You know the type. That's what I've been like for most of my life, thirty-six years of constant mouth. God, I'm old. It frightens me to think of it. How did I get so old? I used to be so young. The problem is that I'm not the type to grow old gracefully: I have these looks, like a middle-aged teenager, with my ear-rings and my pug-dog's nose spreading over my face like a rumour of itself and my veins breaking like threads of puce-coloured cotton and my hair falling out. Sometimes I lie awake at night rubbing my hand over my forehead, here, this bumpy bit, where the hair has receded, pretending I can feel the positive results of the latest transplant.

I've been in movies for seventeen years now, as writer and producer, growing steadily older and uglier and richer and coarser and balder. I reckon that in that time I've been through about a million quid. You'd think you could buy quite a decent life for that

lot, but don't you believe it: I've bought nothing
worth anything: viz, a home abroad; viz, a powerboat
I could never get to work until the day I ran it aground
at Hastings; viz, a small collection of Duchamp lithographs discovered later to be forgeries; viz, an op for
an ulcer, and several more for my hair; and, finally,
viz the usual, the several thousand bottles of vodka,
the countless cigarettes, and a few odd divorces.

No wonder I've aged so quickly. It's boredom. My
life's been like one of my films alright, strong on plot
and weak on character; I've sat through it with my
eyes glazed over, hardly noticing when the video
cassette is changed and a new cast of actors takes up
the impossible story. That's the way I see it now,
anyway. Since two days ago, when my life went freeze-
frame, and for the first time I wondered what I'd been
doing for the last thirty-six years.

My life. It's the story of an obsession. I remember
being seven years old and nasty. I had short, fluffy
hair, and buck teeth enmeshed in metal. No one liked
me because when I spoke spit bubbled in the dark
gaps between my silvery teeth. I used to sit at the back
of the class and kick whoever sat in front. I mention
this because, when I think about it, this nastiness is
what I associate with being in films, being rich, being
a writer – getting my own back. Since I was very
young I wanted to write, in the sense that I wanted to
be known as a writer, not necessarily a *great* writer
but to be famous and wealthy and influential. At
fourteen that involved getting drunk and screaming
obscenities at astonished schoolteachers who found me
on the pavement outside school and tried to help me
up. At fifteen I quietened down, and took up mild
narcotics. By sixteen my style had changed again,
matured, and I was a jaded, chain-smoking alcoholic

[277]

with a surreptitious passion for observing everyone around me. 'Observe perpetually, never cease from observation,' wrote Henry James. I obeyed his dictum fanatically. By the time I was seventeen I had a detailed dossier on each of my schoolfriends, listing not only their appearance, habits, speech characteristics, prejudices, fears, ambitions and so on, but also suggestions for their alternative lives; in other words what I could do to them. I was as ruthless as I possibly could be. Already it was plain to me that if I wanted to be famous and wealthy I would have to write for film or television, which, in literary terms, requires less talent but more instinct, and the special abililty to blend convoluted storylines with a large range of simplistic characters. Mannikins, robots, galley slaves, that's what film and TV characters are, that's what my schoolfriends were about to become.

When I left school at the age of eighteen, with my dossiers of other people's half-formed counter-lives, I made contact with an uncle of mine, name of Mel Thorpe. You won't have heard of him. He was a producer with ITV. His forty-five-minute dramas were low-grade sentimental guff about housewives or salesmen, very English sub-Pinter confrontations in boarding-houses or bus-stations. Occasionally, however, he would make something slightly racier for the big screen. I cared nothing for Uncle Mel's work, it belonged to the curling-at-the-edges generation I was trying to subvert, but he had one or two useful contacts. The result was that I joined a company called Expo Products to assist with the writing of a number of new films for limited release. When I accepted the job I wasn't exactly sure what type of films Expo made, I only knew that they specialised in overseas markets: Japan, Germany, Scandinavia. I soon found out. The name of the first film I worked on was 'Bangkok Bonanza'.

Porn. Blue movies. Adults only. At first they were the jerky one-reelers shown on snowstormed screens in gloomy private clubs from Amsterdam to Helsinki: later, those brown-enveloped videos sold under the counters of a thousand retailing outlets, along with rubber knickers, wind-up willies and bull erection cream. It was a good time to get into porn, especially export. When the UK was tumbling arse over tit into international debt, exports were to be given all possible encouragement.

In 1977, the year The Sex Pistols foul-mouthed their way to fame, I got backing to make films of my own, for my own company, International Entertainments Corporation. Cue the boom-time. Within a year I had a house in Tunisia, a powerboat in dry-dock, and a new wife. I was twenty-three, and already I felt about fifty.

I was a real bastard too, I don't pretend otherwise. But I was good at my work. Delving deep into my schoolday dossiers, I churned out character after character for the usual fleshly routine (depicted a dozen times a film: our working average); the teenagers I had once studied and smoked with I turned into bankers and politicians and nurses and nuns, all of them engaged in the mad scramble of sex, and the Japanese and Germans and Finns bought them by the video-load.

In this way I used all my former schoolfriends. Getting my own back? It was purely mechanical. Until recently I never even considered the matter. Me, I'm a professional knocker-out of knocking-shop scenarios: the tangled relationship certain highbrow writers have with their characters was simply not an

[279]

occupational hazard for me. Once my former friends were rematerialised as Sven the priapic car-mechanic or Mary-Jane the bored but ruttish millionairess, I was free of them and owed them nothing. They were appeased.

But, as I discovered over the years, there was one exception.

Her name was Maria Krizove, and I knew her briefly in my fags-and-apathy period at the age of seventeen. She was a quiet, enigmatic girl of Czecho-slovakian extraction, who could be found most days in the sixth form common-room, sitting on a faded red sofa by the canteen hatch, staring out of one of the windows. (There were precisely two windows in the room, and both were permanently misted over with cigarette smoke and hot adolescent breath.) Maria K acted as if she could see out of it, a physical impossi-bility. One stockinged leg would be crossed beneath her, one arm stretched along the back of her seat, and her head would be languidly tilted as if she were squinting to bring whatever she was pretending to look at into focus. She looked as if she was gazing into the future, dreaming up schemes for the rest of her life.

As a chain-smoker, her features were constantly blurred by plumes of rising smoke, but she wasn't beautiful anyway; her face was too pinched, her movements too reserved, her hair too severe. The only two expressions she possessed were serious and quizz-ical, the latter a variation brought on by her squint. Nor was she companionable enough to be popular. Her one close friend was a girl even quieter than herself who talked only of pure mathematics, a conver-sational hazard few were bold enough to attempt.

Whoever did attempt it was faced with Maria's quizzical frown. I once saw someone cadge a cigarette off her. She asked him to repeat the question, then thoughtfully took her packet from a bag. 'Do you like Czechoslovakian cigarettes?' she asked. The cadger nodded brazenly. 'I also,' said Maria Krizove quietly, and handed him a Benson and Hedges. 'But I cannot find them anywhere.'

Despite her lack of popularity, or perhaps because of it, Maria Krizove exerted a kind of fascination over me. And not only me. Rumour, always a technique close to my heart, periodically transformed her: into an orphan or heiress or diabetic or criminal or something else sufficiently implausible. More than once I was told, with an almost desperate glee, that she was an out-and-out nymphomaniac, several of my friends claimed to have detected a tell-tale trembling of desire behind her look of anvil-faced indifference.

There was certainly something odd about her, something indefinably out of place. But what it was no one could put their finger on. Mostly people were inclined to give up the mystery after a few days' fruitless effort, call her a stuck-up bitch, and have done with her. Me too, at first. Not later.

For the last two days I have been re-reading her dossier. It's thinner than most of my dossiers, more confused and scrappier, but the memories it evokes – I mean, for once, memories of the real person, unadulterated – are sharper.

I remember meeting her one time out of school. Actually, meeting's the wrong word: I observed her. Near school there was a park on a hill and I was slouching along the bottom of it one evening, smoking something or other, when I glanced up, and saw her. She was sitting on a bench with an elderly couple,

[281]

about twenty yards away under a large sycamore. A dachshund in a ludicrous knitted waistcoat was tetchily standing guard on the grass in front of them. Maria K's pose was so characteristic I recognized her at once: her arm was stretched along the back of the bench, one leg was tucked beneath her, and her head was tilted back, with her hair falling to the vertical like dark water. Round her head, like a halo, I could see a small hanging cloud of smoke. I slouched past, puffing like a bastard on my own fag, then changed direction and approached the quartet stealthily from behind. Partly it was writer's instinct, partly I didn't know what the hell I was doing. If I had wanted to hear what they were saying to each other, I was disappointed; they were talking in a language full of coughs and clicks which I assumed to be Czechoslovakian. Maria K's elderly companions were doing most of the work, strenuously gesticulating as they spoke in rapid bursts at the girl who reclined between them. I don't think I'd realised how slightly built she was until I saw her between those two squat old hulks. Occasionally Maria K would say something in English; I remember a weary 'what does it matter?', and 'it's too late for that now'. All the time she kept her eyes fixed ahead of her, gazing down the hill beyond the park boundary as if she could see more than just the street lamps coming on, pinky-yellow pinpricks in the deepening blue above hedges and roofs.

Those lights. Her gaze. There was a feeling of . . . I don't know what, of *timelessness*, as if nothing had ever happened, ever would happen, except this slow diurnal procession of light and dark through all the infinitesimal gradations in between; and then as I turned to go there was a flurry on the bench in front of me and the elderly man struck Maria K across the face.

The dachshund yelped and immediately fell silent. The two old wrecks, who looked too frail for violence, were staring intently at Maria K; Maria K was still staring out across the valley, her position hadn't altered. One cheek turned red. A minute passed without any of them moving, not even the dachshund, then Maria turned to the old man. Somehow, in my curiosity, I must have strayed out from behind the sycamore, because when she turned I found her looking straight at me. She held my gaze for a second or two with those cold eyes of hers, then, without the slightest expression crossing her face, she took the old man's hand where it lay clenched against his knee, lifted it to her lips, and kissed it. She said something to him, too softly for me to hear, and, as if this was a cue, the three got to their feet, stretched, and made their way down the slope towards the park gates, the dachshund waddling irritably after.

It was almost the last time I ever saw Maria Krizove, but that single, inexplicable incident was enough for me, it was all the encouragement I needed. Over the last seventeen years I have portrayed Maria K in some form or other in about twenty-five films. Compared to her all my other schoolfriends have had bit parts; she has been the star – if you can call such characters stars: the moody temptress and willing secretaries, the nuns and hookers and barmaids and nurses and teachers and check-out girls. The videos she appears in have been my absolute best-sellers. Yes, Maria Krizove has brought out the best in me, and, although she doesn't realise it, she's done more than anyone to make my fortune.

At first I was delighted with my ingenuity; I seemed

to be able to turn Maria K into anything I wanted. But as time went by, and as I kept up a steady production rate of celluloid stripteasing Maria Krizoves for the Nips and Krauts and Scandies, I became more and more dissatisfied. Guilty is what I should have been (guilty – for instance – for abusing that moment in the park which, somehow, she had shared with me). But, no, I didn't feel guilty. At the time that wasn't my style. It was something more selfish that was bothering me, an uneasiness, a suspicion that I couldn't actually get rid of Maria K, couldn't *stop* creating these nubile pneumatic versions of her. It was as if the original impressions of her – the outstretched arm, the tucked up leg, the tilted head and smoke-wreathed faraway gaze – persisted in my memory despite what I did to them, and my writing became a game to try and obliterate them. Gradually the game became an obsession. And Maria Krizove, the real Maria Krizove, remained in my memory unaffected by each new facile invention of her. I couldn't shake her off. For seventeen years she dogged my steps, and then, two days ago, I met her again, her real self, in the flesh.

II

Before I start on how it happened, I should say (for the sake of my pride as much as for anything) that I haven't worked exclusively in porn. About five years ago I moved into television, a fairly common move to make. You'd be surprised how many TV writers and producers honed their talents on a blue fuck or two.

[284]

I've done quite a few things for packagers – shorts, docudramas, features, and so on – and last year ITV screened one of my plays, *Last in, First out,* a 'portrayal of life in the age of redundancy'.

It sounds like pure gritty realism, but it had such a high sex content that ITV achieved the best ratings for a play they'd had since the newly-discovered Joe Orton adaptation of *The Two Gentlemen of Verona.* A week ago it won the John Taylor Award for Television Drama (usually given for pure – as opposed to impure – gritty realism).

So, two days ago, I went along to one of those self-congratulatory booze-ups that always accompany awards. It was a typical telemakers' wank: lots of sweaty, stubbly men in creased tracksuits looking like well-used pyjamas and bottle-blonde women with fag-ridden faces, all engaged in fractious agreement with everyone around them. Television people have this basic need to argue, but as they all share the same views, argument's difficult; they get angry agreeing instead.

The party was held – impromptu-style though it was no such thing – in one of the recording studios, a cavernous box tall and narrow. Surreal isn't the word. We occupied the small set of a quiz show filmed that afternoon set out with contestants' desks, giant clock and score-board. The scoremaster's podium had been turned into a makeshift bar and bristled with bottles. Round the edge of the set, against the curtains that soundproofed the walls, the TV cameras stood idle like enormous metal birds frozen on one leg, their vacant eyes trained in on us. Above, racks of dead lights hung down from the girders of the ceiling, throwing the set into shadow. Up above them, dim in the gloom, wires and cables hung in loops like jungle

[285]

creepers. In front of us, the tiered seating for studio audiences reared up and away, fading against the black curtains that disappeared up to the distant ceiling. What I thought of then, in true scriptwriting fashion, was a bunker; that's what the place looked like with its museum-pieces of a lifestyle thrown together with some scuffed metal relics of technical hardware, and a few specimens of humankind persisting in their usual shabby way. I could imagine how the boredom would get to them, how they would drift away, in pairs, to the shadowy corners of the studio. That's what kind of a professional mind I've got.

But by no stretch of the imagination could I have foreseen what actually happened that evening, though this too seemed like a scene from a film, it was as luridly unreal. When I think of it now (and for the last two days I've thought of little else) it's like I'm watching myself on screen.

It's eight o'clock and the loudly-underdressed people (in dayglo tracksuits and Bridget Riley artist's smocks) on the small, dark set are growing steadily rowdier. I'm drinking heavily with my leading lady, a nervous brunette in a cat-suit, when my co-producer, a small, dark, hirsute man, lays a hairy hand on my shoulder and introduces me to two women he has with him. One is thirtyish, plump but well-kept, and overdressed in a shiny black gown; she is also, rather archly, smoking a cigarette in an ebony holder. Her head, which she holds on one side, seems weighed down by an elaborate chignon. The other woman is younger, tall, with blonde hair, a very clear skin and a slightly snub nose. She is also elegantly dressed, in a smart grey blouse and skirt. She'd be my number one choice.

The older woman says something which I don't catch, though I bob forward like a jack-in-box, then adds, with a gesture towards her friend, 'And this is Alicia.' Smilingly they both hold out their hands for me to shake, how quaint.

I smile too. It's smiles all round, how quaint and corny, like a scene in a film.

'Lager or vodka?' I say. 'Or I could do you a mix of the two. There's nothing else. It's all we people in television drink. You get used to it after a while. Wish I could say the same for television,' I add, gesturing round the studio with my fag. The elegant out-of-place women smile politely and ask for vodkas.

'I must warn you,' says the older woman, when I return, 'I'm a television addict. We both are. We've seen all your work.'

If only they knew all my work. *That'd* be something worth barking about. I scrutinize the younger woman, who looks away, into the gloom above the tiers of empty seats in front of us.

'Yes, we've seen everything you've done,' her friend goes on in her precise voice, looking evenly at me, 'We're great fans of yours, aren't we, Alicia?' Her friend smiles briefly and sips her vodka, hiding her mouth with her glass. Her smile is incredible. Haven't seen anything like it for weeks, maybe months. Might just save the situation, I think.

'What do you like best?' I ask Alicia, bobbing forward and putting in some fag-work. 'I mean which film.' There is a certain sickening coyness about the way I ask this, I admit. Her friend replies for her.

'We like *Ave Maria* best, don't we Alicia?' and for some reason they both break out giggling. Watching Alicia's mouth, I try to figure this out. *Ave Maria* is a thing I did for TV in about 1987. It's set in Dublin

[287]

where I camped out for a year after my last divorce. Maria Krizove stars in it as the nun Maria O'Donnell who falls in love with a boy dying of leukaemia, and has to choose between him and her religion. Sounds cheap, doesn't it? Well, it is. But it isn't funny; it's definitely not funny. Why it should amuse Alicia and her friend I can't imagine.

'What about another drink?' I say. They stop laughing, and both shake their heads.

'But there is something we'd like,' says the older of the two. She rummages in her handbag and produces a camera. 'Your photograph.'

I don't like this. I'm the one who does the pictures for Christ's sake. It is explained that they want a photograph of me 'where I work', which certainly isn't on this quiz game set, but the two women won't take no for an answer.

'We'll take it round the back of the set then,' says the woman, squinting into the shadows, 'by one of those TV cameras.' Alicia nods and glances at me.

'Please?' she says, smiling.

Everything's in a mess round the back of the set: the floor is strewn with cables and tool-boxes; rough-edged timber props and joists which hold up the quiz game's fancy screens stick out like ribs. We're behind the scenes, where a kind of real life, with all its crap and compromises, takes over from the chocolate-boxy set in front.

'There,' says the woman, directing me with her cigarette-holder, 'over there. One of you alone, and then one of you with Alicia.'

I stand with one arm draped awkwardly over the cold metal casing of a camera, and the other aggressively stuck out at my hip, trying to look thoughtful.

[288]

'Good,' says the woman. The flash goes off and I, like a tit, give an enormous idiot's blink.

'Now with Alicia,' says the woman. Alicia hardly looks at me, but she presses against me and puts her arm round my shoulder. Fancy perfume rises from her neck and hair. Coincidently I become much cheerier about this business with the photographs, I even crack a few jokes; Christ, I'm almost jovial when I slip my arm round Alicia's waist and – coincidently – feel through her thin blouse the warm ripple of flesh covering her ribs. Above my hand I can sense – skin prickling – the soft weight of her right breast. It's a very long time since I experienced emotions like these. Days. As the flash goes I squeeze Alicia tightly and give a broad grin. The other woman is staring at us.

'No more pickies?' I say.

Alicia slips free and says to her friend, 'One with you now.' But the woman with the camera shakes her head.

'There is no need,' she says, 'I already have such a photograph.'

'Pardon?' I say. 'A photograph of me and you?' She is giggling, and I feel suddenly afraid; I don't like being here surrounded by half-completed carpentry and dormant machines and this woman. But the woman acts as if she's enjoying herself.

'I wanted to see if you would recognise me,' she says. 'How funny. You don't, I see.' She walks up to me, six very smart clicks of her heels on the concrete floor, and holds out her hand again. Oh fuck it, I think, it's a friend of one of my ex-wives.

'Sorry,' I say. I can feel myself going pale. She smiles. Keeps on smiling.

'Maria,' she says, with her hand held out to me as if

[289]

she is offering me something, 'Maria Krizove. It has been a very long time. Do you remember me still?'

Did I remember her? Don't make me laugh. Actually I didn't laugh. Couldn't. To have her there, in front of me — holding my hand for Christ's sake — wasn't exactly funny.

I've already mentioned how frequently, how profitably I've brought Maria Krizove to mind over the last fifteen years; and in what ways I've enlivened the memories. Well, when I met her in that TV studio I had this sudden feeling that her actual presence was somehow a travesty, like a mistake, as if her real life were taking liberties with my fictions. I felt almost angry. I know what this was now: it was a sense of guilt, the long-awaited thing, coming home to roost. At the time I was well pissed off.

For the first time that evening I had a good look at her. She was no longed pinched and pale; far from it, she had a smooth look about her as if she had lived comfortably. Her complexion was richer, deeper, and the skin of her throat was ringed with shiny creases. A freckle above her left eyebrow which I remembered had blossomed into a mole. Facing me, she stood in a confident pose, her weight relaxed, and she seemed . . . what shall I say? She seemed dignified, there's no other word for it.

It all horrified me. Partly, to be honest, I was embarrassed in front of Alicia. I was aware of her hovering by the TV camera where I had left her, and I wonderd what she thought of it all, I wondered what I looked like fumbling for a fag while I stared pop-eyed at Maria K with a cartoon grin slapped on my stubbly, sweaty face.

I was embarrassed, certainly I was; but more than just that, I was disorientated, I was swamped by memories, glimpses of the seventeen-year old Maria Krizove suddenly superimposed over the mature version in front of me, reels of archive footage running wildly in my mind. It was nineteen years since we had last met. That was in May 1971. It suddenly came back to me.

It was only a few days after I saw her that time in the park. I was leaving school one evening and I bumped into her in the street outside. She was standing on the pavement underneath a street lamp, her hair and shoulders almost incandescent in the bright yellow light, her face and the rest of her body invisible in darkness, with the exception of the tip of her cigarette which glowed red at her hip. Somehow I knew it was her straightaway.

It must have been late for it to be so dark, ten o'clock or something like that; at the time I was knocking off this girl who used to stay behind after school to practice the piano. Naturally I was surprised to see Maria Krizove hanging round so late.

'What's up?' I said. 'Need someone to walk you home?' (I was forgetting that she lived about ten miles away.)

She told me she wanted to speak to me and we walked together towards the bus-stop.

'I'm leaving,' she said, without preface, when we were about half way there. Her voice was like a small electric shock in the still air.

'What do you mean?' I asked.

'Leaving school. My grandparents want me to go to America, to my uncle who lives there now, but I think I will go to London and get a job. I do not like relying on family,' she said. 'Or anyone else.'

[291]

I thought it was pretty strange that she was leaving school when there was still about a year and a half to go before her A levels, but I just nodded. There was no accounting for her strangeness.

She began to cough; she had a cold, she said, and some slight sickness. I said I was sorry, but I don't think she heard me. She was barking like a seal, with her head lowered into her hand and her hand scrubbing her mouth as she shook. She coughed for about a minute, and then she said,

'I don't know if I want you to forget me or to remember me. Or even if it matters.'

At that, I began to cough, and, cursing my fag, I threw it on the floor and stamped on it.

'But I wished to say goodbye,' she said, as we reached the bus stop. 'Goodbye.' She held out her hand and I took it.

'Hey,' I said. 'I'll remember you. Don't worry.'

I did. Certainly I did, I made a career out of it for Christ's sake. Here's a memory for instance: two months before we said our goodbyes, Maria Krizove and I had bumped into each other at a party. In those days, like everyone else, I used to think of myself as quite a stud. Anyway, at this party Maria arrived alone, quite late when I was already drunk and over-talkative. I asked her what she was drinking, and she just shrugged.

'Anything will do,' she said. In two minutes she had in her hand the most powerful screwball I've ever made, which for the next half-hour she sipped while I ranted about myself. Occasionally she smiled. Once she laughed, I remember that. It was a game. I was testing the rumours – though I'm afraid to say I had

been responsible for some of them. I was showing off.
When the party was at its loudest and crudest I asked
her if she believed in love, and she shrugged again,
and said 'Why talk of what we don't know? Ask me
again when I'm a hundred.' Ignoring her, I reported
that I myself did not believe in love. I said I believed
in one-night stands.

Maria Krizove smoked her cigarette down to the
butt, dropped it into her glass, and said, 'Prove it.'

After that night I had hardly anything to do with
her. That was my style in those days. I think it was
Maria Krizove's style too. Of course I allowed myself
a few smug remarks when the same old tired rumours
about Maria K came round again, but I moved on
pretty quickly to other concerns, the piano-player for
instance. Once, as I've said, I exchanged glances in
the park with her, and once shook hands with her in
the street outside school, and then, bequeathing me a
few disconnected memories of herself and a pretty
bloody thin dossier, she left my life forever.

Until I shook hands with her nineteen years later in
that TV studio.

To be honest with you I haven't changed much since
I was at school; I still drink too much at parties and
make a tit of myself; it makes up for being so po-faced
all the rest of the time. The way I see it, it's a simple
matter of disillusionment: it's always the disillusioned
who want to be the last of the all-night ravers.

'This calls for a celebration,' I said, still grinning
like a bastard. Auto-enthusiatically I ushered both
Maria and Alicia back on to the set and over towards
the drinks.

*

[293]

Don't ask me to explain in any detail what happened after that. I got into a bit of a state. From the studios we went to a restaurant, somewhere swanky; it was my treat. I remember massed foliage, glossy and fleshy, towering out of terracotta tubs, and skinny waiters with even glossier hair, dressed in DJs, and Maria laughing and Alicia smiling at something I had said. I remember laughing myself, but inside I was dead. It hurt me every time I caught Maria K's eye, and in the end I just stopped looking at her and concentrated on the drinks. I remember little properly until we arrived back at my flat.

My bachelor flat. However many times I marry I seem to end up back here, or something like it. It's my home, my spiritual home, with its shag-pile and stuccoed ceilings and leather-and-aluminium Van Klein suite.

In my studio where I generally live there is a cinema screen and video, some of those fake Duchamp lithographs propped against an art-nouveau drinks cabinet and a cheap array of awards along the mantelpiece. Magazines are everywhere, like litter. Upstairs, where I sometimes venture, the master bedroom is an equal mix of black vinyl and black shag and mirror. Most nights I fall asleep on the sofa in the studio.

We arrived about midnight and I hit the dimmer switch and zap-started the stereo and poured us all a big drink. There were some videos of my earlier films lying around, and Maria and Alicia wanted me to play one.

'What's this about?' asked Maria, reading a label out loud, *'I'm Not Feeling Myself Tonight.'* I waved my fag in the air dismissively.

'Boring,' I said. 'Dead boring, honest.' I thought

[294]

for a second, still waving my fag. 'All about the menopause,' I said inspirationally.

But this was my come-uppance. Having her here in my room, matronly in her black gown, a *decent* woman, reading out the titles of films in which she sucks and fucks. Even I could see it wasn't right. Something that had never occurred to me before occurred to me now: I had betrayed her trust. *Trust* was the word. I still didn't give a toss about the others, but Maria Krizove was different, I had slept with her, and the thing itself, the fuck, I had taken and twisted a thousand different ways (a dozen times a film).

I knew it, but I kept it at bay by drinking, instinctively like an animal. We were all drunk by that stage, lying on the leather bits of the Van Kleins, drinking and smoking cigarettes. I toyed with the idea of bringing out some Lebanese hash I had in the fridge, but thought better of it. Instead, talking like a bastard to keep myself from thinking, I told the two women a lot of lies about my career in the movies, and – also a matter of instinct – began to give Alicia the eye.

She sat quietly, gazing at her friend or at me out of big blue eyes. The intensity of her gaze reminded me (though I fought it) of the seventeen-year old Maria Krizove, sitting on that faded red sofa, outstaring that misted-up window. Once or twice Alicia smiled at something I said, smiles she threw off with a dainty nonchalance. Like gobbets of meat tossed to a hungry dog, as I ducked and weaved among my cheap awards, crushing out fag after fag on the top of the TV.

Yes, it was Alicia now who occupied me rather than Maria, which is where, emotionally speaking, I'd started. After all, I was on my home territory now: whenever I'm at home with female company I get this

[295]

Pavlovian reaction. I was working myself up to the usual state of frenzy.

At some point in the proceedings Alicia left the room to go to the bathroom, and after a short pause I followed her, determined to rescue something from the otherwise naff evening.

'Hold on,' I said to Maria, who was talking of our brief common life when she was a real person, 'Hold on a minute, I think I can hear the cat trying to get in.'

I have no cat, no real cat, just an imaginary one. Leaving the studio, I padded into the hallway, and to the foot of the stairs. I heard the flush go, a whoosh and an apologetic dribble, and then Alicia reappeared.

Yes, we've been here before; this is where the film stops. This is the frozen frame.

When I say she looks like a movie-star coming down the stairs, I mean it. I'm hypnotized. She's like a smooth, elegant ripple barely making contact with the vulgar cascade of black shag. And even as I block her way with a bow and a wave of my fag, and give her the guff, I know she's somehow different from all the other mincing women I've stopped on those stairs with the same thing on my mind.

After I've done the bit about the Hollywood walk, I find myself unexpectedly lost for words. That's one thing that's never happened to me before, not even with old Maria K. I panic.

'Look,' I say suddenly. 'I'm making you an offer for Christ's sake. You're perfect, honest. Do me a favour. Let me at least give you an audition.' I must look a right plonker, pop-eyed and balding, in my maternity-stretch-fabric tracksuit, touting my fag like something I've just that moment picked up and don't know whether to keep or throw away; but I've got to keep at it now. Mouth dry. Forehead wet. Fag-hand going berserk in the space in front of my face, so I can hardly make her out, gazing back at me quizzically.

'Look,' I say desperately, 'Will you give it a go? This film, it's personal, understand? Written from here.' I bang my chest and there's a small explosion of ash down the front of my tracksuit. 'And it's going to be great, I know it is. It's going to be just fantastic.' Alicia looks at me with curiosity. She's got such a kind, soft face. I'm almost there, I think.

'What's it about?' she asks.

'What's it about?' I cry, my mind a blank, 'What's it about?' I wave my fag wildly. 'It's about . . . well, it's about . . . well, it's got everything. It's got . . .' I catch her eye and falter.

'You know, you're not what I expected,' she says suddenly. 'After all this time.' Her glance goes along the hallway to the shut door of my studio, where Maria Krizove is waiting.

'Oh, right, I get it,' I say, with a small laugh that feels like grit, 'your friend's been talking about me. Listen, it was ages ago we knew each other. I hadn't seen her for *nineteen years* before tonight.' As I speak I notice, with vague unease, that Alicia has a small, dark freckle above her left eyebrow.

Her eyes grow wide and bluer than ever, and she steps back from me.

'My *friend*?' she says. 'You mean my mother.' My fag flies from my hand, a small firework, spraying ash in the air. 'Didn't you know that?' she says, with a hint of a giggle.

III

I knew nothing. I know nothing now. I have lived my life in utter ignorance. Of so many things.

When Alicia and I returned to my studio, Maria was standing by the door with her coat on. They must be getting on their way, she said. It was late. They were catching a train early the next morning.

They went, and I was left with nothing but two goodbye kisses, one on each cheek, Maria's moist, Alicia's dry. I saw them out of the flat, they stepped side by side into the elevator, turned and waved, and then I shut my door on myself.

It wasn't until the next morning, waking up on the nauseating Van Klein, that I realised what I had done. I took a taxi to the station, abusing the driver all the way, but I was too late; they must have left hours earlier. The same taxi took me to the TV studios where I spent the rest of the morning locating my co-director, but he told me he'd never seen the two women in his life before he introduced them to me. He said, with a wink, he'd supposed they were friends of mine.

Two days ago I might have agreed with him, more or less. Not now.

Today I realised that things will never be the same again. There's been a change of scriptwriter in my life. Look at me now, pacing up and down my studio, taking a couple of puffs on a fag and crushing it out, mixing a drink and putting it down after a couple of gulps; rubbing my forehead, scratching my beard; all

[298]

the time pacing. I've beaten a path in the shag from door to window. If only I could concentrate, focus on the problem, but other things fly in and out of my mind: my three ex-wives, my unsuccessful trans-plants, the bloody awards on the mantelpiece. I snatch up my dossier on Maria Krizove, but all I can think about is Maria O'Donnell the nun and the Maria in *I'm Not Feeling Myself Tonight* and all those other Marias, the prickteasers and the call-girls and the deep-throat speech-therapists. They're my only com-pany now, the only Marias I'm fit to keep. The other Maria's lost forever. Already I'm starting to forget what she looked like. There's one or two disconnected images I can't put together and a disembodied voice, and that's all.

'Observe perpetually, never cease from observation.' What a quotation to have banging in your head when you've been stone-blind all your life. It's only now I realise that when I saw Maria Krizove in the park, and when she said goodbye to me outside school, she knew she was pregnant.

I've got to find them. As soon as I can think straight, tomorrow or the day after, I'll start looking. First I've got to sort myself out. Stop pacing. Finish a cigarette or two. At the moment I feel so weird it's as if I'm on the outside of myself, looking in. I can see this short, fat guy in a rumpled tracksuit with the looks of a decrepit teenager shuttling nervously up and down his ugly room, looking lost and lonely, and I wonder what he's done with his life, and I wonder what I think of him. He's still worrying about the success or failure of his life, but I'm trying to imagine what kind of part, what minor part, what pathetically insignificant bit-part he has played in the lives of those two great fans of his, Maria Krizove and his daughter.

[299]

BIOGRAPHICAL NOTES

CLARE COLVIN was born in London and grew up in England, Germany, South Africa, the Lebanon, and India. She has worked as a journalist for a number of national newspapers in various fields, from political and foreign reporting to dramatic and literary criticism. She has had a number of short stories published, including two in previous *Winter's Tales*, and is at present working on a novel and a collection of short stories.

PETER BENSON was born in 1956 and was educated in Ramsgate, Canterbury and Exeter. He worked at a variety of jobs before his first novel *The Levels* was published in 1987 and won the Guardian Fiction Prize. His following novels were *A Lesser Dependency* (1989) and *The Other Occupant* (1990). This is the third year he has contributed to *Winter's Tales*.

DAVID PLANTE is a Franco-American, born in a small Quebecois parish in New England. He has, in his Francoeur novels, tried to document a culture as unique to North America as a strange wild bird that has evolved over centuries and is found only in the forests of that vast continent. These novels include *The Family*, *The Woods*, *The Country* and, his last, *The Native*.

PATRICK ROSCOE was born on the Spanish island of Formentera in 1962 and spent his childhood in Tanzania, East Africa. He was educated in England and Canada, and later lived in California and Mexico. A collection of short stories, *Birthmarks* will be published in 1991. Patrick Roscoe currently lives in Seville, Spain.

LAURA KALPAKIAN is the author of many short stories published on both sides of the Atlantic, as well as three previous novels: *Beggars and Choosers* (1978, USA only), *These Latter Days* (1985) and *The Swallow Inheritance* (1987). Her collection *Dark Continent and Other Stories* will be published in 1991. A native Californian, she lives in Bellingham, USA.

ISIDORO BLAISTEN has worked in advertising, both as a photographer and writer; in journalism; and as a bookseller. Now a full-time author, he also holds writing workshops. His first book, *Sucedió en la Lluvia* (1965) was poetry, which he still writes but does not publish. His story collections include *La Felicidad* (1965), *La Salvación* (1972), *El Mago* (1974), *Cerrado por Melancolía* (1982), and *Carroza y Reina* (1986). He is also the author of a volume of essays and reviews, *Anticonferencias* (1983). Among other awards, Blaisten received a Municipal Prize in 1974, the Third National prize for fiction in 1983, and the Second National Prize for essay and criticism in 1986. Born in 1933, Blaisten lives in Buenos Aires.

JANICE ELLIOTT was born in Derbyshire. After Oxford, she worked as a journalist and left the *Sunday Times* when her first novel was published. She has been a regular reviewer for national newspapers for many years and has also broadcast frequently, published articles and distinguished short stories and five highly successful children's books. Of her previous novels,

[301]

Secret Places won the Southern Arts Award for Literature and was made into a prize-winning film, *The Buttercup Chain* was filmed by Columbia, *Private Life* was short-listed for the Yorkshire Post Book of the Year Award, and both *Heaven and Earth* and *The Honey Tree* were New Fiction Society choices. Her latest novel, *Necessary Rites*, was published in 1990. She has one son and lives with her husband in Cornwall.

JOYCE CAROL OATES is the author of twenty novels and many volumes of short stories, poems, and essays, as well as plays. She has been honoured by awards from the Guggenheim Foundation, the National Institute of Arts and Letters, the Lotus Club, and by a National Book Award for Fiction. She is a three-time winner of the Continuing Achievement Award in the O. Henry Award Prize Stories series, and is a member of the American Academy and Institute of Arts and Letters. She lives in Princeton, New Jersey, where she is the Roger S. Berlind Distinguished Professor in the Humanities of Princeton University.

RASAAD JAMIE was born in 1954 in Cape Town, South Africa, and was educated at the Michaelis School of Fine Art in Cape Town and at Goldsmiths College, London. He has had stories published in *London Magazine* and *Artrage* magazine. He lives in North London and earns his living as a temporary office worker.

PAUL SAYER was born and brought up in South Milford, near Leeds. His first novel, *The Comforts of Madness* published in 1988, won the Constable Trophy for fiction, the Whitbread First Novel Prize, and the Whitbread Book of the Year Award. It has been translated into eight languages. His second novel, *Howling at the Moon*, was published in 1990. He is married, with a young son, and lives in York.

ANITA MASON read English at Oxford, and worked in journalism and publishing and at being a 'Sixties dropout before starting to write fiction. Her second novel, *The Illusionist*, was short-listed for the 1983 Booker Prize. Her fourth novel, *The Racket*, was published in 1990. Born in Bristol and resident for many years in Cornwall, she now lives in Leeds, a city for which she developed a liking during a two-year Writer's Fellowship there.

HAYDN MIDDLETON was born in Reading in 1955. He was educated at Reading School and New College, Oxford, where he read Modern History. Since graduation he has worked in advertising, publishing, teaching, and lectured for Oxford University's Department for External Studies on Celtic myth and legend. His novels, the most recent being *The Collapsing Castle* (1990), deal with the magical history of the island of Britain.

CARLO GEBLER was born in Dublin in 1954 and graduated from the University of York and National Film School. He has written and directed a number of films for both BBC and independent television. His published work includes numerous short stories, a work of non-fiction, *Driving through Cuba* (1988), and four novels, the most recent of which is *Malachy and his Family* (1990). His latest novel, *Life of a Drum*, will be published in the Spring of 1991. He currently lives in Co. Fermanagh, Northern Ireland.

[303]

FRANCIS KING was born in Switzerland and spent his childhood in India, where his father was a government official. While still an undergraduate at Oxford, he published his first three novels. He then joined the British Council, working in Italy, Greece, Egypt, Finland and Japan, before he resigned to devote himself entirely to writing. Until recently he was drama critic of the *Sunday Telegraph*, and he reviews fiction each fortnight for the *Spectator*. He is a former winner of the Somerset Maugham Prize, of the Katherine Mansfield Short Story Prize, and of the Yorkshire Post Novel of the Year Award for *Act of Darkness* (1983). His latest novel, *Visiting Cards*, was published in 1990. He lives in London.

SIMON MASON was born in Sheffield, the son of a professional footballer. He became one of the first male undergraduates at Lady Margaret Hall, Oxford, and graduated with a double first in English. His first novel, *The Great English Nude*, was published in 1990. He is now a Senior Editor with the Oxford University Press.